Coaching: Ideas and Ideals

Coaching
Ideas & Ideals
Second Edition

Arthur J. Gallon
University of California, Santa Barbara

Houghton Mifflin Company • Boston
Dallas / Hopewell, New Jersey / Geneva, Illinois / Palo Alto / London

Printed in the U.S.A.

Library of Congress Catalog Card Number: 79-90061

ISBN: 0-395-28693-X

Cover photograph by Alan Orensky

To my wife June,
whose patience, understanding, and assistance
made this revision possible.

Contents

PREFACE *xi*

LETTER TO TOMMY *1*

1 **The Nature of Coaching** *5*

Educational Value of Interscholastic Athletics *6*
The Roles of the High School Coach *12*
Qualifications for a Successful High School Coach *14*
Types of Coaches *19*
Win or Else *22*

2 **Background for High School Athletics** *25*

Development of Interscholastic Athletics *26*
Girls' Participation in Interscholastic Athletics *28*
State Athletic Associations *31*
National Federation of State High School Associations (NFSHSA) *32*
National Council of Secondary School Athletic Directors
    (NCSSAD) *34*
Association for Intercollegiate Athletics for Women (AIAW) *35*
National Association for Intercollegiate Athletics (NAIA) *37*
National Collegiate Athletic Association (NCAA) *38*

3 Motivation in Athletes *43*

Psychometric vs. Perceptual Method of Discovering Personal
   Motivation *44*
Motivational Incentives *51*
Some Motivational Factors *53*
The Importance of Attitude *56*
Motivational Techniques in Coaching *58*
The Importance of Tension Levels *62*
Mental Preparation *64*
Competition and Motivation *65*
Practice Sessions and Motivation *65*

4 Principles of Conditioning *73*

Variance among Conditioning Programs *75*
Strength, Flexibility, and Endurance *75*
Medical Examinations *79*
Warm-up Procedures *80*
Effects of Prolonged Training *82*
Off-season Conditioning *83*
Pre-season Conditioning *85*
In-season Conditioning *85*
Post-season Conditioning *86*
Nutrition *87*
Positive Mental Attitudes of the Athletes *91*

5 Methods of Conditioning *95*

Isometric Exercises *96*
Isotonic Exercises *98*
Isokinetic Exercises *115*
Plyometrics *118*
Cardiorespiratory (C.R.) Fitness *119*
Circuit Training *123*
Combination of Methods *124*

6 Purchasing and Caring for Equipment *127*

Equipment, Facilities, and Supplies *128*
Purchasing Procedures *129*
Purchasing Policies *133*
Care and Maintenance of Equipment and Supplies *139*

Player Responsibility in Caring for Equipment and Supplies   *144*
Care and Maintenance of Artificial Surfaces   *145*
Some Suggested Sources for Sporting Goods   *149*

7   Managing a Budget   *153*

Definition and Purpose of Budgets   *155*
Budget Control and Responsibility   *156*
Criteria for a Good Budget   *157*
Methods of Budget Construction   *159*
Approval of the Budget   *163*
Periodic Appraisals   *164*
Sources of Financial Support for High School Athletics   *164*
Athletic Guarantees   *167*
The Effects of Title IX on Athletic Budgeting   *168*
Data Processing Techniques   *168*

8   Drug Use and Abuse   *185*

The Influence of Drug Use by Professional Athletes on High School
    Athletics   *187*
The High School Coach's Responsibility to Know the Effects of Drug
    Use   *190*
Legal and Ethical Implications of Drug Use in High School
    Athletics   *191*
Drugs Commonly Used in Athletics   *191*
Blood Doping   *198*
Pain and Drugs   *198*
Physical and Psychological Drug Dependence   *199*
Drugs Commonly Abused   *200*
The High School Coach's Obligation to Educate Players About Drug
    Abuse   *206*

9   Legal Education for High School Coaches   *211*

Governmental Immunity for School Districts and Teachers   *212*
Formation of Legal Judgments   *213*
Tort Liability and Negligence   *214*
Defense Against Negligence   *215*
Contributory Negligence   *216*
Prudence   *216*
Supervision   *218*

Equipment and Facilities   *221*
Transportation   *225*
Medical Examinations and Waiver Forms   *226*
Medical Assistance   *226*
Dangerous Coaching Practices   *229*
Failure of Students to Conform to Rules and Regulations   *231*

10   Public Relations   *237*

Public Relations Defined   *238*
Developing a High School Athletic Public Relations Program   *239*
Public Relations and the School Community   *242*

11   Women's Competition   *263*

Title IX   *264*
The Female Image   *266*
Conditioning for the Female Athletes   *268*
Weight Training for the Female Athlete   *270*
Menstruation and the Female Athlete   *272*
Some Unique Problems of the Woman Coach and the Female
   Athlete   *273*
Some Unique Problems of the Male Coaching the Female
   Athlete   *275*
Mixed Competition   *276*

12   Ethics in Coaching   *282*

The Need for Ethics   *284*
Society's Influence on Ethics in Coaching   *285*
The Definition of Ethics: Morals   *286*
Characteristics Influenced by Ethical Standards   *287*
Professional Codes of Ethics   *290*
The California Interscholastic Federation   *291*
The National Council of State High School Coaches Association   *292*
The Association for Intercollegiate Athletics for Women (AIAW)   *292*
National Association of Intercollegiate Athletics (NAIA)   *294*
Win-or-Else Pressures   *296*
Unethical Practices   *297*

13   P.S.   *303*

Index   *314*

Preface

Coaching: Ideas and Ideals, Second Edition, attempts to put forty years of experience in coaching and teaching into written form so that the prospective interscholastic coach can learn the full range of knowledge needed in this profession. In presenting the principles of coaching, this book does not focus on the particular techniques and theories of play of any one sport. Rather, the text explains the principles of coaching through discussion of the techniques that encompass the philosophical, psychological, and moral issues involved in the administration of athletic programs. The text is suitable for use as a core text in principles of coaching or administration courses, and as a supplementary text in a wide variety of other related courses. We hope that *Coaching: Ideas and Ideals,* Second Edition, can also serve as a convenient, comprehensive handbook for the on-the-job interscholastic athletic coach.

More than ever, today's coach is in a position of leadership. This leadership transcends the mere coaching of an activity and requires professional knowledge about subjects such as legal aspects of athletics, motivation, conditioning and training methods, drug use in athletics, public relations, educational values of athletics, managing a budget, purchase and care of equipment, organizations concerned with interscholastic athletics, dealing with college recruiters, travel policies, awards, interaction with game officials, and communication with fellow staff members on a professional level. In addition, since the interscholastic coach is frequently faced with the handling of administrative tasks that normally should be the responsibility of an athletic director, he or she must know how to perform this job, as well.

These diverse topics made up the core of the first edition of *Coaching: Ideas and Ideals.* Their treatment has been updated in this edition. The information presented applies equally to those coaching men or women. Two chapters have been added to the second edition to provide coverage of subjects of vital concern to today's coach: ethics and women in competition.

The entire text has been revised to take into consideration the increased participation of women in sports, as both athletes and coaches. In addition, the chapter on ethics attempts to bring common sense into the long-neglected area of ethics in coaching. It is hoped that *Coaching: Ideas and Ideals,* Second Edition, will serve as a valuable guide and resource for coaches, and others in closely related vocations, beginning their professional careers.

At this point, it is appropriate to acknowledge and thank the following individuals, who reviewed the manuscript at various stages and offered many helpful suggestions: Professor Bruce Rolloff, Western Illinois University; Professor March Krotee, University of Minnesota; Dr. G. Hal Chase, State University College, Oneonta, New York; Dr. Sherman Button, Boise State University; Dr. Boyd Baker, University of Arizona; Dr. Leon Griffin, University of New Mexico; Dr. Frank Mach, College of St. Thomas; Dr. Mary Roby, University of Arizona.

Coaching: Ideas and Ideals

Dear Tommy,

It's been six years since you graduated from high school. I've followed with real pride your accomplishments at college and in the army. There was never any doubt in my mind that you would succeed because of the tremendous enthusiasm and ability you displayed on the playing field.

Soon you'll be getting married, and now you are looking for a job. I'm most pleased to learn that you want to become a high school coach, and I'd like to share with you some of my own ideas about coaching. In this position you'll find a challenge and many responsibilities, but there are few professions in the world as interesting and exciting as high school coaching. You'll have a real opportunity to help in the development of young people. You must give to all the athletes who come in contact with you not only technical training in a sport, but also a great deal of help in fulfilling their needs and interests, and in realizing their innate abilities.

Let me point out that not everyone who has participated in athletics enjoys the challenge of coaching. Pressure from the community, competition, or lack of understanding by the student athletes can cause dissatisfaction. Should you find yourself in this position, my advice is to give up coaching while you are still young enough to make a change. Billie Moore, the U.S. women's Olympic basketball coach in 1976, in an interview made these comments about coaching:

> Mentally, you have to be careful. It can be a task, to come to practice. When you lose your enthusiasm as a coach, your players can lose their enthusiasm for the game. I think if you don't enjoy it and it becomes a job for you, you've probably stayed in it too long. I'd hate to think what it would be like if it were a job.

Perhaps you remember the long discussions we had in my office and on trips to away games. Those sessions may have helped you become a good quarterback, but I think they contributed something else, too. If you can take advantage of opportunities to help your students grow and develop in many ways, you'll experience the ultimate success of coaching. This doesn't show in wins or losses but, rather, in the trust, respect, and friendship you have with each individual you are privileged to teach.

At this point in your life you probably feel there is no challenge too great or obstacle too high for you to conquer. Confidence in your own ability is a fine thing. But let me offer a word of caution. Don't go flying off like a Roman candle, expecting the world championship in your first outing. You'll find that there are still many things to learn. Become a professional. Join associations and attend clinics. Learn all you can from those who are already successful coaches. I'm certain your technical knowledge is adequate, but let me remind you that there is always something new to learn.

1

Figure A *Winning should be just one of a coach's primary objectives.*

Coaching requires great patience with young people and an understanding that teenagers are seeking their identities. A fellow coach, Harold Zeitz, of Simon Gratz High School in Philadelphia, tells an interesting story that I'd like to pass along to you.

John was a student who came from a ghetto neighborhood and had the usual amount of absenteeism, conflicts with authorities, and lack of interest in school. For some reason he decided to try out for junior varsity football. He did not show a great deal of talent, but the coaches noticed his tremendous desire to participate. They gave him encouraging comments on the football field and in the locker room, halls, and classrooms. Suddenly, John acquired an identity, and this spurred in him a general desire to improve himself. Eventually he not only made the varsity team but his school attendance became habitual, and that paid off in better grades. John found himself through athletics. Coach Zeitz believes that all youngsters are crying out, like John, "Love me, hate me, praise me, scold me; but don't ignore me!" When you are a coach, remember that young people crave understanding and guidance from someone they trust.

As a coach you will be expected to live a life of example. The position you fill will make you a personality in the community. Everything you do and say will be observed, and a large number of teenagers will choose your example as the one to follow. The citizens of the future are under your tutelage. Society's charge to you is enormous. Parents and followers of athletics will always be watching you and expecting things from you. Do not disappoint them. *Stand out.* Be a strong example, a symbol on which your players may pattern their lives. You have this opportunity because of your position as coach. The philosophy of "Do as I tell you, not as I do" won't work; you must live the life of "Do as I tell you, and do as I do."

Tommy, you will be surprised at how important a faculty member your position will make you. I doubt if any other member of the faculty is subjected to the close and constant scrutiny that you will experience. Few other individuals on the faculty will have the opportunity to exert the degree of leadership given to your position. Because you will be the focus of much attention, you can encourage reasonable and honest effort in the classroom. Remember how I used to encourage all the team members to study? Many school principals and superintendents believe that a coach's words and actions can influence the morale of the faculty and the student body. This is a responsibility you will not be able to ignore.

You will be accepted as part of the regular faculty by the administration and your teaching colleagues if you share with them such responsibilities as participating in faculty meetings, handling noon-hour duties, and serving as a chaperon at student affairs. True, you will spend many extra hours after school and on weekends coaching, but you must avoid feeling that your job is more demanding than those of other faculty members. The only difference is that you will be observed by the public; the others will spend many extra hours working in private.

Winning should be just one of your primary objectives as a coach—not your only goal. You should have a genuine concern for the total education of your students and must never lose sight of the educational opportunities you can realize through athletics. While it is true that in some situations your tenure as coach might be influenced by your team's record, you should think of your students' welfare first.

You might be tempted to envy college coaches because of the prestige attached to their position. However, if you take the time to listen to a college coach discuss all the problems associated with recruiting, you will realize how fortunate you are in being a high school coach. You don't have to recruit in the same way, but you do have to recognize and encourage raw talent. Watching people blossom into competent performers will be your greatest satisfaction, I think. A college coach is often denied the opportunity you will have to help individual players; he or she recruits excellence and is concerned primarily with team performance.

Don't neglect public relations. This aspect of your job is not easy and will present more perplexing problems than you might anticipate. You'll be at the hub of a lot of relationships: players, parents, officials, recruiters, teachers, and the news media. However, you can be successful in this area if you handle it in a professional way.

One last word of advice. To achieve success you must be willing to pay the price. Lee Bickmore, as president of the National Biscuit Company, listed four criteria for success in business. I have always regarded them as essential for success in coaching, too. They are:

1. *Painstaking preparation.* Only practice brings perfect skills.
2. *Helping others to grow.* I've already mentioned this as a basic tenet of coaching. Your team's success will depend on how responsible your athletes are in carrying out their assignments. Remember that you won't be able to play the game for them.
3. *Aiming high.* It's easy, once you've established yourself, to fall into the trap of self-satisfaction. Improvement or the continuation of excellence must always be one of your goals.
4. *Long days and sleepless nights.* There is no such thing as an eight-hour day for a coach. With your title you will assume a position of leadership and constantly must be aware of your responsibility: You will never know when you will be called on to help someone. The rewards in doing a good job provide great compensation.

I've said a lot in this letter, Tommy, and have implied much more. I want to congratulate you on your decision to enter the high school coaching profession and wish you the best of success.

Good Luck,
Your Old Coach

The Nature of Coaching   **1**

If you don't care whether we win or lose, why'd you buy a new scoreboard?"

Athletics hold an important place in American culture because they dramatize physical and mental courage in a way that is significant and understandable to almost everyone. Interscholastic athletics, in particular, are important for their powerful influence on high school youth. The interscholastic coach is in a position that is both challenging and rewarding; it carries a great deal of responsibility. The coach has a unique opportunity to contribute to the development and education of young people. In performing coaching duties, he or she is constantly teaching.

Objectives ────────────────────────────────

This chapter examines the nature of interscholastic coaching, the coaching of high school athletics on the highest competitive level (not recreation, intramurals, or physical education). It describes:

1. The educational value of interscholastic athletics
2. The roles of the high school coach
3. The qualifications of a successful high school coach
4. The types of coaches
5. The "win or else" philosophy in athletics

Educational Value of Interscholastic Athletics ──────────────

Role in Education

Interscholastic athletics provide an opportunity for young peoples' development; they must be truly educational in nature to justify the necessary expenditure of money, time, and energy. What, then, is the role of interscholastic athletics in the total education of the nation's youth?

Physical fitness contributes to one's performance in all aspects of life. In a message to the youth of the nation, former President John F. Kennedy pointed out that "strength, stamina, and energy . . . are the keys to human progress" (14). He called on the young to dedicate themselves to fitness. Because of the physical requirements for participation, competitive athletics contribute greatly to a player's overall fitness; when a person realizes the importance of conditioning and learns how to get it, he or she will always believe in its value. Athletics can promote improved physical health, impart ideals of hygiene, and develop skills essential to the well-being of Americans who find themselves with more and more leisure time.

Former general of the army and president of the United States, Dwight D. Eisenhower, in commenting on the benefits derived from competitive interscholastic athletics, said:

> . . . they foster among the student body a feeling of loyalty and sportsmanlike competition. They develop the latent qualities of leadership. Because of these advantages our students normally become better citizens of our country; better prepared to carry out the responsibilities and enjoy the privileges of freedom. Athletics are an important part in the maturing process of our young people (16).

Other outstanding Americans have commented on the important educational role of athletics. United States Supreme Court Justice Byron R. White, who was an all-American football player at the University of Colorado and then a professional player with the Detroit Lions, expressed a conviction that it is not at all incongruous for a person noted for athletic feats to aspire to a significant role in society. He said, "Sports and other forms of vigorous physical activity provide educational experiences which cannot be duplicated in the classroom. They are an uncompromising laboratory in which we must think and act quickly and efficiently under pressure, and they force us to meet our own inadequacies face to face . . . as nothing else does" (25). Marcus A. Foster, an outstanding black educator, became principal of Simon Gratz High School in Philadelphia in 1966. On assuming his position, he called the school's athletic director and coach into his office and commented, "Hal, we're down, and I want you with all the support I can give to help pick us up. There is no single phase of school life that can do more to elevate us than can athletics" (27). Marcus A. Foster was slain in 1973 while serving as superintendent of the Oakland, California, school district.

Another positive effect of athletics is its ability to keep young people interested in school. A study of dropouts was conducted from 1966 to 1969 in fifteen schools in the New York City system. The results showed that only about 1.3 percent of athletes left school, whereas the percentage of nonathlete dropouts ranged from 3.5 to 25 percent (1). Dr. Paul W. Briggs, superintendent of the Cleveland Public Schools, in 1970 had his research staff conduct a study on the holding power of athletics in the Cleveland system. The results were startling. In one school where over 50 percent of the students dropped out prior to graduation, not one of the 161 boys who participated in football left school. In another institution with over 400 boys in athletic activities, all stayed on to graduate (2).

Interscholastic athletics provide a special arena where young people can realize their own strengths and weaknesses. In competition, they not only can display their physical strength and stamina, but also may be motivated to develop special skills, learn to control themselves under emotional stress, and learn how to interact with others. Bernie Saggau, executive secretary of the Iowa High School Association, in an address to the Central States Secondary School Athletic Directors Conference in 1972, remarked that interscholastic athletics is one of the few areas left in high school that demand discipline, self-denial, loyalty, and hard work and that are able to persuade young people to sacrifice immediate personal pleasures for long-term benefits (22).

A unique role that interscholastic athletics play in education is providing communication between a school and its community. Schools need community support, and most people understand athletics. Athletics can bring about good relations between the citizens of a community and the schools, which will result in citizens' support for the total educational program.

Contribution toward Personal Values

Gary Cokins, an honor student and athlete at Cornell University who addressed the first national meeting designed especially for secondary school athletic directors, spoke of the importance that athletic competition has for him and many others: "I feel the biggest break a kid can ever get is when he makes a decision to go out for the team. . . . I speak for the tens of millions of athletes past and present. . . . It is you who have helped mold us with your hands. If we are the backbone of America, you have helped create us" (4).

The notion—sometimes considered old-fashioned—that athletics provide men and women with physical, intellectual, moral, emotional, and social benefits is still a valid justification for their inclusion as an educational opportunity at the high school level.

We have discussed the role of interscholastic athletics in other aspects of education; what are some of the specific personal values that athletics can teach? It is very difficult to be specific in listing such benefits, because what is true for one individual is not necessarily applicable to another. In many ways the personal values learned depend on the coach and the leadership provided. As shown in Table 1.1, some values can be listed under each of the five educational categories because of the nature of the contribution.

Table 1.1. *Some personal educational values in athletics*

Physical	*Moral*
Active use of leisure time	Self-discipline
Understanding of physical well-being	Cooperation
Determination and perseverance	Respect for the rights of others and for
Realization of self-limitations	authority
Courage	Ethics
Wholesome release of physical energy	Character development
Self-discipline	Self-knowledge
Acquisition of motor skills	Self-sacrifice
Aggression	
	Emotional
	Self-discipline
	Emotional control
	Aggression and initiative
Intellectual	Self-knowledge
	Courage
	Self-motivation
Understanding of physical well-being	Ability to handle stress
Self-discipline	Character development
Respect for rules	Humility
Realization of self-limitations	
Self-knowledge	*Social*
Knowledge of skills	
Communication	Healthy competition
Character development	Cooperation
Ability to concentrate	
Development of respect	
Mental fortitude	

Social (continued)

Social competence

Respect for the rights of others and for
  authority

Self-discipline

Sportsmanship

Development of leadership

Communication

Active use of leisure time　Athletics develop motor skills that can increase the enjoyment of leisure time, something increasingly important in a culture that is making available more leisure to most people.

Healthy competition　All people are in daily competition to improve or maintain their positions in society. Interscholastic athletics provide a controlled environment for experiencing the stimulation, humility, and joy of competition.

Self-discipline　A coach imposes external discipline, and a player learns an important lesson in responding. But the lesson of self-discipline is even greater. To participate fully and keep a routine, one must deny oneself pleasure; this trait can carry over into many facets of life.

Understanding of physical well-being　Athletics develop an understanding of one's physical being that allows for improved strength, vigor, and fitness. Physical activity and training methods provide an experience of how the body functions and why regular exercise is needed. This experience best creates a healthy attitude with benefits that can last a lifetime.

Determination and perseverance　Athletic success is built on the concept of never giving up until the last individual is out or until the final whistle blows. Success often depends on persevering in spite of adversity and staying with a task until it is completed.

Cooperation　Team sports require great cooperation among members. It is necessary for each individual to meet assigned responsibility if the team is to function effectively as a unit.

Respect for rules　Society is governed by rules and regulations, as are athletic contests. In both areas failure to follow these rules results in penalties and jeopardizes the chance for success.

Aggression and initiative　Participants soon learn the need for aggressive behavior during a contest if they are to win. The person who sits back and waits is usually overwhelmed. Closely associated with aggression is initiative. Many crises can arise during an athletic contest, and how an individual approaches them will depend on initiative and ability to react under pressure.

Figure 1.1 *Sports are an educational experience that contributes to one's performance in all aspects of life.*

Emotional control   The control of one's emotions is essential in both losing and winning. The individual who loses self-control and responds in anger is often beaten. Winners who control their exuberance earn respect from their opponents. Also, those who lose with dignity earn similar respect.

Realization of self-limitations   Not everyone has the ability to be a "superstar." Some will become leaders and some will be followers; an individual benefits from perceiving his or her abilities and limitations.

Self-knowledge   People react differently under pressure, in the face of adversity, and in winning and losing. Athletics provide many opportunities for a person to learn to deal with many different situations. Individuals who are aware of their own strengths and weaknesses know themselves as total persons and are more sensitive to other people as well.

Courage   The Duke of Wellington's well-known phrase, "The battle of Waterloo was won on the playing fields of Eton," is still true. It has been reported that 87 percent of the Medal of Honor recipients in World War II had been high school athletes (22).

Social competence   Players working together for a common goal establish understanding among themselves and dedication to the team. They learn to act for the good of the team and to strive toward the ideals of cooperative effort, loyalty, and public spirit.

Wholesome release of physical energy   It is essential to have a release from the pressures of studying and the classroom routine, as it is important to escape from the pressures of the business world or a household routine. Athletics provide a wholesome medium for this purpose.

Respect for the rights of others and for authority   The ideals of fair play and respect for the opposition's privilege to compete on an equal footing are paramount concepts in interscholastic athletics. Respecting the authority of the coach, officials, and team captain can foster this valuable personal trait.

Development of leadership   Athletics provide the arena for individuals to experience leadership in striving to reach predetermined goals.

Sportsmanship   This ideal has developed into an essential part of American culture. Development of good sportsmanship should always be paramount in interscholastic athletics. (See Chapter 12.)

Ethics and character development   Individuals are born with varying ethical standards. Athletics can provide those traits and characteristics that society acknowledges as desirable behavior patterns. These should be acquired during maturation.

Self-motivation   Goal setting is essential for success in athletics. To reach certain goals, motivation is important. Athletics provide the medium through which individuals may set their own goals. Achievement of these aims often depends on self-motivation and willingness to strive for desired objectives.

Ability to handle stress   Competitive athletics, whether a team or an individual sport, provide stressful situations for the participant. Athletes must learn to deal with stress during games. This experience helps prepare them to put forth a strong arm in everyday living.

Communication   The ability of the coach to communicate with student athletes very often determines the difference between success and failure. Individuals must be able to understand instructions. Also, communication is essential in team sports requiring signals or play calling.

Concentration and mental fortitude   Mental preparedness for a contest has become recognized as an important aspect of game preparation. The ability to concentrate on the task at hand and to approach it resolved to do well often determines its outcome.

Self-sacrifice   Team sports often demand that individuals, regardless of their aspirations, subordinate themselves to the good of the group. Giving of one's self is regarded as desirable for citizenship in any society.

In addition to the values that the active participant can learn, there are others for the spectators. Loyalty, enthusiasm, and pride are developed in fostering school spirit. Discipline within the school can be improved; a better relationship between students and teachers can be promoted; scholarship standards can be influenced favorably through eligibility requirements.

The Roles of the High School Coach

Example

Those who are charged with guiding high school athletic teams have a great responsibility, because they exert a strong influence on the development of their students' characters. Jack C. Curtice, a former football coach and past president of the American Football Coaches Association, received from the wife of one of his former players a letter illustrating the influence a coach can have. In it were these comments (6):

In the case of this young man, he needed strong guidance and leadership in

Figure 1.2 *Every coach is essentially a teacher.*

helping to build character, determination, and a good set of values. He had no male figure in his life at this maturation stage, an ideal on which to pattern his future, to build and to mold, but you. Whether you realize it or not, you took the place of his father.

He, as a result of what you unknowingly gave to him, was able in turn to give to his own. One cannot give unless one has experienced it himself and so another generation has come under the influence of Jack C. Curtice and from that generation will come another.

Teacher

Coaching is actually teaching, not only because sports are a psychologically educational experience but also because players must be instructed in the proper use of skills. Some coaches teach by the whole method, presenting an entire skill at once and then refining the parts. Others instruct by the part method, teaching separately the different aspects of a skill and then putting them together. In either case, the coach must be concerned with all the student players. As in other teaching, the average student deserves attention as much as the most skilled athletes.

In addition, most school systems hire their coaches primarily as academic teachers and secondarily as coaches. Almost all coaches teach an academic course such as physical education or biology as well as coach, or teach, their sports. It is important for a high school coach to be an integral part of the system and to maintain good relationships with fellow instructors. (Sometimes during a dismal season a coach needs the support of everyone!)

The coach should thoroughly believe in the educational value and dignity of coaching. This attitude can make a positive contribution to the objectives of the total educational system.

School Representative

As professional educators, coaches can strengthen their position by participating actively in organizations dedicated to advancing athletics and education. Also, as ambassadors from their institutions to their communities, coaches should acquaint themselves with all facets of their schools' educational programs so that they can communicate them to the public, when they are called on to speak to service clubs and church groups.

Coach

Of course, a coach is expected to teach athletes the technical aspects of a sport, such as the fast break in basketball or the grab start in swimming. His or her effectiveness is constantly open to public scrutiny. A coach's work is reviewed each time the team appears on the playing field or court. The coach should make every effort to increase basic knowledge and to be aware of innovations in the sport. The grab start, for example, is relatively new in swimming, and the swimming coach must know its advantages over the crouched start. In addition to new techniques, a coach must keep abreast of new equipment and innovative training devices like the "mini-gym" and the "nautilus."

Qualifications for a Successful High School Coach

Coaching involves the pursuit of excellence and not just play for play's sake. Coaching interscholastic athletics requires dedication, sacrifice, and an intensity that is not essential in leisure sports. A coach also must have other qualifications to be successful.

Educational Qualifications

A high school athletic coach should be a graduate of an approved college. His or her preparation for teaching should be the same as that of all teachers and should include formal courses in learning and in child growth and development; training in speech and public relations is also very important. The course of study followed by physical education majors also best prepares potential coaches. In addition, a coach should have specialized knowledge of the techniques and methods necessary for the sport he or she will handle.

In recent years, the increased number of activities in an athletic program and the increased number of coaches needed has made it necessary to employ coaches who can conduct formal classroom assignments as well as coach teams. The American Association of Health, Physical Education, and Recreation set up a task force headed by Dr. Arthur A. Esslinger to study certification of coaches. In 1968, the committee recommended that a coaching minor include the following courses (8):

Medical Aspects of Athletic Coaching	3 semester hours
Principles and Problems of Coaching	3 semester hours
Theory and Techniques of Coaching	6 semester hours
Kinesiological Foundations of Coaching	2 semester hours
Physiological Foundations of Coaching	2 semester hours
	16 semester hours

Few institutions have an athletic coaching major comparable to English or history. A physical education major comes the closest to it; but the coaching minor is taking over in popularity. Students who want to coach may take the coaching minor along with a history major, for example. Since almost all coaches must teach as well as coach, it is an advantage to be qualified to teach an academic discipline.

Professional Qualifications

A coach is obligated to be knowledgeable about all the techniques of a sport. By participating actively in a sport, he or she will better understand the technical and emotional problems encountered by the athletes. However, contrary to the previously held notion that an all-American makes a good coach, it has been proved that many of the nation's outstanding coaches never received such athletic recognition. Often an individual who was not an outstanding player and had to work harder for achievements understands better how to help athletes improve their own skills.

Participation alone, however, does not ensure one's knowledge of a sport. A world-record holder in the shotput probably has had little opportunity to learn much about sprints or related activities of track and field. A guard on a football team might be very aware of the requirements for his particular position but know little about backfield play. The coach must acquire a complete working knowledge of the sport. To become a trained technician, one can take professional coaching courses and attend coaching clinics. As techniques change, one should accept new ideas; it is foolish and self-defeating to continue to extol the virtues of the single-wing formation in a pro-set world.

Physical Qualifications

Coaching requires certain physical qualifications that are not related to size, speed, or weight.

Good health Since physical fitness is one of the objectives of athletics, the coach should set a good example for students.

An acceptable standard of motor skill This does not mean that coaches need above-average coordination or abilities to show that they understand the physical skills required by the sport. They may demonstrate, show visual aids, have a student demonstrate, or use other means to illustrate their understanding.

Good personal appearance This is the least important physical qualification. It is helpful, though, if the coach has some physical qualities the athletes can observe, such as a well-proportioned body structure, a pleasant smile, and a clean appearance. Every coach will not look like the proverbial all-American, but respect can be gained by taking care of personal appearance.

Moral Qualifications

Concern for fellow human beings and such values as honesty and fairness are important. The coach, through his or her approach to fulfilling basic responsibilities, will impart these standards to the athletes.

Personality Qualifications

Certain personality traits can be related to successful coaches. In an address to participants at the Western State Conference in Secondary School Athletic Administration, Bruce Ogilvie, psychologist at San Jose State University, spoke on the personality characteristics of physical educators and

Figure 1.3 *The coach's personality traits should portray a strong, positive character.*

coaches. He accumulated his list as a result of contacts with interscholastic coaches throughout the nation. It included (19):

1. a need for high achievement
2. a need to exert leadership and an ability to get others to follow directions
3. a fair amount of inflexibility
4. aggressiveness
5. a solid sense of right and wrong
6. emotional stability
7. tough-mindedness and an ability to face facts
8. great determination
9. organization
10. a lack of anxiety
11. a willingness to accept blame and pay the physical or emotional price for success
12. a willingness to listen to authorities and acknowledged leaders in the field

There is no special significance in the order in which these have been listed. What is important is the strong positive character these traits portray.

Certainly few coaches will possess all these qualities in the same degree, but there is little doubt that most successful coaches are strong and dynamic leaders who are certain about their responsibilities and goals.

Related Qualifications

There are several important qualifications for good coaching that don't fit any of these categories. Coaches should have a sincere interest in their work and genuinely like people. Because they are constantly in contact with people, they will do a better job if they deal with both athletes and the public in a friendly and cooperative manner.

Also, if they are fair with their athletes, each will feel that he or she has been given a chance to develop to full capacity. As a symbol of leadership, a coach should display maturity in judgment and wisdom in decisions. This maturity will include a quality of humility. A coach must remember that prominence comes as part of the job rather than as a personal tribute; the wise coach will govern his or her conduct accordingly. To receive loyalty from the players, a coach should be loyal to them and to the school administration.

A youthful spirit is necessary, and a positive outlook helps achieve desirable relationships with young people. Because a coach needs to be a disciplinarian and is always dealing with the athlete's intense emotions, a sense of humor is extremely important. It can help relieve tensions and make losses seem less disastrous.

John Ralston, while head football coach at Stanford University, co-authored a book with Mike White and Stanley Wilson entitled *Coaching Today's Athlete—A Football Textbook* (20). In this book, the authors listed some basic ingredients for coaches.

1. An inspiration to students and an ability to command faculty respect
2. Friendly and helpful to team members and students
3. Tireless worker
4. Colorful and imaginative—ability to operate under the public's eye with dignity, gentlemanly appearance, and sportsmanlike conduct
5. Good disciplinarian—helpful attitude but respectful control
6. Capacity for organizing recruiting program if coaching at the college level
7. Commitment to operate program within the rules of the league or conference
8. Ability to fit into the athletic department organization and cooperate in overall program
9. Understanding of the role of students and respect for students in nonathletic activities
10. A good organizer and administrator; must have executive ability to get the most out of those employed by him
11. Flexibility in coaching methods

Types of Coaches

Coaching dictates a position of authority. The coach's personality will determine the treatment of the athletes: whether to bully or coddle, bellow or listen, push or pull. It is essential that a coach be, above all, himself or herself.

In their book *Psychology of Coaching,* Thomas Tutko and Jack Richards place all coaches in five categories: the hardnose or authoritarian coach, the "nice-guy" coach, the intense or driven coach, the easy-going coach, and the businesslike coach (24). Normally, an individual does not fall neatly into one classification but is a combination of types and possesses unique mannerisms and coaching style.

Authoritarian Coaches

These coaches leave no doubt about who is boss. They possess well-formulated goals, know exactly what they are trying to achieve, and expect and demand certain responses from those under them. They take the credit or blame for both achievements and mistakes. The advantages and disadvantages of authoritarianism are the same as those for any dictatorship. Most coaches fall into this category.

"Nice-guy" Coaches

These coaches are the opposite of the authoritarian coach and take pride in using the democratic approach. They want to be "one of the gang" and enjoy a popularity that usually results from their sociability. They basically are interested in people and get along well with them. Because they coddle rather than force, they are often thought of as weak leaders, but they often experience great success because their players are relaxed and self-motivated. For example, the football coach of a high school in California was having a hard time winning games, so he decided to change his strategy. He allowed complete freedom for the players, who decided among themselves who would be the starters of the next game. The system was a success: Team effort doubled, the game was won, and the team continued to be victorious.

Intense Coaches

These coaches share many of the characteristics of authoritarian coaches. They are aggressive and have few interests outside the world of athletics. Intense coaches tend to take things too seriously and to overemphasize situations, and they are constantly worried. They lack emotional composure

Figure 1.4 *Two types of coaches: authoritarian and intense.*

and fly into rages. Because of their intense desire and demand for perfection, their teams are usually well prepared and reach early peaks that cannot be maintained throughout the season. These coaches have trouble handling players who can't approach the game with the same dedication that they do.

Easy-going Coaches

These coaches are completely opposite the intense coaches. They regard sports as just a game, and though the outcome is important to them it is not the paramount issue. Of most value for them is participation. They rarely appear excited, dislike the routine and business procedures associated with games, and seem not to take athletics seriously. Easy-going coaches seldom drive their players, they often are not in condition to play an entire game, and they are ill-prepared to handle competitive situations and pressures.

Businesslike Coaches

Perhaps a more accurate title would be professional coaches. They see coaching as a science and employ a scientific approach to the games, using movies, computers, and television to accumulate information and analyze performances. They are logical in their approach and leave nothing to chance. Because the businesslike coaches rely heavily on their ability to outcoach their opponents, unlike other types of coaches they are willing to share ideas and concepts. They follow new developments of their sport and are eager to learn new techniques.

Because of their thoroughness, these coaches can command respect for their leadership. However, their teams exhibit mechanical perfection and lack enthusiasm; players lose their distinctive styles and become robot-like. Many athletes dislike the businesslike approach to athletics and drop off these coaches' teams.

Regardless of the coach's personality, his or her approach to athletics is reflected in team play. The skilled coach inspires student athletes and encourages them to work a little harder than their competitors. Often a composite of the five types is a sixth category, the creative coach.

Creative Coaches

The creative coach is innovative and a master at blending all the aforementioned approaches. Negation and affirmation can be used in one stroke with excellent effects. This coach uses authority with kindness. This combination produces an easy-going, nice-guy approach, but with the sense of imparting both mental and physical strength. If the mind is strong, then action is also strong and successful. It is the greatness of the creative coach that brings out an innovative question from a player. An alert approach to an individual brings desired results. In a professional way, this innovative coach combines efficiency, authority, and creativity.

Win or Else

Winning is part of our American heritage. It descended from the necessary ability to overcome hardships and has become a prime ingredient in the American way of life. Winners in all areas of society are praised and rewarded; in athletics, especially, champions are openly adored. The age-old saying that "everyone loves a winner" remains true today, and professional sports managers have learned that the paying public will follow winners and shy away from losers. Out of this tradition has grown a win-or-else philosophy in athletic competition. Basically, this philosophy implies that if a coach does not continually have winning seasons he or she will be released. A coach may lead a championship team one year but be released the next.

Unfortunately, this attitude has filtered downward from the professional ranks through the college level and into secondary school athletics. Frequently, a coach's tenure is determined by wins and losses. Consequently, some high school coaches are willing to risk the welfare of their students: Individuals who have been injured in a game continue to play even though they may sustain permanent physical damage. To some coaches, victory becomes more important than the character-building aspects of athletics.

The elimination of this philosophy remains one of the greatest challenges in interscholastic athletics. Winning under the fair rules of competition should be the immediate objective of high school athletics, but it should not be an end in itself.

Summary

Interscholastic athletic coaching is challenging and presents a great opportunity to influence teenage youth in a positive and constructive way. In this position a coach is responsible for technical knowledge of a sport but should also participate in other activities of the school community.

The educational values of interscholastic athletics are unique because a participant finds many opportunities for personal and social development. Individuals can realize their own strengths and weaknesses and learn total fitness better than in any classroom situation.

Perseverance, self-discipline, cooperation, healthy competition, self-understanding, and the development of valuable personal characteristics can all be realized through well-guided sports participation.

Coaching represents the pursuit of excellence. Successful coaches have qualifications such as professional training—both educational and technical—physical fitness, and a strong, positive character.

The high school coach exerts a tremendous influence on the youth of the nation. Therefore he or she must be aware of the school's entire educational program and accept the responsibility of supporting all phases of it.

Coaches tend to be categorized as authoritarian, nice-guy, easy-going, intense, and businesslike. Most individuals do not fit neatly into one category but rather combine the five types into the sixth type—the creative coach.

The win-or-else attitude should have no place in interscholastic athletics.

References

1. "Athletics Make the Difference." *The Athletic Director,* Washington, D.C.: National Council of Secondary School Athletic Directors, 2:2 (December 1970).
2. Briggs, Paul W. "We've Got to Take a New Look." *The Coach.* (August 1970).
3. Cobb, Stanwood. *Patterns in Jade of Wu Ming Fu.* Washington, D.C.: Avalon Press, 1935.
4. Cokins, Gary. "The Privilege of Athletic Participation." *Secondary School Athletic Administration—A New Look.* Washington, D.C.: AAHPER, 1969.
5. Curtice, Jack. Interview. September 1972.
6. ———.Letter from Elaine Horlander (May 6, 1972).
7. Donn, Henry F. "Role of Coach, Physician in Program." *The American School Board Journal,* 153:2 (August 1966), 44–45, 48.
8. Esslinger, Arthur A. "Certification for High School Coaches." *Journal of Health, Physical Education, and Recreation,* 39 (October 1968), 42–45.
9. Forsythe, Charles E. *The Athletic Director's Handbook.* 3rd ed. Englewood Cliffs, N.J.: Prentice-Hall, 1965.
10. Griffith, John L. "Today's Coach Is Dedicated." *The American School Board Journal,* 153 (August 1966), 46–47.
11. Hart, Donald M. Speech given at memorial dinner for Dr. Theodore Harder. Santa Barbara, Calif. (November 7, 1970).
12. Hatch, Robert. "Are Athletics Educational?" *Scholastic Coach,* 44:1 (September 1974).
13. Jerome, W. C. and Phillips, J. S. "The Relationship between Academic Achievement and Interscholastic Participation: A Comparison of Canadian and American High Schools." *Sports Sociology: Contemporary Themes.* Dubuque, Iowa: Kendall/Hunt, 1976.
14. Kennedy, John F. "J.F.K.'s Challenge to Youth." *School Board Journal,* 153 (August 1966), 21.
15. Knicker, Charles. "The Value of Athletics in Schools: A Continuing Debate." *Phi Delta Kappan,* 56:2 (October 1974), 116–120.
16. McCarthy, John. "Athletics and the Cult of the Individual." *The Physical Educator,* 31:3 (October 1974), 157–158.

17. Nash, Jay B. "Character Education as an Objective." *Mind and Body,* 38 (May 1931), 497–499.
18. Newell, Pete, and John Bennington. *Basketball Methods.* New York: Ronald Press, 1962.
19. Ogilvie, Bruce. "Personality Characteristics of Secondary School Athletic Directors." Speech given at Western States Conference on Secondary School Athletic Administration. Las Vegas, Nev. (December 1970), 11–14.
20. Ralston, John, Mike White, and Stanley Wilson. *Coaching Today's Athlete—A Football Textbook.* Palo Alto, Calif: National Press Books, 1971, 15.
21. Sage, George H. *Sports and American Society: Selected Readings.* 2nd ed. Reading, Mass.: Addison-Wesley, 1974.
22. Saggau, Bernie. Speech given at Central States Secondary School Athletic Directors Conference. Cedar Rapids, Iowa (April 9–12, 1972).
23. Smalling, Raymond H. Report written for Central States Secondary School Athletic Directors Conference. Cedar Rapids, Iowa (April 9–12, 1972).
24. Tutko, Thomas A., and Jack W. Richards. *Psychology of Coaching.* Boston: Allyn & Bacon, 1971.
25. White, Byron R. "Educational Value of Physical Fitness." *School Board Journal,* 153 (August 1966), 21.
26. Youngert, Eugene. "College Athletics: Their Pressure on the High Schools." *The Atlantic Monthly,* 202 (October 1958), 35–38.
27. Zeitz, Harold. "Athletics: Its Holding Power in the Inner-City Schools." *Scholastic Coach,* 38 (January 1969), 5, 82.

Background for   2
High School Athletics

'01 Coach Publications ©1966 by Ray Franks Publishing Ranch

"I'm thinking of making a comeback."

Fundamental to an understanding of the objectives and problems of high school athletics is an awareness of their history and related organizations. In the past eighty years, educators' attitudes toward the importance of athletics in education have changed from disapproval to support. With this change and the increased scientific and medical knowledge about athletic conditioning, the concepts of what high school athletics are, what they should provide, and for whom have changed too, producing big differences in facilities, programs, finances, and the professional career of coaching. High school athletics is now in a new stage of evolution because of tightened budgets and the emergence of girls' athletics. The role coaches will play in choosing goals for this latest change depends on their knowing the past and present contexts of high school athletics.

Objectives

This chapter decribes the contexts of interscholastic coaching by presenting:

1. The development of interscholastic athletics
2. The expansion of girls' participation in interscholastic athletics
3. The role of state athletic associations
4. A brief history and the purposes of:
   a. The National Federation of State High School Associations (NFSHSA)
   b. The National Council of Secondary School Athletic Directors (NCSSAD)
   c. The Association for Intercollegiate Athletics for Women (AIAW)
   d. The National Association for Intercollegiate Athletics (NAIA)
   e. The National Collegiate Athletics Association (NCAA)

Development of Interscholastic Athletics

Unlike most secondary school offerings, interscholastic athletics were initiated by students and forced on administrators. At first, students participated with little or no supervision, and there were few rules regulating participation. It was not uncommon for individuals who were not enrolled in a school to play as members of its team. Natural rivalries developed, and in the desire for superiority, unbridled adolescent enthusiasm ran wild. However, athletics brought such pleasure and generated such loyalty that eventually they could no longer be ignored or considered unwanted. At the beginning of the twentieth century, school authorities unwillingly accepted this activity as something to be tolerated but not necessarily encouraged.

At this time in America, the philosophy of education was undergoing a dramatic change. Educational leaders like John Dewey emphasized concentration on the individual and on experiences that would prepare him or her for society (23). Physical education emerged as a new discipline under the guidance of physicians and was accepted as part of the secondary school curriculum. Early physical education programs were designed around activities such as gymnastics and physical training, which involve

Figure 2.1 *After World War I, interscholastic athletics increased greatly in popularity.*

strict discipline. When competitive interscholastic athletics were introduced into school programs, many physical education instructors resented the intrusion; others, like Dudley A. Sargent, recognized that competitive athletics provide educational opportunities for students (22). Many leading school superintendents also supported interscholastic athletics (4). The activity was placed in the hands of the physical education instructors because of the prevailing concept that athletics were in actual practice "education of the physical" (23).

Until the end of World War I, the physical education program in the schools remained primarily one of gymnastics and formal exercise: Instructors had been trained in this way, and facilities for any other sports were minimal. Interscholastic athletics flourished, but regulations began to be imposed. Local faculty control was initiated, and league or conference policies were set to determine procedures and standards for activities. As interscholastic athletics increased in popularity and transportation facilities improved, voluntary statewide associations appeared in an effort to establish uniform regulations and equal opportunities for competition. One important result of the formation of these state associations was the imposition of controls on all levels of high school athletics. To join the association, for example, individual institutions had to give up their arbitrary ideas about the proper age for participation; this ended the unfair practice of allowing twenty-one-year-olds to play football against fifteen-year-olds or of holding students back academically so they could play for six years instead of four. Any group could impose stricter rules, but it had to follow the generally established minimum regulations. Eventually, in the 1920s, a national association composed of state organizations was established. This national association is not a regulatory body but concerns itself primarily with policy matters and interstate competition. Its authority for such matters is delegated to it by member state associations (16).

Because many young Americans failed to pass the physical for induction into the armed services for World War I, physical education became a compulsory subject after the war. Leaders in the development of interscholastic athletics like Jesse F. Williams and Jay B. Nash believed that athletics should be an integral part of the high school educational program instead of a side show for students and interested adults (12). Sports and athletics began to occupy more and more time in physical education classes. The concept emerged in the 1920s that interscholastic athletics represent the essence of physical education and that those who participate in athletics are actually the honor students of the discipline. Many physical education leaders today agree with this contention.

During the depression years of the thirties, school activities that were considered "frills" were cut from the curriculum. Interscholastic athletics were drastically curtailed: The number of activities and teams was greatly reduced, and competition involving extensive travel often was eliminated entirely. However, there was one bright spot for high school athletics in this otherwise bleak picture. Government funds were available for construction of school buildings, including gymnasiums and athletic playing fields (4). Also, to fill the idle time of the American people, sports programs were initiated under the sponsorship of Work Project Act (WPA) Recreation Projects. It was only natural that when the nation's economy recovered sports activities increasingly would be included in high school physical education and athletic programs.

Athletic programs again were curtailed sharply during World War II, but following this period interscholastic programs grew quickly as an attempt was made to extend the educational opportunities of athletics to more and more students. The typical school program just before World War II included an average of three or four sports at the varsity level, whereas today a typical program includes nine to ten sports with teams at the varsity, junior varsity, and sometimes sophomore and freshman levels (13).

Although the future of interscholastic athletics is unclear because of recent cutbacks in financial support and the sharing of available funds between boys' and girls' programs, they currently are more popular than ever. They have become an integral part of the American secondary school program and the nation's culture.

Girls' Participation in Interscholastic Athletics

The historical development of competitive sports reveals participation among girls and women in organized programs as early as the middle of the nineteenth century (29). However, as with the men's programs, there were those educational leaders including women physical educators who frowned on women's involvement in athletics. Despite this, organizations

Figure 2.2 *Girls should have an equal opportunity for educational development through interscholastic athletics.*

were formed during the early twentieth century by women physical education leaders to meet the continuing demands for help in solving problems associated with girls' and women's athletics (5).

During the 1920s and 1930s, some women leaders felt that women athletes were being lured into competition without regard for their well-being. These leaders condemned women's participation in competitive athletics. Emphasis was placed on intramural programs and "play days," which provided sports for all girls. New leaders emerged during the 1950s who felt that there should be an opportunity for the highly skilled girls to engage in competitive athletics. Throughout the various stages of its growth, the organization now known as the National Association for Girls' and Women's Sports (NAGWS), a division of the American Alliance for Health, Physical Education and Recreation (AAHPER), has been the recognized proponent for girls' interscholastic athletics. In 1963, this organization expressed a major change of policy that included "interscholastic and intercollegiate athletics as acceptable forms of extramural competition" (5). NAGWS supports the National Federation of State High School Associations to serve as a governing body for interscholastic athletics. The Association for Intercollegiate Athletics for Women (AIAW) serves as the leading body for controlling women's intercollegiate sports.

The passage in 1972 of Title IX, a law prohibiting sex discrimination in education, had a tremendous impact on both interscholastic and intercollegiate women's athletic programs. The opportunity for women to participate in organized competitive athletics has significantly increased. Speaking of girls' participation, E. W. Cooley, executive secretary for the Iowa Girls' High School Athletic Union, said in 1972, "It is the most significant movement in athletics today" (3).

The dramatic increase in women performing in the Olympics reflects this trend. In 1900, only six women competed; in 1972, of the eight thousand athletes at Munich one-third were women, who participated in ten different events. The strength of America's women's contingent was in track and swimming (7). The 1976 Olympic games in Montreal, Canada, had a total of 6,189 participants. Of this total, 1,274 were women. The women increased their participation from ten sports in 1972 to fourteen sports in 1976. The three sports with the largest number of women participants were track and field, swimming, and rowing (19).

The increased participation by women in competitive athletics is due in part to a reversal in the attitude of the people who administer and control athletic programs. They have begun to relinquish the notion that competitive athletics should be only for men and are beginning to realize that women should have equal opportunities for educational development and a chance at the values high school athletic competition offers. In the following comment, Peggy Peterson Tyler, former all-American and U.S. basketball player, expresses how important participation has been for her: "There is no doubt in my mind which was the most rewarding to me, it was of course the opportunity I had to compete because the thrill is not reached in any other way. Only through the experience of competing yourself do you really ever know not only victory or defeat but all the other qualities to be attained through competition" (28). As women have shown through their performance in the Olympics and in other nationally publicized sports, one's sex does not determine whether one is an able athlete.

Of the problems involved in the growth of girls' participation in interscholastic athletics, facilities and finances are probably the greatest. Many schools don't have adequate facilities for two programs; some don't even have adequate facilities for one. And because of this lack of facilities, scheduling can be a problem. As money for interscholastic athletic programs becomes more difficult to secure, many male coaches will object to subtracting any—much less half—the funds that traditionally have supported their boys' activities. It is important for high school coaches to remember that *all* students should be given the opportunity for a total education. Also, they should consider that the citizens who finance the school athletic program with taxes are parents of girls as well as of boys.

The leaders of high school athletics in many states have begun to recognize the importance of girls' athletics. Iowa has a separate state athletic association for girls, with its own executive secretary. Minnesota and Colorado also recently have appointed such directors. Organizations in many other states, have established separate rules and regulations for girls' programs but have not yet begun to promote women's activities at the state level. As girls' athletic programs are accepted and promoted at the national level, it is reasonable to assume that all states will provide the leadership required by the expansion of girls' participation in interscholastic athletics.

State Athletic Associations

State athletic associations play a very important part in governing high school athletics. Their primary purpose is to establish uniform controls and regulations governing interscholastic competition. Within such guidelines, students are assured of equal competition under sound educational guidance.

State athletic membership is voluntary. However, because of the popularity of these organizations, schools that want to compete find they must join the association to have a program.

Most state athletic associations are outside the jurisdiction of the state Department of Education, but since the primary responsibility for education rests with the state, there is a close relationship between the two. Some state associations, notably in New York and Michigan, are affiliated with their state departments of education because of legislation allowing state funds to be spent for interscholastic athletics. In a few states, such as Texas and South Carolina, the association remains closely tied to the respective state university (11).

It should be noted that all state organizations impose minimum regulations in such critical areas as eligibility, scholarship, supervision, safety, length of season, age, tournaments, awards, conduct, playing regulations, travel, use of officials, and relations between schools. In some states like California, further restrictions may be imposed by districts, conferences or leagues, and institutions; however, the minimum restrictions imposed by the state organization may not be changed. Violation of regulations can result in suspension of contestants or schools. Every coach has the responsibility to keep informed of regulations and to educate all the athletes on matters directly pertaining to their participation.

National Federation of State High School Athletic Associations (NFSHSA)

By 1920, most states had some organization to promote and control high school athletics. Yet many universities, colleges, clubs, and private promoters ignored regulations and exploited high school athletes. In 1920, L. W. Smith, secretary of the Illinois High School Athletic Association, invited representatives of neighboring states to discuss with him mutual problems concerning high school athletics. Representatives from Illinois, Indiana, Iowa, Michigan, and Wisconsin attended. They decided an organization should be established to ensure effective control. In 1921, Iowa, Illinois, Michigan, and Wisconsin formally ratified the constitution establishing the Midwest Federation of State High School Athletic Associations. George E. Marshall of Iowa was elected president, and L. W. Smith of Illinois became secretary-treasurer (16). Representatives from eleven states attended the 1922 meeting of the federation in Chicago. At this time, the organization expanded and the name was changed to the National Federation of State High School Athletic Associations.

Since then, this organization has grown to include representation from all states in the nation. Eight provinces of Canada—Alberta, British Columbia, Manitoba, New Brunswick, Nova Scotia, Ontario, Prince Edward Island, and Saskatchewan—are affiliated members. Also, the association of the Republic of the Philippines is an affiliate member. In 1940, a national office was established, and H. V. Porter was appointed as the first executive secretary.

The headquarters for this office are at 11724 Plaza Circle, Kansas City, Missouri, 64195.

The federation publishes a handbook that includes pertinent information on the organization's origin, growth, and function. In summary, the stated purposes of the federation are (16):

To secure proper adherence to the eligibility rules of the state associations in interstate contests for high schools

To promote high school athletics through the exchange of experiences and pooling of interests

To protect high school athletes from exploitation

To promote high school athletics so that they reflect the objectives of the institution and become an integral part of the curriculum

Since its beginnings in 1920, the Federation of State High School Athletic Associations has made many contributions toward the improvement and control of interscholastic athletics. It has cooperated with other national organizations, such as the National Collegiate Athletic Association, that are dedicated to the "sane control" of athletics. It has shared in developing suggested national minimum standards of eligibility for interscholastic athletics. Areas covered are age, scholarship, semesters in school, enrollment, transfers, recruiting, awards, and amateur status. The federation has helped develop national high school rules for some sports activities, notably basketball. National track and field and swimming records established by interscholastic athletes are verified and approved by the national organization, which also serves as a depository for these records.

In other areas, the federation's functions have been to promote uniformity among sports within each state; help in developing sports equipment best suited for the protection of the teenage athlete; promote safety programs for schools; establish standards for interstate athletic contests; resolve national policies about contractual agreements between professional and high school athletics; produce visual aids for use in rules-training programs and student assemblies; establish a national code of ethics for interscholastic coaches and of cardinal principles for the purpose of high school athletics; work to eliminate an overemphasis on high school athletics and promote their educational benefits.

A national council, which is composed of one representative from each state association, is the legislative body of the organization. The executive committee, which handles the organization's business, comprises seven members who are elected at the federation's annual meeting. This committee elects its own president and vice-president and appoints the executive secretary. Membership in the national federation is limited to state associations.

National Council of Secondary School
Athletic Directors (NCSSAD)

In the past, the high school athletic director's position had little substance. It was primarily a title handed to a coach who had decided to give up active coaching; as athletic director, individuals found themselves with many announced responsibilities and not much authority.

This situation is changing rapidly. Today secondary school athletic directors are usually in an accepted administrative position. They are the speakers for the interscholastic athletic program and responsible for all the administrative details of the program. They must understand the total educational program and be well versed in current trends that can influence athletics. As the heads of the entire athletic programs, they must work with all areas of the school community in making certain that interscholastic athletics are understood and not abused.

In recent years, state athletic directors' associations have been formed. Their primary function has been to promote an understanding of the high school athletic director's role and to encourage the exchange of profitable experiences. The American Alliance of Health, Physical Education, and Recreation (AAHPER), through its division for men's athletics, sponsored a National Council of Secondary School Athletic Administration in the fall of 1967. One of the outgrowths of this meeting was a recognition of the need to upgrade the athletic director's contribution and position. In the fall of 1968, a new national council was approved by AAHPER. A second national meeting of interscholastic athletic directors was held in Washington, D.C., in January 1969. At that time, the National Council of Secondary School Athletic Directors was formed.

The council is administered by an executive committee whose members serve on a rotating basis. Members are elected at the national council's annual meeting. In addition to the six elected members, representatives in an ex-officio nonvoting capacity express the views of the National Federation of State High School Athletic Associations and the American Association of School Administrations, and the vice-president of AAHPER speaks for the Division of Men's Athletics.

The stated purposes of the National Council of Secondary School Athletic Directors are (25):

Improve the educational aspects of interscholastic athletics and their articulation in the total educational program
Foster high standards of professional proficiency and ethics
Improve understanding of athletics throughout the nation
Establish closer working relationships with related professional groups
Promote greater unity, goodwill, and fellowship among all members
Provide for an exchange of ideas
Encourage the organization of state athletic directors' councils

Assist and cooperate with existing state athletic directors' organizations

Provide a national forum for the exchange of current practices and the discussion of evolving trends in the administration of athletics

Make available to members special resource materials through publications, conferences, and consultant services

Establish and implement standards for the professional preparation of secondary school athletic directors

Membership in this organization is open to anyone who has a primary responsibility for directing, administering, or coordinating the athletic program at the junior or senior high school level. Further information is available through the AAHPER offices in Washington, D.C. The address is NCSSAD, ℅ AAHPER, 1201 16th St. N.W., Washington, D.C., 20036.

Association for Intercollegiate Athletics for Women (AIAW)

The Association for Intercollegiate Athletics for Women (AIAW) was formally organized during the 1971–1972 school year and became operative July 1, 1972. It grew out of the Commission on Intercollegiate Athletics for Women (CIAW), which was a branch of the Division for Girls' and Women's Sports (DGWS). The CIAW was organized in 1967 (1). DGWS eventually changed to become the National Association for Girls' and Women's Sports (NAGWS), but continues to serve as a division of the American Alliance for Health, Physical Education, and Recreation. The AIAW was organized as one of eight sections under NAGWS.

At the 1979 general meeting in Los Angeles, the assembly empowered the executive board to negotiate and complete all steps in establishing the AIAW as a separate and legal entity by July 1, 1979. Its programs and administration will retain continuing ties with both AAHPER and NAGWS.

"The AIAW provides a governing body and leadership for initiating and maintaining standards of excellence in women's intercollegiate athletics" (1). Upon its inception, it included accredited institutions of higher learning, such as junior or community colleges as well as small and large colleges and universities. The nation is divided into nine geographic regional governances whose titles are as follows:

Region 1. Eastern (EAIAW)
Region 2. Southern
Region 3. Southeastern
Region 4. Southwestern
Region 5. Midwestern (MAIAW)
Region 6. "Region 6" AIAW
Region 7. Intermountain
Region 8. Western (WAIAW)
Region 9. Northwest College Women's Sports Association (NCWSA) (1).

The purposes of the AIAW are stated in the 1978–1979 handbook:

1. To foster broad programs of women's intercollegiate athletics which are consistent with educational aims and objectives of the member schools and in accordance with the philosophy and standards of the NAGWS.
2. To assist member schools in extending and enriching their programs of intercollegiate athletics for women based upon the needs, interests, and capacities of the individual student.
3. To stimulate the development of quality leadership for women's intercollegiate athletic programs.
4. To foster programs which will encourage excellence in performance of participants in women's intercollegiate athletics.
5. To maintain the spirit of play within competitive sports events so that the concomitant educational values of such an experience are emphasized.
6. To increase public understanding and appreciation of the importance and value of sports and athletics as they contribute to the enrichment of the life of the woman.
7. To encourage and facilitate research on the effects of intercollegiate athletic women and to disseminate the findings.
8. To further the continual evaluation of standards and policies for participants and programs.
9. To produce and distribute such materials as will be of assistance to persons in the development and improvement of intercollegiate programs.
10. To hold national championships and to sponsor conferences, institutes, and meeting which will meet the needs of individuals in member schools.
11. To cooperate with other professional groups of similar interests for the ultimate development of sports programs and opportunities for women.
12. To provide direction and maintain a relationship with AIAW regional organizations.
13. To conduct such other activities as shall be approved by the governing body of the association.

The AIAW shall not have any purpose nor engage in any activity which would be inconsistent with the status of an educational and charitable organization as defined in Section 501(c)(3) of the Internal Revenue Code of 1954 or any successor provision thereto, and none of the said purposes shall at any time be deemed or construed to be other than the public benefit purposes and objectives consistent with such educational and charitable status. And provided further that the AIAW will not adopt purposes nor engage in any other activity inconsistent with the purposes and policies of AAHPER and its NAGWS (1).

Membership in this organization is open to any accredited institution of higher learning that provides an intercollegiate program for women and is willing to abide by the AIAW's stated policies. To be eligible for regional qualification and national championship play, an institution must have an active membership in its region. The address is AIAW, 1201 16th St. N.W., Washington, D.C., 20036.

National Association for Intercollegiate
Athletics (NAIA)

Under the direction of Mr. Emil S. Liston, Dr. James Naismith, and other recognized basketball leaders, a tournament to decide a national championship for small colleges was held in Kansas City, Missouri, in 1938. This
tournament was the forerunner of the National Association of Intercollegiate
Basketball (NAIB), which had its organizational convention on March 10,
1940, in Kansas City. The current name of National Association for Intercollegiate Athletics (NAIA) was adopted in 1952. Along with change of name,
"the first all-encompassing rules and standards were adopted" (26). Besides basketball, national championships in track and field, golf, and tennis
were established. Since that time, eleven national championships have
been added that include two for football under the titles Division I and II.

The primary purpose of the organization, since its inception, has been to
champion the cause and provide national championships for four-year collegiate educational institutions with moderate enrollment. The average enrollment among members is about fifteen hundred students.

A distinguishing mark of the NAIA has been its firm belief that intercollegiate athletics should be part of the overall educational program for
member institutions and controlled by those responsible for the administration of the college or university. The NAIA is divided nationally into thirty-two
districts embracing the entire United States. The affairs of each district are
handled by elected representatives of their intercollegiate conference or independent member institutions. Membership in the association is open to
any four-year college or university approved by its regional accrediting
agency. Membership fee is based on institutional enrollment.

The objectives of the organization as stated in its handbook are:

1. To assist member institutions in the development of a sound philosophy of intercollegiate athletics which shall include:
   a. A broadly based program of physical education for all students which includes
      prescribed physical education courses, intramural and extramural activities
      and intercollegiate athletics.
   b. The development of the individual to the fullest extent of his capabilities, both
      as an individual and as a citizen.
   c. A plan of evaluation so that all organized activities which take place on the
      campus will be evaluated in terms of the educational purposes of the college
      or university.
   d. Intercollegiate athletics which are an integral part of the total physical educa-
      tional offering of a college and not a separate organization with different prin-
      ciples, aims, and objectives.
   e. The department of physical education, which should have a place in the in-
      stitutional structure comparable to any other department, should be subject to
      the same institutional policies, budgetary provisions and controls, as are all

other departments of the college; and members of the faculty of the department should be selected in the same manner and have the same rights, privileges, and responsbilities as other faculty members of comparable rank.

2. To assist member institutions in providing a program of intercollegiate activities which places priority upon such items as:
   a. A program of intercollegiate athletics which is instrumental in educating participants and other students in moral and ethical values inherent in the program.
   b. A program of athletics which is so conducted that the educational and ethical status of the college will be enhanced.
   c. A program of intercollegiate athletics which offers the participants valuable educational experiences not provided in other phases of the physical education program.
   d. A program of intercollegiate athletics which is controlled by those responsible for the administration of the college.
   e. Competition with other colleges having similar educational philosophies, policies, and practices.
3. To assist the student-athlete to attain his educational goals:
   a. All students participating in intercollegiate athletics should be admitted to the college in the same manner as other students and should be regularly enrolled students making normal progress, both quantitatively and qualitatively, toward a degree.
   b. All financial aid to any student in money or in kind, except that which comes from members of his immediate family or from those upon whom he is legally dependent, should be administered by the college under policies and procedures established by the college for administration of scholarships and grants-in-aid to students having special abilities.
4. To provide leadership to member institutions in attaining worthwhile goals in their own athletic programs. The NAIA and the member institutions each have a role:
   a. The role of the association is that of working cooperatively with members and providing leadership which will assist in the realization of such objectives as have been stated in Article III.
   b. The role of the member institutions is to strive toward the attainment of NAIA objectives; and, to work cooperatively with the NAIA and other member institutions to improve programs of intercollegiate athletics (26).

Further information is available through the NAIA offices at 1205 Baltimore, Kansas City, Missouri, 64105.

National Collegiate Athletic Association (NCAA)

The National Collegiate Athletic Association (NCAA) was founded because of abuses in intercollegiate football at the start of the present century. Deaths attributed to football prompted President Theodore Roosevelt, in the fall of

1905, to call several collegiate leaders to the White House where he gave them an ultimatum: "Either clean up football and I will give it the sanctions of my office or let it remain as it is and I'll ban it from the American sports scene" (10).

On December 9, 1905, thirteen institutions responded to an invitation from New York University's Chancellor MacCracken to meet and consider three basic questions. These were:

1. Shall football be abandoned?
2. If not, what reforms are necessary?
3. If so, what substitute can be suggested in its place?

On December 28, 1905, sixty-two colleges and universities met in New York City, a meeting that led to the formation of the Intercollegiate Athletic Association and a formal adoption of its constitution and bylaws March 31, 1906. The first annual meeting was held December 29, 1906. The present name of NCAA was adopted at the annual meeting on December 29, 1910.

The original purpose of the organization was to formulate policies that would govern intercollegiate athletics. It was hoped that these policies would provide *sane control* of collegiate sports. Enforcement of standards was left to individual institutions or conferences.

Among the organizations' first responsibilities was the establishment of rules committees for various intercollegiate sports. The number of such committees has increased over the years and currently represents all sports except baseball, which uses the rules of the professional game (27).

The first NCAA-sponsored national event was in track and field in 1921. Today it conducts national championship meets in all sports except football.

The NCAA remained an advisory body until 1948 when it adopted the "sanity code." This code provided monetary fines for known violations. It soon became evident that it was ineffective, however, and it was dropped in 1951. At that time, a full-time executive director, Walter Beyers, was appointed and machinery was established to handle violators. This machinery included the present practice of placing institutions on probation, thus making them ineligible to participate in NCAA events.

The purposes of the NCAA are:

To uphold the principle of institutional control of, and responsibility for, all intercollegiate athletics in conformity with the Association's Constitution and Bylaws.

To serve as an overall national discussion, legislative and administrative body for the universities and colleges of the United States in matters of intercollegiate athletics.

To recommend policies for the guidance of member institutions in the conduct of their intercollegiate athletic programs.

To legislate upon any subject of general concern to the membership in the administration of intercollegiate athletics.

To study all phases of competitive athletics and establish standards therefor, to the end that colleges and universities of the United States may maintain their athletic activities on a high plane.

To encourage the adoption by its constituent members of eligibility rules in compliance with satisfactory standards of scholarship, amateur standing and good sportsmanship.

To establish and supervise regional and national collegiate athletic contests under the auspices of the Association and establish rules of eligibility therefor.

To stimulate and improve programs to promote and develop educational leadership, physical fitness, sports participation as a recreational pursuit and athletic excellence through competitive intramural and intercollegiate programs.

To formulate, copyright and publish rules of play for collegiate sports.

To preserve collegiate athletic records.

To cooperate with other amateur athletic organizations in the promotion and conduct of national and international athletic contests.

To otherwise assist member institutions as requested in the furtherance of their intercollegiate athletic programs (27).

Membership in the NCAA, which numbered over 850 in September 1977, is open to any college or university accredited by its regional accrediting agency. An institution that accepts membership in the organization must sponsor at least "four intercollegiate sports with one sport in each of the three traditional seasons of the academic year" (27). It also must agree to comply with the rules and regulations of the organization and to recognize the enforcement program. "Through the process of self-determination, each member institution places itself in Division I, II or III for purposes of championship competition" (27). Further information is available through the NCAA offices at P.O. Box 1906, Shawnee Mission, Kansas, 66222.

Summary

Competitive high school athletics began outside the academic world. But, through the interest of students, alumni, and merchants, school superintendents were eventually forced to include athletics in school programs to ensure faculty control and equal opportunities for participation.

The expansion of girls' participation in interscholastic athletics has recently begun and will continue to be an important development in the years ahead.

State and national athletic associations have developed to supervise and improve interscholastic athletics. The National Council of Secondary School Athletic Directors (NCSSAD) was established in 1968 to promote the athletic director's role and to further this position as a profession. Intercollegiate organizations, such as the Association for Intercollegiate Athletics for Women (AIAW), the National Association for Intercollegiate Athletics (NAIA), and the

National Collegiate Athletic Association (NCAA), which influence interscholastic athletics, have developed in the current century.

References

1. Association for Intercollegiate Athletics for Women, *Official Handbook, 1978– 1979.* Washington, D.C., 1977.
2. Coleman, James S. "Athletics in High Schools." *Annals of the American Academy of Political and Social Science,* 338 (November 1961), 33–34.
3. Cooley, E. Wayne. "Girls' Athletics." Speech given to Central States Secondary Schools Athletic Directors Conference. Cedar Rapids, Iowa (April 9–12, 1972).
4. Cozens, Frederick W., and Florence Stumpf. *Sports and American Life.* Chicago: University of Chicago Press, 1953.
5. Deatherage, Dorothy, and C. Patricia Reid. *Administration of Women's Competitive Sports.* Dubuque, Iowa: William C. Brown, 1977.
6. DeBacy, Diane L., Ree Spaeth, and Roxanne Busch. "What Do Men Really Think about Athletic Competition for Women?" *Journal of Health, Physical Education, and Recreation,* 41 (November–December, 1970), 28–29.
7. Dosti, Robert. "Number of Women in Olympic Games Continues to Grow." *Los Angeles Times,* part 3 (August 24, 1972), 1.
8. Ewers, James R. "Move Over Men: The Women Are Coming." Speech given at 74th Proceedings of the National College Physical Education Association for Men, 1971.
9. Forsythe, Charles. *The Athletic Director's Handbook.* Englewood Cliffs, N.J.: Prentice Hall, 1965.
10. Gallon, Arthur J. "Commissioner Form of Intercollegiate Athletic Administration." Unpublished Thesis. University of California, Berkeley, Calif., 1954.
11. George, Jack F., and Harry A. Lehmann. *School Athletic Administration.* New York: Harper & Row, 1966.
12. Hackensmith, Charles W. *History of Physical Education.* New York: Harper & Row, 1966.
13. Jones, Frank B. "Intercollegiate and Interscholastic Athletic Programs in the 1970s." *Sportscope,* 15 (June 1970), 1–19.
14. Magnusson, Lucille. "The What and Why of AIAW *Journal of Health, Physical Education, and Recreation,* 43:3 (March 1972), 71.
15. McFadden, Karen. "Our Unwanted Athletes." *Scholastic Coach,* 37 (March 1968), 42–44.
16. National Federation of State High School Associations *Official Handbook, 1977–1978.* Elgin, Ill., 1977.
17. Neal, Patsy E. *Coaching Methods for Women.* 2nd ed. Reading, Mass.: Addison-Wesley, 1978.
18. Neal, Patsy E., and Thomas A. Tutko. *Coaching Girls and Women: Psychological Perspectives.* Boston: Allyn & Bacon, 1975.
19. *Olympic Review,* 113 (March 1977), 166.
20. Sabock, Ralph J. *The Coach.* Philadelphia: W. B. Saunders, 1973.
21. Sage, George H. *Sport and American Society.* Reading, Mass.: Addison-Wesley, 1970.

22. Sargent, Dudley A. "The Place for Physical Training in the School and College Curriculum." *American Physical Education Review,* (March 1900), pp. 1–17.
23. Scott, Harry A. *Competitive Sports in Schools and Colleges.* New York: Harper & Row, 1951.
24. Scott, Phebe M., and Celeste Ulrich. "Commission on Intercollegiate Sports for Women." *Journal of Health, Physical Education, and Recreation,* 37:8 (October 1966), 10, 76.
25. Smith, Rex B. "The National Council of Secondary Schools Athletic Directors." *Secondary School Athletic Administration–A New Look.* Washington, D.C.: American Association for Health, Physical Education, and Recreation, 1969, 121–122.
26. National Association of Intercollegiate Athletics. *Official Handbook,* 1974. Kansas City, 1974.
27. National Collegiate Athletic Association. *General Information Pamphlet.* Shawnee Mission, Kansas, 1976.
28. Tyler, Peggy P. "The Challenge of Girls' Athletics." Speech given at Central States Secondary Athletic Directors Conference. Cedar Rapids, Iowa (April 9–12, 1972).
29. Von Borries, Elaine. "History and Functions of the National Section on Women's Athletics." Washington, D.C.: American Association for Health, Physical Education, and Recreation, 1941.

Motivation in Athletes

"Despite what you think, you don't have a complex.
Actually, you are inferior."

Physical ability is, of course, a key element in athletic performance; but an even more necessary ingredient for achievement is motivation. One of the coach's primary responsibilities is to inspire each player with the desire to realize his or her full potential. The coach must be sensitive to each athlete's particular needs and interests, help set goals, and encourage optimum performance. Athletes are spurred on by many different factors, and these incentives make the difference between an average performance and a superior one.

Objectives

The following chapter presents the aspects of motivation a high school coach should understand:

1. The psychometric vs. the perceptual method of discovering personal motivation
2. Motivational incentives
3. Some motivational factors
4. The importance of attitude
5. Motivational techniques in coaching
6. The importance of tension levels
7. Mental preparation
8. Competition and motivation
9. Practice sessions and motivation

Psychometric vs. Perceptual Method of Discovering Personal Motivation

Psychometric Method

During the 1960s, many psychologists became interested in using a psychometric approach to discovering personality traits and motivational factors in athletes. Bruce Ogilvie, Leland Lyon, and Thomas Tutko, directors of the Institute for the Study of Athletic Motivation at California State University, San Jose, developed the Athletic Motivation Inventory (A.M.I.), a questionnaire that is filled out by athletes and then analyzed by psychologists. The inventory provides information about the attitudes and probable behavior of the athletes. The factors measured are: drive, aggressiveness, determination, responsibility, leadership, self-confidence, emotional control, mental toughness, coachability, conscientiousness, and trust. Each athlete's answers to the questions are computed and presented on a profile sheet as percentile scores. Comparisons are made against a composite score for successful athletes of similar sex who are competing at a comparable level. Evaluations of each factor are provided. These interpret the athlete's score. Included are descriptions of the athlete's probable behavior in a situation and some suggestions for helping the individual develop desirable attitudes. A typical profile report is shown in Figure 3.1.

Psychometric assessment forms can be very beneficial in helping a coach understand each athlete's capabilities and limitations. They can also reveal personality traits a coach should be sensitive to in dealing with a student. There is a danger in relying too heavily on the information these forms provide, however, and a coach must be careful not to form biased opinions or prejudices about a player. This information should be kept in its proper perspective and, of course, absolutely confidential.

ATHLETE'S REPORT

PREPARED: JUNE 78

**ATHLETIC
MOTIVATION**

```
                    ATHLETIC MOTIVATION PROFILE


          PERCENTILES 0   10   20   30   40   50   60   70   80   90   100
---------------------------------------------------------------------------
DRIVE                  XXXXXXXXXXXXXXXXX   43
---------------------------------------------------------------------------
AGGRESSIVENESS         XXXXXXXXXXXXXXXXXXXXXXXXXXXX   67
---------------------------------------------------------------------------
DETERMINATION          XXXXXXXXXXXXXXXXXXXXXXXXXXXXXXXXXXXXX   90
---------------------------------------------------------------------------
RESPONSIBILITY         XXXXXXXXXXXXXXXXXXXXXXXXXXXXX   72
---------------------------------------------------------------------------
LEADERSHIP             XXXXXXXXXXXXXXXXXXXXXX   54
---------------------------------------------------------------------------
SELF CONFIDENCE        XXXXXXXXXXXXXXXXXXXXXXXX   59
---------------------------------------------------------------------------
EMOTIONAL CONTROL XXXXXXXXXXXXXXXXX   41
---------------------------------------------------------------------------
MENTAL TOUGHNESS       XXXXXXXXXXXXXXXXXXXXXXXXXXXXXXXXXXXX   88
---------------------------------------------------------------------------
COACHABILITY           XXXXX   11
---------------------------------------------------------------------------
CONSCIENTIOUSNESS XXXXXXXXXXXXX   30
---------------------------------------------------------------------------
TRUST                  XXXXXXXXXX   25
---------------------------------------------------------------------------

REFERENCE GROUP: FEMALE, HIGH SCHOOL, BASKETBALL


                        REPORT RELIABILITY


ACCURACY:  You experienced some difficulty in completing the
AM inventory accurately.  You basically understood the
questions, however, and this report should be representative
of your attitudes toward athletics.



DESIRABILITY:  You did not attempt to present a favorable or
unfavorable impression of yourself in completing the AM
inventory.  Your trait scores, unaffected by a desire to
impress others, should be reliable.
```

Figure 3.1 *Coach's report on an athlete's motivation.* (From *The Athletic Motivation Program, Preliminary Technical Manual* by Thomas A. Tutko, Ph.D., Leland P. Lyon, M.A., and Bruce C. Ogilvie, Ph.D. © 1977, 1975, Science Research Associates, Inc. Reprinted by permission of the publisher.)

ATHLETE'S REPORT

PREPARED: JUNE 78

**ATHLETIC
MOTIVATION**

DRIVE
You like athletics, even though it isn't the most important
thing in your life. You want to be good in your sport and
are willing to work at it. You tend to set high goals when
there is a good chance of success. You accept challenges
well, like competing, and don't give up simply because the
chances are even or are slightly against you.
DEVELOPMENT: You will benefit from having specific,
measurable goals to work toward. Set up a system that will
tell you how much progress you're making. Check your
progress at regular times: every day, every week, or every
contest. Your coach can help you with this. Since you
probably prefer challenges only in areas where you are
already competent, you may have to push yourself to work on
areas where you are least competent.

AGGRESSIVENESS
You are a very aggressive athlete and believe that
aggression is important to winning. You don't like to be
pushed around, freely show anger toward those who defeat
you, and will probably be eager for a second chance to win.
You release aggression readily, don't let others take
advantage of you, and don't back down from an argument. You
are a self-assertive athlete who makes things happen.
MAINTENANCE: You could serve as a model for your fellow
athletes in drills and competition because of your ability
to release aggression easily. It would be helpful to match
yourself in practice against opponents who are at least as
aggressive as you. Your aggressiveness will be very
important to you in improving your talent. Maintain it, but
be sure it's used constructively for yourself and your team.

DETERMINATION
As a competitor, you are extremely persistent and determined
in pursuit of your goals. Once you start something, you
rarely give up. You do not stop when you are tired or
having trouble. You believe in hard work and are willing to
give extra time to develop your skills. Your ability to
sustain effort will be a great help to you in realizing your
athletic potential.
MAINTENANCE: Continue to accept with confidence any tasks
or positions that require extra stamina and energy. You
should also serve as a model to fellow athletes for staying
on an assignment. You must, however, beware of working so
hard that you forget physical capacity has a limit. This is
particularly important to remember when you're recovering
from an injury.

DATA-COPYRIGHT   1977   SRA

Figure 3.1   *(Continued)*

ATHLETE'S REPORT

PREPARED: JUNE 78

**ATHLETIC
MOTIVATION**

RESPONSIBILITY
You are a highly responsible athlete. You accept criticism
in a very positive way. You are willing to work very hard
to develop skills and keep yourself in good condition; you
don't let minor injuries keep you from competing. Sometimes
you feel too responsible and punish yourself too harshly.
MAINTENANCE: Your nondefensive attitude toward criticism is
important to an athlete. It contributes to easy
communication with your fellow athletes and your coach. You
should be careful, however, not to be too hard on yourself
after losing a contest. Seek out the opinions of others
before taking too much blame. Even if your mistakes
contributed to a loss, you should spend your energy on
correcting them, not on punishing yourself.

LEADERSHIP
You accept leadership roles in sports when stronger or more
active leaders are not present, but you don't seek them
otherwise. You accept responsibility for others, are
pleased when others look to you for help or direction, but
do not see yourself as having definite leadership ability.
When you have strong personal opinions, you can be forceful
and convincing.
DEVELOPMENT: The ability to dominate others is an important
quality in an athlete--whether that athlete wants to be a
leader or not. This is because dominating an opponent is an
important factor in winning. It would be valuable for you
to seek out those situations in which you are willing to
accept leadership. Do so gradually; don't be overwhelmed.

SELF-CONFIDENCE
You have an average amount of confidence in yourself and
your talents as an athlete. You handle new and unexpected
situations well, though a strong challenge to your self-
assurance shakes your confidence. You do speak out when the
issue is important to you. You aren't intimidated easily,
and you consider yourself equal to most opponents.
DEVELOPMENT: In athletics, there's almost no such thing as
having too much self-confidence. The self-confident athlete
makes more of opportunities and trusts his or her abilities
to the limit. You could benefit from taking more chances
and letting your natural abilities take over. When you lose
self-confidence, notice what happened to cause it. Work
closely with your coach, record your progress, and check it
out with fellow athletes.

Figure 3.1   *(Continued)*

ATHLETE'S REPORT

PREPARED: JUNE 78

ATHLETIC MOTIVATION

EMOTIONAL CONTROL
You generally control your emotions well as an athlete. You may get nervous before an important contest or be upset by a bad break. But in general you don't let your feelings get in the way of your concentration. Therefore your performance is fairly even and consistent.
DEVELOPMENT: Emotional control is something you can't have too much of as an athlete. It intimidates opponents and contributes to general confidence. Even though emotional control is not a problem for you, you can benefit by strengthening it. You probably already have ways of relieving tension and clearing your mind during competition. Practice them and develop others until they become habits. Practice stopping negative feelings before you have trouble controlling them.

MENTAL TOUGHNESS   *Cooky*
You are an extremely tough-minded athlete who responds to the stress of athletics in a direct, positive manner. You feel completely at ease with your coach and fellow athletes. You don't need their encouragement to continue to improve yourself as a competitor. You accept criticism at face value and can take rough coaching. You take defeat in stride and keep on going.
MAINTENANCE: Your mental toughness is a help not only to you in your continued growth as an athlete but to others as well. Because you always face situations as they are, your fellow athletes look to you in a crisis. When things are not going well, your steadiness can help to steady others. Your positive response to failure can be an important morale booster after a defeat.

COACHABILITY
You have little respect for the coach and coaching. You resent the demands of the coach and often pay too little attention to coaching suggestions. These characteristics may lead you to be uncooperative with the team captain as well. You feel strongly independent.
DEVELOPMENT: It's important for you as an athlete to re-examine your attitude toward coaching. Maybe you feel capable of developing your ability without the help of the coach. Perhaps a former coach let you down and you refuse to trust another. Or you may simply be very independent and reject help. Whatever the reason, it would be well for you to adopt a more open attitude. The coach's experience and insight can contribute to your growth. Talk with your coach.

DATA-COPYRIGHT   1977   SRA

Figure 3.1 *(Continued)*

ATHLETE'S REPORT

PREPARED: JUNE 78

**ATHLETIC
MOTIVATION**

CONSCIENTIOUSNESS
You tend to be casual in meeting commitments to the coach,
your group, and yourself. You respect team rules only when
they make sense to you. You justify breaking a rule by
saying that it doesn't apply in every situation, that
breaking it one time won't matter, or that it is unfair.
DEVELOPMENT: Keep in mind that the obligation to stick to
rules was not forced on you; it's something you took on when
you became an athlete. It is necessary for sports groups to
have regulations in order to stay together and to win. If
you don't see the point of a rule or think it's unjust,
don't just ignore it. Ask the coach why it's important.
The coach doesn't expect blind, unthinking obedience; the
coach knows that you'll be more likely to follow a rule if
you understand why it matters.

TRUST
You are not sure you can trust your coach and fellow
athletes. You sometimes feel cut off from others, and you
will take sides when the group is split. You are careful
about what you say, for you don't trust others to listen
with care.
DEVELOPMENT: The fact is that the more open you are, the
more likely it is that others will be open to you. It is
easier to trust someone who is being candid. Distrust may
just be a habit you developed--one you can break. Make an
effort to communicate openly with others. If you are
disappointed, you still have lost nothing. If not, you will
have taken an important first step toward building better
relationships.

CONCLUSION: This report is based on extensive research with
thousands of athletes. Study this report and strive to
understand the objective information and recommendations
presented. This report can provide a foundation for your
personal growth and development in the field of athletics.
Consider sharing your report with the coach and others whom
you trust, if you are able to do so comfortably. Although
the eleven traits are important contributors to athletic
success, other factors must also be taken into consideration
in evaluating your athletic performance. Finally, please
remember that this report was prepared specifically for
athletics and may not be applicable to other areas of your
life.

DATA-COPYRIGHT   1977   SRA

Figure 3.1 *(Continued)*

Perceptual Method

In 1949, Arthur Combs and Donald Snygg, leading proponents of the perceptual method of assessing personality traits, wrote a book titled *Individual Behavior: A Perceptual Approach to Behavior* (10). Many of their ideas have been widely accepted and practiced. Though perceptual methods of assessment do not conflict directly with the psychometric approach, in practice the system can prove quite different.

Basically, under the perceptual method behavior is observed, the situation in which the behavior takes place is considered, and the cause for the behavior is determined. The observer may ask such questions as "Why is this person acting that way? What is she thinking? How does he feel?" Emphasis is placed on each individual's self-perception. A person's behavior is generally dictated by needs, which take a variety of forms. If these needs can be determined, they often reveal the source of motivation. Behavior patterns can be altered by influencing emotional needs; however, a coach must be able to perceive special problems of the athlete and help discover the causes to improve performance. The following example illustrates how the perceptual method of assessing motivation can help in high school coaching.

A football coach had a halfback who seemed to have trouble carrying the ball through openings in the line. Instead of hitting a hole with force, the player would veer away at the last minute and circle one of the ends. He had terrific speed and often made good yardage, but some teammates and fans branded him as "yellow." The coach talked with the boy and discovered that this behavior resulted from a fear of being hit on the head, which he associated with a parental method of punishment. The halfback didn't mind bumps or hits on any other part of his body.

The coach convinced this player that he could excel in football, and the boy was determined to overcome his fear. Together they agreed on a method: Every day the player stayed after practice and ran with the ball to a designated area, where the coach was standing. As the player went by, the coach slapped and hit him on the head. The boy obviously was suffering, but after two weeks he began to accept the slaps as something other than punishment. From then on he was able to go through the holes without hesitation, and because of his innate ability and speed he became an outstanding player. The coach learned later that the boy's teammates were aware of what the halfback had been going through and had encouraged him to continue in his efforts. Undoubtedly, this peer support was instrumental in the player's success; but the coach's perception of an emotional difficulty, and his encouragement, helped the athlete overcome this motivational problem.

Coaches have always dealt with motivation by using their own experience, intuition, and common sense. Part of their job is to have insight into the psychology of their players and to determine the extent to which motivational problems may be caused by personality traits.

Motivational Incentives

If coaches are to understand why athletes compete in a particular sport, they need to have some understanding of the various incentives impelling an athlete to action. David Birch and Joseph Veroff, in their book on motivation, list seven incentive systems that account for some motivational behaviors. They call these the achievement, affiliative, aggressive, curiosity, independence, power, and sensory incentive systems (7). Athletes who consistently enter competition knowing the adversity they face are regarded to be driven by positive incentives. Those athletes who avoid such situations are thought to be impelled by negative incentives. Although incentives are hard to measure, psychologists and coaches know through both intuition and experience that some incentive systems are more powerful than others.

Achievement Incentives

Achievement is the major incentive in team sports today. The more arduous the task and the more public the evaluation, the greater will be this incentive. Many athletes depend greatly on external standards and have little awareness of their own capabilities. As they become more capable, they should be encouraged to judge their own performances. Many coaches prefer to set the external standards of winning and of publicity as the criteria for excellence. Athletes with low achievement motives probably do not remain long in a sport. They are the ones who become the dropouts.

Three response systems influence the achievement of athletes. The first is competence. Comparisons are always being made about an athlete's performance. Hence some athletes may experience both success and failure. This directly affects their motivation. To generate success in the athlete, it becomes necessary for the coach to make precise assessments of exactly what kinds and levels of competence the sport requires. Competence and the prime motive to achieve are very closely related.

The second response system is effectiveness. If athletes can be helped to sense the potential of their own effectiveness, their achievement motives can be greatly enhanced.

The third response system involves the tendency in our culture to ascribe a masculine identity to successful athletic performance. This masculine identity has created a dilemma for women athletes, for often their life goals are incompatible with the masculine orientation of achievement motivation.

Thus, to retain their feminine image, some women modulate their efforts. Conversely, many male athletes draw on a strong masculine image of achievement.

Affiliation Incentives

The urge to affiliate with teams on which one's teammates are similar in age, ability, and sex is an incentive in two ways. First is the distinction of performing well on one's team. Good performance has strong affiliative incentive values because of the esteem, support, and social respect it engenders. Second is the love and affection that one may establish with the coach and one's teammates. In present-day culture, this use of the word *love* may have a perplexing aspect. Strictly speaking, to love one's coach and teammates is not to love their persons, but the good in their characters.

Aggression Incentives

Injuring or harming the other person is not the goal of an athletic program. It is the aggressive behavior in attaining goals unconnected to the aggression that is important. For example, one uses aggression in getting the majority of rebounds in a basketball game.

Curiosity Incentives

The inherent complexities of games like football, basketball, and baseball satisfy the curiosity incentive of trying something new or different. Athletes who participate in more than one sport have inquiring minds with strong curiosity motives, but, once these incentives are satisfied, the sport must have other major attractions.

Independence Incentives

Independent athletes enjoy being on their own and accomplishing an activity without help. They like to train by themselves, to succeed by themselves, and, if necessary, to fail by themselves. They are generally highly competent. If they were not, they would have to rely on those more qualified for help. Constitutionally, they are generally very responsible. The combination of independence, competence, and responsibility is qualities of excellence to be sought not only for participation in individual sports, but also in team sports.

Power Incentives

These are the incentives associated with influencing and controlling other people's attitudes. The ego-tripping coach who is motivated by power needs to have control over his players. It becomes extremely gratifying to teach a skill to a player who then becomes a champion. The more prominent the competition, the more powerful the incentive becomes. Players attain a power incentive when they can change spectator opinion from one of derision to one of massive approval.

Sensory Incentives

The pleasure or pain one receives from bodily contact in sports is a sensory value. Pain is the negative value and pleasure the positive value of the incentive. The harder and longer one plays, the more quickly one becomes drained of the desire to continue in a certain activity. This explains staleness and boredom in athletes as well as slumps in sports.

Some Motivational Factors

Motivational factors and incentives may coexist or mingle to a different degree in each individual. They not only influence athletic participation but also influence attitudes that govern all phases of action. The intensity with which an athlete participates may depend on the force of incentive factors. These factors may also merge with the various needs and drives influencing teenage athletes. The following sections describe some important motivational factors.

Recognition

In our culture, we place great emphasis on success. Athletics provide an opportunity for a person to be recognized publicly for superior performances. According to Abraham Maslow, a leading psychologist in the field of motivation, gratification of the need for recognition may represent the greatest single stimulus underlying personality development (24). Steve Garvey, Los Angeles Dodgers baseball player, reinforces this contention when he says, "All sports are based on the ego of the athlete . . . he lives for the applause" (20). James Counsilman, Indiana University swimming coach, contends that recognition is of primary importance for athletes. He says, "Recognition is important to all individuals, but it is essential to a hardworking athlete. It satisfies the ego drive"(11). There are three major categories of recognition:

Peer recognition   Admiration from peers exerts a powerful force on adolescent behavior. In many high schools, the male athlete is regarded as a "big man on campus." This prestige is a great incentive for young boys to want to excel in athletics.

Parental recognition   For the most part, teenagers want to please their parents. Most parents are proud when their children do well; young people realize this and feel great satisfaction when they know they have given a good performance. Adults consider athletics wholesome and important in many phases of development. A young person's athletic achievements often ensure receiving parental praise.

Public recognition   Since success is important in North American culture, individuals who excel are considered important. Superior athletes enjoy more recognition and fame than most other outstanding members of society. Many athletes' names are truly household words. Commenting on his first year of coaching a professional football team, Tommy Prothro expressed surprise at the players' determination to succeed and their willingness to work to achieve this goal. When asked why they did it, Prothro replied, "For the recognition, I think, more than the money. . . . To the players, football is essentially a search for identity" (28). In high school football, too, this public acclaim is definitely a motivational factor.

Ego-reinforcement

When one wins an athletic contest, he or she gains status—and hence a sense of confidence and importance. The qualities of a successful athlete such as confidence, perseverance, tolerance of pain, and a winning attitude have been well publicized in books, magazines, television, films, and the sports pages of newspapers. By participating in sports, many young people try to achieve an image that includes the following characteristics:

Self-respect   Athletic participation provides the individual the opportunity to develop and refine abilities such as coordination, speed, reaction time, and strength. Success in athletics can bring a player self-respect and a sense of fulfillment.

Sense of adequacy   Athletics are an area where good performance brings personal rewards: A player will know he or she has fulfilled a responsibility to the team or has perfected skills to the point of outdoing an opponent.

Display of masculinity   Many boys are motivated to try out for a team because they want to prove their masculinity or maybe impress a girlfriend.

Fear of Failure

Fear is a strong motivating force. A coach can use it effectively with the players, but must be aware of the impact, both positive and negative, it can have. Teenagers need authoritative direction and guidance, which give security and a sense of what is expected. Fear of failure and of the loss of security serves as a strong motivational factor for an athlete. Team members want to belong and to do well; if threatened with expulsion from the team, they will work harder to adhere to training rules and to improve performance.

Material Gain

Some people are motivated by material proof of achievement. Athletic scholarships, trophies, and letters are rewards that a high school athlete may strive for as indicators of success. One danger of material gain as a motivating force is that objects can become ends in themselves, and a player may lose sight of the other values of athletic participation. Another danger is that the individuals who are not rewarded may receive negative motivational reinforcement and become demoralized.

Need for an Emotional Outlet

Pressures of daily life build up emotional tensions. Both participants and spectators use athletics as a means of emotional release. One athlete may experience a thrilling release of energy in a well-executed vault in gymnastics or track and field; another may get the same release from the physical contact of football or wrestling. Regardless of the sport, a typical comment after a vigorous workout is "I feel so much more relaxed now than when I started." Many spectators who release pent-up emotions by yelling at the game officials are models of behavior away from the sports arena.

Need for Physical Movement

People have an inherent need for developing motor skills. They are excited by movement and rhythm. Sports that require a great deal of action can provide much satisfaction: skiers are exhilarated by their speed in a good run down a mountain, and a halfback's fifty-yard run for a touchdown is truly thrilling. Roger Bannister's description of a childhood memory involving the joy of movement effectively describes this motivational drive. He wrote of the joy and happiness he experienced walking barefoot on a sandy beach:

> In this supreme moment I leapt in sheer joy. I was startled and frightened by the tremendous excitement that so few steps could create. I glanced around uneasily to see if anyone was watching. A few more steps—self-consciously now and firmly gripping the original excitement. . . . I was running now, and a fresh rhythm entered my body. . . . I had found a new source of power and beauty, a source I never dreamed existed (4).

Physical fitness   Physical exertion brings a feeling of well-being and is necessary for good health. Coaches and physical educators have always believed in the need for physical fitness and in the benefit of active participation in sports. President Kennedy's emphasis on the importance of physical fitness helped increase it as a motivating force in athletics.

Stress addiction   Some individuals are driven to participate in activities that by their nature involve risk or danger. Examples of these sports are sky diving, hang gliding, mountain climbing, surfing, automobile racing, and aerobatic piloting.

Personal pride   Dr. Bruce Ogilvie adequately describes this motivating factor when he says, "People talk about external rewards motivating the athlete. But external rewards are all secondary to the answering of one's personal pride. The money, acclaim, press notices, and pats on the back from friends are nice but they're only echoes in the canyon. They won't sustain an athlete. I mean really sustain him—if he has any character" (20).

The Importance of Attitude

Attitude forms the basis for motivation in athletics. This opinion is shared by successful coaches like John Ralston, former football coach at Stanford University; John Wooden, U.C.L.A. basketball coach; Henry Iba, Oklahoma State University and Olympic basketball coach; Brutus Hamilton, University of California at Berkeley and Olympic track and field coach. Coaches Pete Newell and John Bennington point out in their book, *Basketball Methods,* that "the mental attitude of an athlete on a team can often be the difference between two teams on a given night" (26). Psychologists Tutko and Richards have written: "Before really effective learning can take place, the player's interest and desire must be stimulated to the point where he is not only more receptive to instruction, but actually desirous of it" (37).

A good attitude should be developed through positive rather than negative instruction, since positive methods have proven more beneficial and effective as teaching techniques (34). Coaches should adopt the "this is how you do it" approach and eliminate the "this is the wrong way to execute this skill" method. The athlete should be encouraged to replace "I can't" with "I can" and "I'm not sure I can do that" with "I know I can do it." Successful coaches must be perennial optimists and should transmit this attitude to their athletes. Several factors combine to create a positive attitude toward athletic achievement.

Goal-setting and Plans

Coaches should help an athlete establish realistic objectives
so that the athlete feels he or she has truly accomplished son
so high that he or she can't come close to reaching them. Pla
cedure for attaining objectives helps a player's attitude beca
will be able to observe progress and thus be motivated to c⸱⸱⸱⸱⸱⸱⸱ toward
the ultimate goal. Athletes should be presented with the question "What do
you want to achieve not only as an individual but also as a team?"

Desire

Desire can be defined as enthusiasm and an intense wish to attain or overcome something. Often this quality involves a great deal of personal dedication. When the late Rocky Marciano, undefeated heavyweight boxer of the
world, started boxing, his arms were so bulky that by the end of a third round
he lacked the strength to hold them up. To overcome this he sat in a swimming pool for hours swinging his arms against the resistance of the water.
Eventually he was able to develop his arms and lungs so as to achieve his
goal—the world title. An often-repeated cliché in athletics—"he was willing
to pay the price"—indicates an athlete's positive attitude and strong desire
to succeed.

Confidence

Confidence can be developed with repeated assurance in one's ability.
When she was only fourteen years old, Peggy Fleming represented the
United States in the winter Olympics because the figure skaters who were
supposed to participate had been killed in a plane accident. She did not
win, but she left the games with confidence and a knowledge that in the future she could win. She returned to the Olympics four years later and won
a gold medal for the United States. Her attitude of confidence encouraged
her to spend the endless hours of practice needed to perfect her ability.

Determination

Determination involves the desire to succeed. If a player is really determined, he or she can suffer pain and exhaustion and still fight for a personal
goal. Dick Roth, who swam for the United States in the 1968 Olympics, experienced severe abdominal pain just before his event. His trouble was
diagnosed as appendicitis, but, although the doctor recommended an operation, Roth refused: He had worked and trained for four years and was

determined to swim. He won a gold medal and set a new world record. Fortunately, his determination did not cause any serious physical after-effects.

Motivational Techniques in Coaching

Because athletes are motivated by different drives, a coach's motivational techniques and styles will vary. The coach constantly must be alert to different methods of accomplishing his or her aim of guiding athletes to achievement. There are several recognized techniques a coach should be aware of such as: praise, threats of punishment, diversion from failure, gimmicks, love and affection, use of voice, individual and team discussions, and pep talks.

Praise

Praise for accomplishment and effort offers a great deal of psychological reinforcement. The coach always should be looking for things to praise sincerely. A player who realizes that a performance is just average might resent tributes given as if he or she were a superstar, and would probably regard the coach as hypocritical—or worse, incompetent—and lose respect for him or her (6). A coach should offer praise judiciously and also encourage students in areas where they are weak. Too much praise can be dangerous: It can make athletes so content that they will not expend the effort necessary to continue their development.

Threats of Punishment

Fear, as pointed out before, can be an effective and powerful motivating force. Some authoritarian coaches rely almost exclusively on threats—or on actual punishment—as their motivational technique. When players or teams do not perform up to expectations, they are ordered to undergo extra practice sessions. Extra laps, push-ups, or sprints are demanded as punishment for mistakes; a player might be demoted in squad placement or even threatened with expulsion from the team. Threats and punishment can defeat a coach's purpose by creating resentment and fatigue among the players.

Though the threat of punishment can be a powerful motivating technique, it usually works only when a team is winning. If a team is losing in spite of its effort, the impact of penalization is decreased, because the players have already failed to achieve their primary goal.

Diversion from Failure

When individuals or teams fail they sometimes become depressed and cease trying. If left unchallenged, failure tends to impede future perfor-

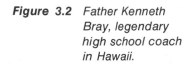

Figure 3.2 *Father Kenneth Bray, legendary high school coach in Hawaii.*

mances (21). Coaches have a major responsibility to hide their own feelings about an unsuccessful effort and try to divert attention from that failure. They should not avoid pointing out errors and mistakes, but also should recognize superior performances and use them to encourage renewed effort.

Use of Gimmicks

Coaches have long used gimmicks to motivate their players. They put slogans like "When the going gets tough, the tough get going" and "There is no *i* in *TEAM*" in the dressing room or other appropriate places. Soon the players have absorbed the sayings subconsciously. Football coaches sometimes put decals on their players' helmets to display the number of pass interceptions or touchdowns the athletes have made. Father Kenneth Bray, legendary high school coach in Hawaii, was a master of psychology in handling his players. He used a horseshoe from a famous racehorse in motivating them to give extra effort. Prior to practice sessions, he read stories of the horse's great courage, and before a game each player was allowed to hold the horseshoe to receive some of the horse's hidden strength! This gimmick may seem unusual, but it provided a tangible rallying point for the players; the phenomenal number of victories they recorded is a matter of history.

Love and Affection

James E. Counsilman, swimming coach at Indiana University who has also served as a head coach for the U.S. men's Olympic swimming team, cites love and affection as a primary motivational technique (11). He points out that these are basic needs in all individuals. To receive both, coaches must first give both. They must feel genuine concern for the athlete. Those coaches who feign affection are soon labeled as phonies and lose the respect of the athletes. Counsilman's advice to all young prospective coaches is, "If you do not genuinely like and understand young people, do not try to become a high school coach" (11).

It is also important for the players to have some affection for each other. Vince Lombardi, the epitome of the authoritarian coach who once said winning isn't . . . the only thing, attributed the success of his Green Bay Packer teams to the players' love and affection for each other.

Use of Voice

A coach's voice can influence the performances of athletes: It can calm an individual player or prod a team to greater efforts. If a coach shouts all the time, reprimands become worthless; if the coach's voice is never raised, words may lack strength. By contrast, a scornful tone can express displeasure and spur the athletes to try harder. Coaches who are masters in using their voices seldom shout at players, but when they do raise their voices they get an instant reaction.

Individual and Team Discussions

There is tremendous value in a coach's discussions with individual players. He or she becomes better acquainted with each athlete, learns of personal ambitions, and can give advice on particular strengths and weaknesses. The coach can help players establish goals for personal achievement. When he was at Stanford University, Coach John Ralston met individually with every player during spring football practice. During these sessions, he assumed the role of a counselor and discussed anything the player wanted to talk about. He felt strongly that he was able to establish closer relationships with all his athletes (30). High school coaches may claim that they don't have the time to conduct such sessions, but they should be able to plan their daily schedules to turn wasted minutes into productive time. Certainly nothing else a coach does can have a greater effect on the players and help him or her to know them better than these personal discussions.

In team discussions, the coach can explain rules and regulations and the reasons behind them. The coach can also explain the philosophy behind his or her coaching and playing techniques and can develop team aspirations. Also, such discussions keep open lines of communication: When supported by fellow team members, a player can bring up problems that might otherwise go unmentioned and inhibit performance.

Figure 3.3 *Pep talks, if not overused, are an effective technique for motivating athletes.*

Pep Talks

Pep talks are an important technique for motivating athletes, and a coach should give them at appropriate times. If they are not given as a matter of course before and after each game, and at every halftime, pep talks can be very effective.

The legendary tale of Knute Rockne and his plea of winning the game for the "Gipper" is part of the romance associated with a coach's ability to stir the players. George Gipp, whom Coach Rockne called his greatest player, was the leader of the 1919 and 1920 undefeated Notre Dame football teams. He was known as a superstar and became an all-American in 1920. During the 1920 season, he became ill with pneumonia and was hospitalized. Without permission, he left his hospital bed while running a temperature of 102°, and appeared for a game against Northwestern (where his talents weren't really needed because Notre Dame won easily, 33–7). Because of the clamor of the fans he was allowed to participate. Playing, however, aggravated his illness so that he died a few weeks later at the age of twenty-three. During the 1928 season, Notre Dame was experiencing one of its few poor seasons. The team had lost two games prior to its traditional game with Army, then undefeated and heavily favored. In the pregame talk, Coach Knute Rockne tearfully related what George Gipp had said on his deathbed: "Sometime when the going is real tough, win just one for the Gipper" (9). Notre Dame won, 12–6. In another famous pep talk, Rockne prodded his players to "charge through that door to victory." The first players through the door ran directly into the swimming pool.

The coach must evaluate the purposes of pep talks and use them accordingly. When a team is getting ready to meet a traditional rival, a pep talk will do little good, for the athletes are usually excited sheerly by the approaching contest. In some cases, it is necessary for a coach to reverse the usual tone of his talks and calm the players; in other instances, when a team is lethargic or has a casual attitude about a game and needs to be jolted into action, the coach may find it necessary to berate the players for their lack of effort. On special occasions, the coach can help the athletes by having a former star player return and speak to the team members.

As an adjunct to motivational techniques, a coach might find it helpful to keep a diary of how certain situations were handled and their success. This information might prevent a repetition of mistakes and loss of valuable time when working with a future team or player.

The Importance of Tension Levels

"They were high as kites" or "they were flat as pancakes" are expressions that coaches have used for years to express their athletes' levels of tension or emotion before a contest. In all sports, a certain amount of tension is essential for an athlete to realize the best possible performance. Thus practice sessions too must create tension for players to acquire a high level of skill. However, extreme tension can hinder a player's drive toward a goal and cause a breakdown in performance. Too much tension has been compared to a thief in the night. It can steal the skill of the individual who is not mentally prepared. Thus an important decision for a coach to consider is the optimum level of tension for a particular sport.

Sports that primarily involve simple motor skills—and the elements of strength and power—normally are performed best when there is a high level of tension. The opposite is true for those sports that involve a great deal of finesse and fine muscle coordination (31). In following these general rules, of course, a coach must consider that individuals react in different ways: Some players might need the level of tension reduced; others might perform better under greater stress.

Also, a coach must be sensitive to the tension build-up that takes place in athletes before a game and be able to recognize the ways players individually achieve the proper mental approach. One might need solitude and a chance to think deeply about the task at hand; another may have to be around fellow teammates and engage in some horseplay to release tension. A coach's pregame plans and conduct must take these differences into consideration. The coach who has insight into players' individual needs can help the team perform at its highest ability.

Vince Lombardi was a coach who dealt beautifully with the differences in his team's personalities and tension levels: Some players he berated unmercifully, while he ignored others. He gave some performers lavish praise, but others received merely an approving glance. Lombardi's approach resulted in each athlete giving a superior performance.

It is valuable for a coach to realize that inexperienced players generally approach games with a great deal of personal tension, and he or she should try to allay their fears and reduce the tension level. Experienced players may have a casual attitude about a game and therefore may be too relaxed to perform up to expectation. In this case, the coach must arouse their competitive urge by creating more tension for them.

A coach can increase the level of tension by quoting to his team derogatory statements made about the team or an individual by opponents or opposition coaches. Focusing on the abilities of the opponent also can achieve the same result—an increased desire to fight and win. Too much emphasis on the opposition's strength may make a team feel beaten before it even plays, but a coach may feel that some goading is necessary to create in the team the determination to prove its own superiority.

Tension levels can be decreased by maintaining a sense of normality. Familiar game plans and plays usually lower tension levels, since players feel comfortable with them. Introducing a new play or a special technique generally increases the players' emotional stress. One famous coach has often commented that he doesn't worry about his opponent's playing style or preparations for a game against his team. He is concerned mainly about perfecting his own team's abilities and the variety of techniques they can use to meet any situation (40).

Mental Preparation

One of the common expressions voiced by professional athletes after a losing effort is, "We weren't ready mentally for this contest." Mental preparation should be a major concern for coaches at all levels of competition.

George Haines, a very successful head coach for the U.S. Olympic men's and women's swim teams, declares, "The approach to an effort goes hand in hand with being 100 percent physically prepared. After a swimmer is in top shape, winning is close to a 90 percent mental effort" (15). Dick Jockums, former coach at California State University at Long Beach indicates, "Winning is 90 percent mental and 10 percent physical, just as training is 90 percent physical and 10 percent mental. The barriers are always psychological in meets as well as in workouts. Without conquering the barriers in workouts, one can never conquer them in a meet" (15). Don Sutton, a star Los Angeles Dodger pitcher contends, "In a business like major league baseball, most of us have similar athletic abilities. The differences are mental and emotional, and the big thing is mental preparation. That's where everything starts: the poise, the confidence, the concentration" (27). Patti Johnson, the nation's leading woman hurdler in 1974 said, "Once you're physically capable of winning a gold medal, the rest is 90 percent mental attitude" (27). Charlie Cowan, a star tackle for the Los Angeles Rams, in commenting about mental preparation said, ". . . you can have good practices and pay close attention to the films and still play a bad game if you don't nail things down mentally. The mental part is the most important thing in football or any sport" (27).

Mental preparation involves the athlete's attitude toward good technique, temperament, self-confidence, concentration, motivation, and goals including intrinsic and extrinsic achievement. Confidence and concentration seem to be the key factors. These can be implemented by the coach who provides a suitable learning atmosphere, one that allows both physical and mental rehearsal by the athlete. Physical rehearsal is part of the automation needed for the complex series of movements when executing a given technique. The details are taught on the practice field. Mental rehearsal is essential because it augments the key intangibles that make up the athlete's mental attitude and allows for adjustment in the event when adversity takes place. This rehearsal is especially important for those who participate in individual sports such as golf and those who are expected to be leaders of an activity such as a football quarterback.

John Ralston, former head football coach at Stanford University and the Denver Broncos, sums up the importance of mental preparation by saying, ". . . assuming the size, speed, and willingness to hit other people 'is equal,' the mental part is the winning edge. Whatever you vividly imagine, ardently desire, sincerely believe and enthusiastically act upon must come to pass" (27).

Competition and Motivation

The American dream was built on the concept that individuals, through their own efforts, should be able to achieve whatever status, privileges, or power they want. No feature of American culture has been treasured more highly (18). This philosophy, coupled with an individual's innate need to succeed, forms the arena of athletic competition. Athletes have been glorified as individuals who are able to master great challenges and succeed against overwhelming odds.

In an individual sport, an athlete is strictly alone, competing against both the skill of an opponent or a previous score or mark. The athlete in an individual sport is always in competition with self and is motivated by self-improvement. Team sports involve cooperation as well as competition. A coach may comment that a particular player is a "team player and not concerned about individual achievements." Actually, within the team, there is strong competition for each position. This competition should be as intense as possible to make players perform at a high level. But team members must cooperate and work as a unit if the team is to compete successfully against opponents.

Athletic competition provides an arena for individuals at all levels to realize some of their ambitions and be motivated to other achievements. In competition against their own previous score or against other skilled athletes, players learn how to react to stress, how to evaluate strengths and weaknesses, and—occasionally—how to lose. Competitive athletics teach young people that defeat can bring feelings of frustration and inferiority, thus a coach must impress the athlete that success it measured, not by victories or losses, but by whether one has performed to maximum ability.

Practice Sessions and Motivation

Young people who participate in athletics generally possess a great deal of vigor and above-average motor skills. But they also show differences in maturation—in height, weight, strength, coordination, and speed—characteristics that a coach can easily recognize. A coach also must realize that individuals differ in such qualities as temperament, emotional maturity, and the "fighting spirit." In planning practice sessions, a coach must consider all these variables and adopt methods that provide the incentive for each athlete to work at his or her maximum level of performance.

A coach planning football practice sessions is faced with a problem when one of the starting guards is a mature, quick seventeen-year-old weighing only 140 pounds and whose key attribute on the field is aggressiveness, and the other guard is a large, undeveloped fifteen-year-old weighing 210

Figure 3.4 *The athlete in an individual's sport competes. Team sports require cooperation as well as competition.*

pounds and possessing a jovial nature that tends to be passive on the playing field. Obviously, the same practice plans will not work for both players. But each player can receive the practice and coaching suitable to him, if the

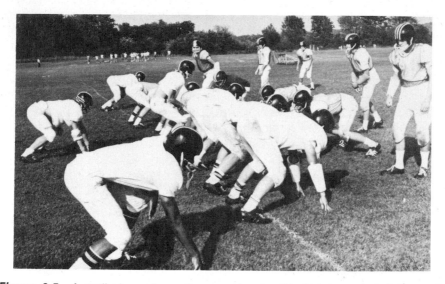

Figure 3.5 *A well-planned practice session is directed toward definite goals, which a coach should tell his players beforehand.*

coach puts the smaller, more aggressive guard with other quick, naturally tough players for practice and puts the large, more passive guard in a group of players with whom the coach can spend more time teaching skills and vocally encouraging more effort. In this way, each guard can get what he needs to improve without interrupting players of different abilities.

During practice sessions it is the coach's right and responsibility to demand excellence from the players, for only by making demands on them will he or she be able to motivate the athletes to improve their performances. Two primary ingredients of excellence are discipline and dedication to purpose (2). Discipline can be dictated by the coach, or it can be self-imposed by an athlete; all members of a team must be dedicated not only to specified team goals but also to their personal aims. A coach should conduct practice sessions in an atmosphere that fosters these ingredients and allows each athlete to use his or her potential most effectively.

To perfect athletic skills often requires endless repetition, practicing until certain actions and reactions become automatic. This sort of drill becomes very tedious, and the level of motivation can drop drastically unless a coach provides new approaches and circumstances that foster the same skill development. It is important for a coach to remain sensitive to this situation and plan practice sessions that are interesting. A good basketball coach varies the shooting drills by adding contests between groups of players, spot shooting, and games such as basketball golf, which is played with eighteen spots to shoot from. (The player who takes the lowest total number of shots to make the eighteen baskets wins.) The coach should also keep in mind the need for tension in order to motivate the players, and although practice sessions should be fun, they should not be conducted in such a relaxed mood that incentive disappears.

Well-planned practices are directed toward definite objectives, which a coach can announce beforehand. After each session is over the coach should discuss with the players whether and how well these objectives were achieved. In football, for example, a coach might ask every player to achieve the objective of five clean open-field tackles within a practice session; after each tackle, the coach can say whether it was good or bad and explain why. Practice objectives should be within the reach of all players, and when they are realized each athlete's motivation to succeed remains high. Everyone—not just the first team—should be involved so that no player becomes bored and loses enthusiasm for the sport and the team activity.

One of the most successful coaching techniques for conducting a practice session is to provide variety and not dwell on any one item too long. Normally, a well-planned session for any sport takes no more than two hours. Interminable practice sessions, with a coach calling for "just one more play, one more lap, one more jump" achieve little and more often than not end with injuries. Every coach should use a time schedule so that he or she does not place undue importance on an unsuccessful drill. Motivating athletes should be the primary objective.

Many texts on athletics written by successful coaches contain examples of planned practice sessions that can be very helpful to inexperienced coaches. Basically, the plans involve a practice outline that encompasses an entire season and gives detailed daily schedules according to the development of the squad members as individuals and as a team. (See Figure 3.6.) In his book *Practical Modern Basketball,* Coach John Wooden provides excellent samples that can be adapted for most sports (40).

Figure 3.6 *Sample plans for preseason and inseason practice sessions.*

Basketball Season 1975

1. Six weeks of preseason practice sessions; two hours each day.
   a. First week: general conditioning; fundamental skills.
   b. Second week: continued conditioning with all players passing the mile run; more work on fundamentals; introduce the pattern offense.
   c. Third week: reduce conditioning work; increase work on fundamental skills and on pattern offense; introduce the defense.
   d. Fourth week: drills on fundamental skills; separate offense and work on details; increase work on defense by introducing pressing styles.
   e. Fifth week: fundamentals; establish teams; continue work on offense and defense; scrimmage a great deal.
   f. Sixth week: introduce special situations such as jump ball, out of bounds, free throws; continue work on fundamentals; perfect offense and defense.

2. Twelve weeks of in-season practice sessions; one and a half hours a day. Continue fundamental drills; introduce scouting reports and game plans prior to games; reduce hard-driving and fatigue-type practice sessions; work for perfection; increase shooting skills.

Practice session for Monday, second week of preseason

3:00–3:15 Free shooting and warm-up
3:15–3:25 Grapevine weave
3:25–3:45 Introduce basic pattern offense
3:45–4:15 Run players through movements of basic pattern offense
4:15–4:30 Break pattern into basic segments and have the position player perform moves that are part of their responsibilities
4:30–4:40 Lay-in drills
4:40–4:45 Free-throw shooting, one and one
4:45–5:00 Shooting drills
5:00–   Players run mile before shower; no emphasis on time

Practice session for Thursday, second week of season

3:00–3:10 Lay-in drills
3:10–3:20 Grapevine weave
3:20–4:00 Introduce opponents' offense and defense with our reserve team imitating them; set our defense
4:00–4:15 Review our offense against opponents' and run unopposed
4:15–4:30 Shooting drills (including free throwing)

Players dismissed but gym open for those who feel they need more work on shooting. *Save efforts for game night!*

Summary

Motivation is one of the major ingredients for achieving success in athletics. In recent years, some psychologists have developed psychometric techniques to assess personality traits and motivational factors affecting successful athletes. These psychometric assessments can help make a coach aware of players' individual strengths and weaknesses; however, they also possess an inherent danger in that they can create prejudices or mirror failures.

A coach can also use the perceptual method of dealing with the students' motivation. By observing a player's behavior and determining his or her needs, the coach can help the athlete improve performance.

Each athlete has his or her own motivational drive. A combination of incentives can provoke greater achievements. Among the most common sources of motivation in high school athletes are personal recognition, ego-reinforcement, self-realization, development of a sense of adequacy, proof of masculinity, fear, material gain, the need for an emotional outlet, the need for purely physical movement, physical fitness, stress addiction, and personal pride.

If an athlete is to realize his or her potential, he or she should have a positive attitude. This attitude can be developed through setting goals, through encouraging desire, confidence, and determination, and through planning.

Some of the successful techniques for developing motivation at the high school level are praise, threat of punishment, diversion from failure, gimmicks, use of voice, individual and team discussions, and pep talks.

Tension plays an important part in athletic performance. A certain amount of tension is necessary, but an extreme degree hinders achievement. Since each athlete builds his or her own tension level, the coach must be sensitive to these differences among the players. To determine the ideal level, the coach should rely on experience and apply the general rule that sports involving simple motor skills are performed best under greater stress, while complex sports concerned with fine muscle coordination are played best with a lower degree of tension.

Mental preparation has become recognized as an important consideration in the coaching of athletes. Some coaches feel that after an individual is physically prepared, mental outlook becomes 90 percent of the performance.

Competition and a person's desire to improve are basic parts of the American way of life. Competitive athletics provide a player with the opportunity to succeed and to realize his or her own potential. They also help an individual to develop self-awareness and learn how he or she reacts to stress and challenging situations.

Practice sessions in athletics should provide excitement and point out areas that need improvement. These sessions should be well planned and lively and involve all members of a team. During practice it is the coach's responsibility to demand excellence, which is realized through discipline and dedication to purpose. The coach should be concerned primarily with motivating the athletes to perform to the best of their abilities.

References

1. Alderman, Richard. "Incentive Motivation in Sport: An Interpretive Speculation on Research Opportunities." *Sports Coaching,* Australian Government Publishing Service, Canberra, 1976, 129–138.
2. Atkinson, John W. *Motives in Fantasy, Action and Society.* Princeton, N.J.: D. Van Nostrand, 1968.
3. ——— and Norman T. Feather. *A Theory of Achievement Motivation.* New York: John Wiley, 1966.

4. Bannister, Roger. *First Four Minutes.* London: Corgi Special, 1957.
5. ———. *The Four Minute Mile.* New York: Dodd Mead, 1955.
6. Biehler, Robert F. *Psychology Applied to Teaching.* Boston: Houghton Mifflin, 1971.
7. Birch, David and Joseph Veroff. *Motivation: A Study of Action.* Belmont, Calif.: Brooks/Cole, 1966.
8. Bolles, Robert C. *Theory of Motivation.* New York: Harper & Row, 1967.
9. Claassen, Harold, and Steve Boda, Jr. *Ronald Encyclopedia of Football.* New York: Ronald Press, 1960, 19.
10. Combs, Arthur W., and Donald Snygg. *Individual Behavior, A Perceptual Approach to Behavior.* Rev. ed. New York: Harper & Row, 1959.
11. Counsilman, James E. "A Philosophy of Motivating Athletes." *The American Football Coaches Association—Summer Manual,* 1977, 86–90.
12. Cratty, Bryand J. *Psychology in Contemporary Sport: Guidelines for Coaches and Athletes.* Englewood Cliffs, N.J.: Prentice-Hall, 1973.
13. ———. *Psychology and Physical Activity.* Englewood Cliffs, N.J.: Prentice-Hall, 1968.
14. Donohue, J. "Basketball: When Coaching Girls—Are Flowers and Sweet Really Necessary?" *Sport and Fitness Instructor* (February 1974), 5.
15. Finneran, Carolyn. "A Pool of Olympic Resources." *The Olympian,* 4:9 (June 1978), 8–9.
16. Fisher, A. Craig., ed. *Psychology of Sport, Issues and Insights.* Palo Alto, Calif.: Mayfield, 1976.
17. Frost, Reuben B. *Psychological Concepts Applied to Physical Education and Coaching.* Reading, Mass.: Addison-Wesley, 1971.
18. Gardner, John. *Excellence.* New York: Harper & Row, 1961.
19. Goldfast, Joseph. "Motivational Psychology in Coaching." *Scholastic Coach,* 37:6 (February 1968), 54.
20. Green, Ted. There's Nothing Like the Euphoria of Accomplishment." *Los Angeles Times,* part 3 (June 5, 1974), 1, 10.
21. Locke, Edwin A. "The Relationship of Task Success to Task Liking and Satisfaction." *Jr. Applied Psychology,* 5 (1965), 379–385.
22. Maltz, Maxwell. *Psycho-cybernetics.* Englewood Cliffs, N.J.: Prentice-Hall, 1960.
23. Martens, Ranier. "Influences of Participation Motivation on Success and Satisfaction in Team Performance." *Research Quarterly,* 41:4 (December 1970), 510.
24. Maslow, Abraham H. *Motivation and Personality.* New York: Harper & Row, 1970.
25. Neal, Patsy E., and Thomas A. Tutko. *Coaching Girls and Women: Psychological Perspectives.* Boston: Allyn & Bacon, 1975.
26. Newell, Pete, and John Bennington. *Basketball Methods.* New York: Ronald Press, 1962.
27. Oates, Bob. "The Brain Game." *Los Angeles Times,* part 3 (May 7, 1974), 1, 5–6.
28. ——— "Prothro: Recognition as Important as Money." *Los Angeles Times,* Section D (February 27, 1972), 1.
29. Ogilvie, Bruce C., and Thomas A. Tutko. *Problem Athletes and How to Handle Them.* London: Pelham Books, 1966.
30. Ralston, John, Mike White, and Stanley Wilson. *Coaching Today's Athlete.* Palo Alto, Calif.: National Press Books, 1971.

31. Ryan, Dean E. "Competition Performances in Relation to Achievement Motivation and Anxiety." Paper presented at the Annual American Association for Health, Physical Education, and Recreation Convention. Minneapolis, Minnesota (1961).
32. Singer, Robert T. *Coaching Athletics and Psychology*. New York: McGraw-Hill, 1972.
33. Slovenko, Ralph, and James A. Knight. *Motivation in Play Games and Sports*. Springfield, Ill.: Thomas, 1967.
34. Strickland, Bonnie R., and Orsin Jenkins. "Simple Motor Performance Under Positive and Negative Approval Motivation." *Perceptual and Motor Skills,* 19 (October 1964), 599–605.
35. Takeda, Dr. Ken. "Psychological Principles of Coaching." *The American Football Coaches Association Proceedings* (1978), 79–83.
36. Tutko, Thomas A., Leland P. Lyon, and Bruce C. Ogilvie. *The Athletic Motivation Program—Preliminary Technical Manual.* Chicago: Science Research Associates, 1977, 17–19.
37. Tutko, Thomas A., and Jack W. Richards. *Psychology of Coaching.* Boston: Allyn & Bacon, 1971.
38. Veller, Donald. "The Big Question: Praise or Punishment." *Athletic Journal,* 47: 6 (February 1968), 40.
39. Voelz, Chris. *Motivation in Coaching a Team Sport.* Washington, D.C.: AAHPER, 1976.
40. Wooden, John R. *Practical Modern Basketball.* New York: Ronald Press, 1966.

Principles of Conditioning 4

"Bro-thur! Has he seen a lot of kickoffs!"

Development of a sound conditioning program should be a major concern of every high school coach, since physical fitness is essential for a player's successful performance. In preparing athletes for competition, the coach should take into account the nature of the sport involved and the individual conditioning of each player. The coach should know and explain the bodily functions related to the sport and concentrate on techniques that help the athletes achieve their best performances.

Often coaches use conditioning methods that have been handed down—without knowing why they are employed. A good example is the coach who requires a long-distance run for qualification on a team that basically employs short bursts of speed. There is no question that the ability to run a long distance indicates good physical condition, but there is little correlation between this type of fitness and the type needed for sports that do not involve long-distance performance. Many professional football coaches require that the players run a mile or longer within a limited time. Sometimes there is no allowance made for different size or weight. Interscholastic coaches often duplicate such a practice. Traditionally, many high school football coaches conclude their practice sessions with a number of one hundred yard sprints. They claim they want to have all their players in top physical condition, and they want to send them into the showers feeling tired. Yet, how many times does a football player run one hundred yards at full speed during the course of the game? Such a long-distance program often results in poor individual effort, which can only have a detrimental effect. This is especially true for the larger interior lineman. It would be much more meaningful to end the practice with short bursts of all-out speed for ten to forty yards, rather than the traditional one hundred effort. The shorter distance allows the use of correct running form and a total expenditure of energy. The longer distance may produce poor running form and create a feeling of guilt in the player. These individuals know that they are not putting out 100 percent effort the entire distance.

Objectives

This chapter deals with the following aspects of conditioning programs:

1. Variance among conditioning programs
2. Stength, flexibility, and endurance
3. Medical examinations
4. Warm-up procedures
5. Effects of prolonged training
6. Off-season conditioning
7. Pre-season conditioning
8. In-season conditioning
9. Post-season conditioning
10. Nutrition
11. Fluids in conditioning
12. Positive mental attitudes of the players

Variance among Conditioning Programs

It is generally understood that the skills and conditioning necessary for participation in one sport are different from the skills and conditioning required for other athletic activities. For instance, the football player requires strength, endurance, and hard muscles. He must be able to hit and be hit. To achieve this condition, he engages in rough, combative drills. On the other hand the golfer requires strength and endurance. He engages in leg and body exercises that provide strength but not necessarily hard muscles (although it is acknowledged they will be firm). Therefore, conditioning programs also should vary, and the high school coach must design practice programs that help in developing each player's greatest skill and optimum level of physical fitness for a particular sport.

It is important for the coach to understand the various skills involved in the sport (such as shooting, dribbling, screening, defensive play in basketball), what type of efforts are needed for good performance, and how to attain proficiency. Although actual participation in a sport is the best way for a player to learn skills, it does not necessarily develop all the aspects of strength and fitness he or she needs to perform at a maximum level of ability. Basketball involves a geat deal of jumping, but repeated jumps, although they will improve the overall condition of the player, will not necessarily increase jumping ability. To do this, the player must engage in a resistance training exercise to strengthen the legs. Many basketball coaches realize the necessity for such work and design drills that individuals engage in throughout the entire year. This is referred to as "specificity of training."

The conditioning program for a contact sport like football should vary a great deal from the program for a non-contact sport such as gymnastics. Also, within a given activity there may be a wide difference of individual requirements. A gymnast who performs on the rings or highbar must have tremendous arm and shoulder strength. However, development of leg size and strength actually can be detrimental: Overdevelopment and extra weight of the lower body put a greater demand on the upper body. Although the gymnast must have a certain amount of muscle strength in all parts of the body to perform well, he or she should concentrate on developing strength in arms, shoulders, and upper back.

Strength, Flexibility, and Endurance

Although physiologists differ on what they believe is the most important component of fitness, they seem to agree that fitness basically involves strength, flexibility, and muscular and cardiorespiratory endurance. Each of these physical attributes can be improved through judicious training. An

Figure 4.1 *The essentials of physical fitness are strength, flexibility, and muscular and cardiorespiratory endurance.*

athlete's efficiency in each area is essential in developing athletic skill. A person who lacks the degree of fitness required for a certain activity may develop habits that actually hamper performance.

Fitness is defined as "the ability to carry out daily tasks with vigor and alertness, without undue fatigue, and with ample energy to enjoy leisure time pursuits and to meet unforeseen emergencies" (6). This description can be interpreted in many ways within the field of athletics. Athletes who are involved in active sports require a different kind of fitness from those participating in less vigorous activities: the physiological demands on a football player are very different from those required of an archer. Also, although a player is in good condition for one vigorous sport, he or she is not necessarily fit to perform another one that is demanding in another way. When a football player attempts to participate in boxing or wrestling, he soon becomes tired, because his body is not conditioned for other types of strenuous activity.

Strength

Strength is perhaps the most important aspect of fitness; it is not an isolated factor but is related to flexibility and endurance. In conditioning programs today, increased emphasis is being placed on strength, the ability of the muscular system to exert force, which is achieved by contraction of the muscles. Although participation in a sport helps to condition an athlete, it is necessary for him or her to develop strength through a systematic program. The programs coaches currently are using vary in concept and nature, but they generally involve the "overload principle," which means that a player's muscles are required to respond to gradually increased amounts of resistance. An increase in strenuous demand strengthens muscles and enables them to react with greater force. This increase is commonly termed progressive resistance.

There are two basic kinds of muscle groupings involved in the process: agonistic and antagonistic. The agonistic muscles are concerned primarily with the exertion of force. They may be involved in the motion of throwing a weight like the discus or javelin; they also may be used to execute blows such as those given in a boxing match or in a football block or tackle.

The antagonistic muscles are those that oppose the force being exerted by agonistic muscles. To do this, an antagonistic muscle must be able to relax and stretch to a degree equal to the agonistic muscle's contraction. If an antagonistic muscle fails to react properly, it can be torn, and the athlete's performance can be impaired. When an agonistic muscle contracts, an antagonistic muscle must relax; and when an antagonistic muscle contracts, an agonistic muscle relaxes. There is a trading of roles. Contraction and relaxation are best performed when the temperature of the muscles involved is higher than normal. This increase in temperature, which varies according to individual differences, can be created by proper warm-up procedures.

Dr. Nicholas Aspiotis, a physiology professor at the Greek University of Thessaloniki, gave a talk to the International Olympic Academy in 1969. In discussing the importance of strength as related to athletic performance, he made some interesting observations about the use of muscles (1).

1. Muscles that have been inactive for a period of time will not exert the maximum force upon the first contraction. The force of contraction will usually get greater until the fifth or sixth contraction when maximum strength is exerted. Continuous contractions will become progressively [weaker] dependent upon the degree of fitness.
2. Decreasing the quantity of water contained within the muscle cell allows a greater contractibility. [Reducing the intake of salt and water reduces water in the cells, which allows the cells to contract more because they aren't limited by what they contain and this in turn allows the muscle to contract more.]
3. Methodical training procedures allow the muscle's motor cells to be stimulated more easily at the moment an athletic effort is required for performance. [Motor cells stimulated through repetition are more easily stimulated; this is the value of going through an entire movement easily in warm-up before performing an all-out effort.]
4. Anger brings about the secretion of adrenalin. This in turn reacts upon the blood vessels of the muscles, causing them to enlarge. The enlarged vessels thus carry

a greater quantity of blood to the muscles, and this [action] is directly related to fitness and strength [because it increases the efficiency of muscular glycogenolysis].

These facts are extremely important for a coach to know. He or she also should explain them to athletes so they will understand the conditioning process. In many ways high school coaches—and players—should become "athletic scientists" with systematic knowledge of basic body functions. This information results in an intelligent approach to training procedures.

Flexibility

Flexibility is an important part of physical performance. Basically, flexibility refers to the range of motion of body parts. Athletic skills, such as jump shots in basketball, require a free flow of motion and a great degree of pliancy. Each sports activity requires a certain observable level of flexibility. A player who is too stiff may be hampered in performance; also, strange as it may seem, a player who is too flexible may also lack the ability for good performance in certain activities. A basketball player whose wrists and fingers are "double jointed" cannot control his or her shooting well because shooting baskets requires a firmness for the "explosion."

Each person's flexibility depends somewhat on his or her particular body structure. Essentially there are three body types: ectomorph (long and slender), mesomorph (muscular), endomorph (squat and fat). If a sports activity like crew or running hurdles is best performed by a long lean athlete, a coach should be careful about encouraging a short, chunky individual to engage in it. However, flexibility is a body function that can be developed through the judicious use of conditioning techniques. There are many cases of determined athletes who, although they lacked the body structure recognized as proper for an activity, were able to excel in the sport. Rocky Marciano did not have the body structure considered best for boxing. He was short and round, yet he became a world heavyweight boxing champion.

Endurance

Endurance is essential to good athletic performances. It involves both the muscular and cardiorespiratory systems. Endurance is the body's ability to sustain long periods of activity without becoming fatigued. Conditioning of the muscular and cardiorespiratory systems reduces the amount of energy the body must exert to perform a specific task and delays the onset of fatigue.

Muscular endurance is achieved by exercise. It involves basic strength that has been developed by isometric or isotonic contractions. These different methods might develop similar amounts of strength, but they can result in different degrees of muscular endurance. Therefore the two systems should be understood by the coach who is developing a conditioning program.

Cardiorespiratory endurance and efficiency generally are improved by all forms of vigorous activity. When the heart beats faster, it produces a greater stroke volume of blood and thus increases the lungs' ability to exchange more oxygen for metabolic waste materials (such as lactic acid) in the blood stream.

Physiologists are aware of the problems created by the build-up of lactic acid or "fatigue toxin" in the muscles. When the muscles reach their maximum tolerance level of lactic acid, they develop an oxygen debt, and a slowing of activity results. This is basically termed *anerobic* (without O_2) *conditioning.* This oxygen debt can be repaid by an efficient cardiorespiratory system (10). Continuous consumption of oxygen turns a small percentage of lactic acid back into glycogen, which is actually stored energy.

Developing a player's cardiorespiratory systems to high levels of efficiency and endurance should be one of the coach's major concerns in conditioning. A well-rounded running program (jogging, short sprints, long sprints, distance running) can help achieve this endurance (21). The conditioning program should fit the sport.

Medical Examinations

Prior to participation in any high school sport, an athlete should be required to undergo a thorough medical examination, not merely a "cough and temp exam." Many athletes and coaches regard medical exams as nuisances; however, physicals protect both the player and the coach because they can uncover defects (such as a rheumatic heart problem) or problems that could prove harmful to the player under the stress of a vigorous athletic program (21). The examination should cover cardiorespiratory conditions, overweight or underweight problems, and all other aspects that relate to the vigorous activity involved in athletics. If the coach knows a player's medical history and condition, he or she can devise an intelligent conditioning program to help the athlete achieve better fitness. Without such information, the coach may advocate a program that results in damage to the athlete.

Frank Jackson, a basketball player, was found to have a body that burned cells at a high metabolic rate. He constantly lost excess weight during the season and became very weak and subject to illness. When the cause was determined and explained to him and the squad, he reduced his participation in drills. For example, when the squad worked on lay-in drills, he limited his number of turns. Taking his turn and then going to the side of the court was at first a psychological problem, but after a time the change was accomplished with both his approval and the squad's, and his condition improved.

The American Medical Association (AMA) has recognized the need for preventing injuries in high school athletic programs throughout the nation and actively supports the functions of "sports medicine." The AMA also has urged that boards of education and state departments of health establish medical units in every school that has a sports program. In addition, because of the unique nature of athletic injuries, the AMA advocates that medical schools be aware of the need to train health coordinators (trainers) and specialists in athletic medicine. Because some physicians may not be trained to deal specifically with athletic injuries, many doctors advocate the development of a particular curriculum for physicians who want to specialize in the care and prevention of athletic injuries. It is hoped that such training will result in the best possible medical care for athletes.

Dr. Fred Allman and the Atlanta, Georgia, school system have established an ideal system. There is one medical center for all schools. Each school, however, has a training room with equipment and trained personnel to handle it. Athletes on rehabilitation and prevention programs are diagnosed at the center, but treated at their school. Doctors are responsible for all medical problems.

Warm-up Procedures

There is a wide variety of opinion among coaches, athletic trainers, and athletes regarding warm-up techniques. Some feel that short sessions and relaxed warm-up procedures are best. For example, a sprinter might limit warm-up activities to merely stretching exercises (toe touches, trunk bends, squats) and perhaps jogging a bit before actual competition. In contrast to this view is the belief that extensive warm-up procedures are more desirable: A miler who begins with stretching and general body activity (calisthenics) then may run a mile (some run at three-quarters of their mile speed, then allow twenty minutes' rest) to warm up for a race. Although there is controversy about the methods and the extent of warm-up, it generally is agreed that some form of movement prior to competition reduces the possibility of strain or muscle tears (24). The main idea, however, is to flex the muscles about to be used.

Certain conditions ideally result from warm-up activities and contribute to athletic performance: Tendons are stretched and the range of motion in the joints of the body increased; body and deep muscle temperature is raised, which seems to influence the ability of the muscles to relax; blood circulation is increased, and more oxygen is carried to active muscles; muscle resistance is decreased and the ability of the muscles to contract is consequently increased; the athlete is mentally readied for activity through a rehearsal of the neuromuscular pattern to be used.

Though the value of a warm-up session to bring about these conditions is disputed, coaches and athletes generally recognize the importance of mental preparation for maximum performance. If certain warm-up procedures produce nothing more than a confident mental attitude, a coach is justified in using them.

Many teenage athletes fail to engage in enough warm-up exercises because they want to save themselves for actual competition. A high school coach has a responsibility to explain properly the value of an extensive warm-up and to provide players with correct techniques. It is important to remember that the amount of exercise necessary for an adequate warm-up varies with each athlete and with the type of sport.

Recommended Procedures

For most activities, the normal warm-up period is about twenty minutes. Recommended procedures include starting with static stretching, an exercise that involves the contraction and relaxation of muscles and increases the elasticity of muscles and tendons. This preliminary action is needed to prevent muscle strains and tears; it is extremely important in sports like football where athletes are active for a time on a defensive or offensive unit and then relax when the other unit takes over. Muscle tears can be avoided if a player engages in a short period of stretching between periods of activity. A coach should encourage athletes who temporarily are taken out of action to do some stretching exercises before they return to participation.

Jogging or easy running normally follows the static stretching warm-up procedure. This activity stimulates the cardiorespiratory system, which is strained in most active sports. After jogging or running, players should do general body exercises, which usually take the form of calisthenics commonly associated with athletics. Especially in team sports, exercises are most effectively done by the group as a whole. Group pressure makes the individual work harder. (Few individuals can condition themselves completely on their own; there are only a few Jim Ryuns in the world.) This phase of the warm-up should end with an activity that includes the skills needed for competition, like shooting baskets, and that charges up the players for the actual contest.

One way of telling when an athlete is warmed up is whether he or she is perspiring in a light sweat. However, the coach should recognize individual differences among the players, since some people perspire with a minimum of activity, whereas others require a great deal of exertion before they perspire. Warm-ups should be timed so that the athletes do not waste valuable energy.

Also, the coach must deal with the question of how long before actual competition warm-up procedures should take place. He or she should consider the nature of the activity, whether it is to be played indoors or outdoors, climatic conditions of heat or cold, and individual player differences such as maturity, body type, and age. It is generally agreed that an athlete never should start competitive activity with an oxygen debt created by the warm-up procedures. Some rest following the warm-up period produces the best performance. Of course, the type of activity and warm-up procedures dictates the length of the rest period: Most athletes participating in a physically demanding sport need approximately fifteen minutes of rest before they can perform well in active competition.

Judicious warm-up procedures influence a player's endurance and in some instances give an opportunity to get a "second wind." Basically, proper warm-up techniques seem to affect endurance, because they set in motion the whole process of body functions involved in strenuous muscular effort and enable the player to sustain activity for a longer period of time. Keeping basketball players in shape during the week or ten days of exam time, usually in mid-season, is difficult because regular workouts are impossible. But if the players come to the gym for a short, fifteen- to twenty-minute session, just enough to break a bead of perspiration, then their conditioning generally stays with them.

The Overload Technique

Many coaches and athletes advocate the "overload" technique during warm-up sessions. If an athlete practices with an instrument that is heavier than the one actually used, he or she may perform better in competition. Some baseball players warm up with weighted bats, and some athletes in track and field use a heavier shot or discus for practice. Weighted basketball shoes were introduced for practice sessions with the expectation that players would improve their endurance and jumping ability. However, an experiment at the University of California at Santa Barbara proved that the overload technique does not necessarily work. Half of the basketball team used regular shoes and half used weighted shoes. The results showed that those using the weighted shoes did not increase their vertical jumping ability or endurance as much as those players using regular shoes did.

Effects of Prolonged Training

It generally has been thought that excellent athletic performance can be achieved by prolonged periods of training and year-round involvement in one particular sport. Therefore, specialization and dedication to one sport have become an established pattern for athletes who want to excel. Although this specialized involvement is undeniably productive, the attitude tends to deny teenage athletes an opportunity to participate in a well-rounded athletic program. In many schools, it is unusual to find an athlete who has letters in more than one sport; only in schools where limited enrollments demand that students participate in more than one sport are dual letter holders still generally found.

One of the undesirable effects of specialization and prolonged activity in one sport is that the athlete becomes fed up and bored with the sport. Debbie Meyers, one of the outstanding U.S. swimmers at the 1968 Olympic games, was asked the question, "What do you think of training?" Her response showed disgust and distaste for the long periods of endless laps and the lack of any enjoyment in the activity in which she had become so proficient (23). Although training methods had resulted in excellent performance, they had taken all the fun out of swimming.

Any coach who advocates a year-round training program for athletes should realize the need for providing a great deal of positive motivation to make the players want to participate.

Off-season Conditioning

Many high school coaches believe that in the off-season from a major sport an athlete should participate in an athletic activity that is closely related to the one he or she wants to excel in. For instance, some football coaches encourage their players to take up wrestling or a similar sport after the football season is over. Continued activity and exercise maintain fitness throughout the year, and the players are in good shape when football season arrives. Although many coaches advocate participation in other sports because they think athletes will acquire skills that can be transferred to the major sport, this is a faulty concept. The only time a skill from one sport can be transferred to another is when it is used identically in both activities. This again infers the "specificity of training."

Increase of Strength

What then, should be the purpose of the off-season conditioning program? Although it is certainly desirable for an athlete to maintain physical fitness during the off-season, the conditioning merely should be a by-product of the program. The primary objective of off-season conditioning should be to increase players' strength so they can perfect skills necessary for the particular sport.

It is important for the conditioning program to work on developing strength in specific areas and to simulate skills required for competition. A baseball player who wants to increase arm strength should follow a practice routine that resembles throwing, because merely increasing arm strength will not necessarily improve throwing ability. One could use weight (five pounds and then more) in a throwing motion or one could use exergenie or a similar resistance device. Some high school coaches have players throw with a rubber strip (from an old inner tube) nailed to a post or the wall as the resistance. To develop leg strength and improve vertical jumping ability, basketball players should work out in a program that follows the vertical jump, for example, performing jumping exercises while wearing ankle weights or vests.

Strength in itself does not bring athletic excellence. It is meaningless for an athlete to proclaim his or her strength by announcing proudly he or she can bench-press a certain amount of weight, particularly when the movement involved in the bench press does not apply to the sport for which he or she is training. In copying the off-season programs of other sports, football coaches often make the mistake of concentrating on strength for its own sake. They put the entire squad through one conditioning program, regardless of the skills needed for different positions, and express pride in all players' increased strength as an indication of their physiological development. However, this increase in strength often has no relationship to the players' performance during the football season. Each coach must be fully aware of the demands and skills of a particular sport and devise an off-season training program that gives athletes an opportunity to develop strength in specific needed areas.

Adequate Supervision

Adequate supervision should be available at all times during an off-season conditioning program. The coach, an athletic trainer, or some other experienced person, such as a senior athlete who has been through the program, should supervise the activity to correct techniques that might cause injury and to assure athletes that they are doing the proven things to achieve desired results. Teenage athletes need to be encouraged and corrected and generally made to work hard enough to benefit from the conditioning procedures. Inadequate supervision can destroy the purpose of the entire program.

Measurement of Results

A desirable feature of the off-season program is measurement of the results of conditioning techniques. In most programs involving strength, a student can tell if he or she is becoming stronger because the weights become visibly increased. Dynamometers can be used to show increased strength of grip. The athlete working to increase vertical jumping ability can have jump heights measured at regular intervals to note achievement. It is very important for young athletes to know if they are improving; encouragement increases their enthusiasm and stimulates a desire to do even better in the activity.

Pre-season Conditioning

A thorough conditioning program should precede the athletic season so that players are ready for actual competition. In any high school sport, the most dangerous period for possible injury seems to be the first few weeks of the season, when most athletes lack the desirable level of strength, flexibility, endurance, and general good overall condition. Because of this problem, many state high school athletic associations have passed regulations stating the days of training an athlete must have before he or she can participate in competition. In some sports, such as football, a given number of days must be devoted to practice before players can wear contact gear. All coaches should devise drills and activities to improve all aspects of their athletes' condition and thus decrease the danger of injury due to violent contact.

Many coaches request that players report for practice with a certain amount of conditioning obtained from the off-season program. If this level of development truly has been achieved, the athletes can spend more time perfecting specific skills necessary for successful competition. In the absence of such previous conditioning, at least three weeks of training are necessary to develop sufficient strength and endurance for players to tolerate safely the physiological demands of vigorous sports such as football and soccer. Naturally, the amount of time needed and the extent of conditioning differ with each activity; however, it is equally important for golfers, wrestlers, swimmers, and gymnasts to be totally fit to perform well.

In-season Conditioning

Length of Practice Sessions

Once an athlete has attained the desirable level of fitness, he or she no longer needs extensive programs of activity to maintain good condition. Jesse Owens, the United States' track and field hero at the 1936 Olympic games, revealed that he required only approximately forty minutes a day of in-season training (23). Such a limited conditioning program must seem incredible to coaches who believe that prolonged practice periods during the season are essential to maintain proper physiological efficiency. The majority of coaches who advocate extended in-season fitness programs often leave their victories on the practice field.

If athletes are suitably conditioned, once the season starts extensive daily practice sessions are no longer required and actually may produce undesirable physical and mental fatigue. An athlete can maintain muscle tone and general condition if he or she works hard enough to break into a good sweat; if the athlete goes to the showers in a state of complete exhaustion, the practice period has wasted valuable energy that cannot be recovered easily. Practice sessions should be demanding, but they should be designed to produce specific results—perfecting skills, perfecting coordination in team play, and the like. A certain level of achievement must be realized, even if it is only one part of a total program. Overworked and fatigued athletes are subject to a high rate of injury. Those who are properly conditioned have a greater amount of reserve energy and are ready for competition.

The U.S. military academies—Air Force, Army, and Navy—are outstanding examples of how athletic excellence can be achieved with relatively short practice sessions. Because of its full daily schedule, each institution allows only a limited practice time for athletes. Therefore, sessions must be highly organized without long periods of standing around. Although practice time is short, players do not leave the practice field without undergoing vigorous activity if that is what the sport calls for. Coaches and athletes simply make the most efficient use of time and energy.

Strength Maintenance Program

It is important for coaches who are teaching sports that involve a great deal of strength to continue a strength maintenance program during the season. The extent of the in-season program depends on off-season development of strength, the nature of the sport involved, and whether the coach and athletes think the activity will improve performance. Some coaches believe that extensive strength training during the season will "tie up" the athlete, but this is not true. A strength program does have value during the season if athletes limit the number of times they engage in it and the amount of work they perform. Most in-season programs use resistance training no more than three times a week, and workouts take place approximately thirty minutes after the regular practice session has ended. At no time should a strength maintenance session take the place of a regular practice session.

The San Francisco 49ers football team has one of the best strength maintenance programs in professional football. Three times a week during the season players lift weights, using the resistance of their pre-season limit of lifting ability and without trying to increase the weight during season. The strength of all joints is involved in this phase of the players' workout (22).

Post-season Conditioning

This phase of the conditioning program is often neglected. Some coaches and athletes simply are glad the season is over, and many high school athletes do not go on to participate in another sport. It is part of the high school coach's job to explain the importance of the post-season conditioning program.

During the season, an athlete must maintain a high d‹
there is an extraordinary demand on muscles, heart, and
suddenly stops activity, he or she will feel lethargic, and
will deteriorate.

Therefore, the coach should develop a post-season p
ally reduces activity to maintain fitness and good hea
athlete participates in another sport, he or she will keep this good condition
ing level.

Nutrition

Nutrition is closely related to conditioning, since physical exertion of any
kind requires energy that must be supplied by a sound diet. The purpose of
this section is not to present detailed information about the nutritional values
of certain foods; rather, it is to alert high school coaches to their responsibility of explaining to their students the connection between nutrition and
physical fitness.

Most teenage athletes who participate in high school sports are eager to
attain their maximum performances and consequently are happy to learn all
types of information that will contribute to success. Therefore, it should be a
fairly easy task for the coach to encourage the athlete to follow good eating
habits throughout the year, not just during periods of competition.

In addition to explaining the importance of nutrition, the coach should, if
possible, pay attention to problems that might be related to poor diet. If a
player uses more energy than a diet provides, tissue protein may be broken
down to supply the needed energy, and, as a result, there may be loss of
weight and strength. Many coaches use weight charts to record athletes'
weights before and after practice; an unusual loss of weight may indicate
that something is wrong. A coach should take into account the body types,
ages, heights, and general conditions of the athletes at the start of practice
sessions when he or she analyzes the weight charts. A heavy-boned
mesomorph, eighteen years old, six feet two inches tall, with mature sturdy
development, whose weight is 220 pounds without fat, does not need to reduce even if the weight chart indicates a lower weight.

Unfortunately, many high school coaches are not in a position to do much
to correct poor nutritional practices among their athletes. Unlike college
coaches, they generally do not have training tables where they can control
diet. Often the eating habits of an athlete's family, dictated by cultural or
economic factors, may not be nutritionally sound. Also, if a teenager is left to
fend for himself or herself in the morning, often breakfast will be skipped because it is too much trouble to prepare. This habit is dangerous, because
breakfast raises the blood sugar level, which is essential for the body to
function well. Although the coach actually can do little to correct athletes'

diets, every attempt should be made to educate them about nutritional needs and the effect a poor diet can have on total performance.

It is important for the high school coach to be aware of new developments in the field of nutrition and to be open minded about accepting them and explaining them to students and parents. Some of this information is available in *Nutrition for Athletes—A Handbook for Coaches,* which was published by the American Alliance for Health, Physical Education, and Recreation (20). This publication included contributions from the American Dietetic Association and the Nutrition Foundation, Inc. Also, *Nutrition, Weight Control, and Exercise,* by Frank Katch and William McArdle, contains valuable detailed information that can help coaches understand all phases of this important part of their program (16).

Here is some other rather basic information a coach should know about nutrition:

Natural foods   A well-balanced diet of fresh, natural food is sufficient to meet everyone's body needs. Essential vitamins and minerals are provided best by natural, wholesome animal and plant sources. Natural foods supply both known and undiscovered vitamins, plus the minerals and enzymes that are essential to the maintenance of good health. Raw fruits and vegetables are considered by progressive nutritionists to be the true builders of health; they supply an abundance of minerals, vitamins, and enzymes, as well as very digestible carbohydrates. They are also healthful when steamed lightly in their own juices.

Vitamins   Vitamins are essential to the metabolic process. Much is still being discovered about the importance of vitamins, but it is already known that they cannot be substituted for each other and are involved in growth, resistance to disease, and general good health. Basically, if a person is eating the correct foods, he or she should not need to take vitamin supplements; but because agricultural practices often result in impoverished and poisoned soil, an all-purpose vitamin supplement may be beneficial.

Carbohydrates   Carbohydrates are an essential type of food, since they are changed into energy by the body faster than fats or proteins are. Athletes on high carbohydrate diets have shown a greater degree of endurance than athletes on relatively high fat diets (5). In many dietary plans, carbohydrates make up as much as 45 or 50 percent of the diet, but this percentage should be flexible, because nutritionists are still studying carbohydrates.

Superior carbohydrates are supplied by whole grains—oats, barley, wheat, rye—which are rich in vitamins, minerals, and auxones, the vital substance that promotes growth and development. Eating foods composed of whole grains causes conversion of carbohydrates in a sufficiently gradual way to sustain an energy pick-up for a relatively long period of time. Whole grains are most important to an athlete, whose caloric needs are high and whose Vitamin B requirements cannot be met through refined cereals.

Protein A well-balanced diet should include 10 or 15 percent of protein. Protein is essential for athletes because it contributes to the building and repairing of tissues and to the muscle growth that results from increased activity. Many people falsely assume that beef is the primary source of protein; consequently, steak has become the traditional anchor of many athletic diets. But protein is also supplied by eggs, poultry, fish, cheese, milk, and all types of meats, nuts, and beans (6).

Fats Fats provide essential reserve fuel in the form of unsaturated fatty acids, and they allow for the absorption of fat-soluble vitamins. Also, fats contribute to flavor and aroma, which in turn help make foods cooked in them more palatable.

In the digestive process, fats are broken down after carbohydrates to provide energy. It is important for a diet to contain enough fats and carbohydrates so that protein of the muscles is not broken down in order to provide energy needs. The everyday need for unsaturated fats can be satisfied not only by vegetable oil, but also by unroasted nuts and sunflower seeds, avocados, peanut butter, and good salad oils (6).

Water Pure drinking water is essential, since the protoplasm of body cells is composed of about 75 percent liquid. However, it is important to note that foods should not be washed down or diluted with liquids, as this action affects the digestive processes. It dilutes the digestive juices and therefore increases the time needed for digestion. Many young people are guilty of this bad eating habit, and athletes should be encouraged to obtain their water needs between meals.

Milk Milk is important for teenagers because it is a complete food. Many teenagers drink milk in excessive quantities, which they actually do not need. Three or four glasses a day generally provide all the nutritional value milk can supply. At mealtime milk should be regarded as a solid food and sipped rather than gulped.

Tea and coffee Tea and coffee are not advisable drinks for teenage athletes. They contain caffeine, which may act as a stimulant to the central nervous system, and they especially should be avoided on days when games are played because they can add to a player's tensions.

Snacks If a teenager is not overweight, given body type, development, and energy needs, snacks between meals can supply needed additional nutrition. The best snacks are fresh and dried fruits, which provide energy in the form of natural sugars. Manmade sweets and pastries should be avoided.

Pregame meals Pregame meals are regarded differently by different coaches, because players react in various ways to food before a contest. Because they are tense, some athletes cannot tolerate the presence of solid food before a game and therefore should take liquid diet supplements. Other players who by nature are more relaxed perform best when they eat regular meals.

It is generally accepted that four hours should be allowed between the meal and the game. Naturally, this time span will be influenced by the contest and the hour it is held. One common-sense principle is that an athlete should not radically change usual eating habits before a game.

Importance of chewing A coach should encourge athletes to take their time when eating and not to gulp food. Food that is thoroughly chewed is assimilated more easily by the body, because the saliva mixed with the food during chewing initiates digestive action. Therefore, foods that are thoroughly chewed provide the maximum amount of nourishment.

Fluids in Conditioning

Traditionally, coaches have considered it dangerous for athletes to consume fluids while training or participating in contests. This belief derives from observing individuals suffering from stomach or intestinal cramps. Usually, such pains result from overindulgence. Recently, researchers have proved that withholding fluid can be dangerous and under certain conditions lead to death by dehydration (27).

Dehydration Maintaining the proper fluid balance is essential for maximum athletic performance. A serious problem related to excessive exercise during high humidity and temperature is the loss of fluids. Sweating is nature's way of maintaining the proper body temperature. Dr. Jack Wilmore, a noted exercise physiologist, reports that "Man is able to sweat at the rate of two liters per hour for short periods of time" (30). Prolonged activity without fluid intake may produce significant physiological and biochemical changes in the body leading to stress and a reduction of efficiency (25). Body temperature will rise. Blood volume may be reduced, because of loss of water, thus reducing its ability to transport heat from the inner body to the skin and serve the muscles used in exercise. Severe kidney damage is also possible (28).

Water The dangerous practice of denying fluid intake during practice sessions has been well established. Today, most coaches with the proper background stop practice for fluid breaks, providing water or a fluid such as Gatorade. Climatic conditions usually dictate the frequency of such breaks.

In areas of high temperature and humidity, it is recommened that each athlete be given one-half pint of water every fifteen minutes (9). This practice replaces the lost fluid and keeps efficiency at a high level.

Larry Holloway, athletic trainer, reported an experiment conducted with football players in a Texas high school. Saline-fluid breaks were taken after forty-five minutes of activity. The players took salt tablets. Even though this procedure seemed proper, several team members experienced leg cramps, stomach cramps, and pulled muscles. These problems led to the discontinuance of the practice, and buckets of ice were placed at each practice station instead. Players were allowed to have as much ice as they desired during practice. Every fifteen minutes the players were given squeeze bottles of ice water and allowed to drink what they needed. The new method reduced substantially the pulled muscles, cramps, and heat-related problems (13).

Salt   Associated with fluid loss is salt. Many coaches feel that the depletion of salt and related minerals in the body leads to muscle cramps. As a result, they commonly provide salt tablets after practice. Some athletes react negatively to the salt tablets, which may cause nausea or diarrhea. Prolonged use of excessive salt may also relate to high blood pressure. As a result, physiologists are advocating that the loss of salt during prolonged perspiration can adequately be replaced through the normal use of table salt (9).

Positive Mental Attitudes of the Athletes

An essential ingredient in a coach's conditioning program is the development of a positive attitude among the players. They should believe that all training activities are necessary for good performance, and it is the coach's responsibility to instill this understanding in each athlete. Failure to develop a positive approach toward conditioning may result in an athlete's rejecting training procedures and perhaps never realizing his or her potential.

It is important for a coach to deal with each player individually and help each one work on skills that need improvement. When an athlete is given personal encouragement and attention, he or she will respond by trying harder to perform well. In this way, the coach can not only develop physical conditioning but also create in the players positive attitudes toward all activities involved in the athletic program.

Summary

Programs to develop overall conditioning vary according to the skills and fitness needed for different types of athletic activity. Basic to physiological

fitness are strength, flexibility, and both muscular and cardiorespiratory endurance. These attributes can all be improved through a judicious training
program that conditions an athlete for a particular sport.

The physiological demands made by a sport depend primarily on its
nature. Participation in a particular activity conditions the athlete for that
sport, but does not necessarily develop transferable skills. Such conditioning does not generally improve one of the basic ingredients of fitness—
namely strength.

Strength, basically, is the ability of muscles to exert force. The overload
principle, which involves placing increased amounts of resistance on muscles, is fundamental to the various techniques of developing strength. Contraction and relaxation of muscles are best performed after proper warm-up
procedures increase the temperature of the muscles.

Flexibility refers to the range of motion of body parts. It is essential in
activities that require a free flow of motion and can be developed by
conditioning.

Endurance, both muscular and cardiorespiratory, is the ability of the muscles, heart, lungs, and circulatory system to function for sustained periods of
activity without undue fatigue.

Before participation in high school sports, all players should undergo
thorough medical examinations that reveal any problems and thus help the
coach devise a program for the student's fitness.

There are a wide variety of opinions about the necessity and nature of
warm-up procedures. However, most coaches and athletes agree that some
physical and mental preparation is essential to allow maximum performance
with a minimum of injury.

If a coach advocates a year-round training program, he or she should
provide a great deal of positive motivation so that athletes do not get tired of
specialized practice activities.

An off-season conditioning program should be concerned primarily with
the building of strength in a way that also helps players perfect skills necessary for their major sport.

Pre-season conditioning should be thorough so that athletes are totally
ready for competition.

In-season conditioning programs should be concerned primarily with
maintaining good overall condition, including strength. Prolonged periods of
activity are not essential to meet this need and may even deprive an athlete
of essential energy.

Post-season conditioning programs are necessary for a winding down of
the bodily processes so that a player's good condition can be maintained.

Nutrition is closely related to conditioning, since energy is provided
through a well-balanced diet. This balance can easily be achieved by reducing the refined carbohydrates—white sugar, white flour, and all the "junk"
products made from them—and also by eating a wide variety of meat, fish,

poultry, eggs, dairy products, fresh fruits and vegetables, plus real whole grains, nuts, and seeds. The high school coach must stress the *simplicity* of good eating habits and explain the importance of nutrition to athletes.

Physiologists have disproved the traditional approach of denying fluid intake during training or competitive participation. Frequent breaks with the consumption of a small amount of liquid have proved to be the most effective way of keeping up energy and preventing dehydration.

A positive mental attitude toward conditioning is essential if players are to perform well. The coach should work individually with each player to encourage positive attitudes toward all activities involved in the athletic program.

References

1. Aspiotis, Nicholas. "Strength and Performance." In *The International Olympic Academy Ninth Session at Olympia Greece.* Athens, Greece: M. Pechivanidis, 1970, 94–98.
2. Bentysen, C. "Heading into the Stretch." *Los Angeles Times,* part 3 (November 27, 1974), 1, 6.
3. Bentysen, C. "Shape of Things to Come: Staying in Shape Year Around." *Los Angeles Times,* part 3 (November 26, 1974), 1, 7.
4. Bergstrom, J., and E. Hultzman. "Nutrition for Maximal Sports Performance." *Journal of American Medical Association,* 221:9 (August 28, 1972), 999–1006.
5. Burton, Benjamin T. *The Heinz Handbook of Nutrition.* New York: McGraw-Hill, 1965.
6. Clark, H. Harrison, ed. "Basic Understanding of Physical Fitness." *Physical Fitness Research Digest.* 2:1 (July 1971), 1–20.
7. ———. "Toward a Better Understanding of Muscular Strength." *Physical Fitness Research Digest.* 3:1 (January 1973), 1–20.
8. Davis, Adele. *Let's Get Well.* New York: Harcourt, Brace, Jovanovich, 1965.
9. Gisolfi, C. V. "Exercise, Heat, and Dehydration Don't Mix." *Rx Sports and Travel* (May–June 1975), 23–25.
10. Gould, Adrian G., and Joseph A. Dye. *Exercise and Its Physiology.* New York: A. S. Barnes, 1932.
11. Gutherie, Helen A. *Introductory Nutrition.* 2nd ed. St. Louis C. V. Mosby, 1971.
12. Hatfield, F. C., and M. L. Krotee. *Personalized Weight Training for Fitness and Athletics.* Dubuque, Iowa: Kendall/Hunt, 1978.
13. Holloway, L. "Water Breaks—Good, Bad, Indifferent." *Athletic Journal,* 56:1 (September 1975), 30.
14. Karpovich, Peter V., and Creighton J. Hale. "Effects of Warming-Up upon Physical Performances." *Journal of American Medical Association,* 162 (November 1956), 1117–1119.
15. Katch, F. L., and W. D. McArdle. *Nutrition, Weight Control, and Exercise.* Boston: Houghton Mifflin, 1977.

16. Lombardi, Vince. *Run to Daylight*. New York: Grosset & Dunlap, 1968.
17. Moore, J. W. *The Psychology of Athletic Coaching*. Minneapolis: Burgess, 1971.
18. Moorehouse, Larry, and John M. Cooper. *Kinesiology*. St. Louis: C. V. Mosby, 1950.
19. Moorehouse, L., and A. Miller. *Physiology of Exercise*. St. Louis: C. V. Mosby, 1976.
20. *Nutrition for Athletes: A Handbook for Coaches*. Washington, D.C.: American Association for Health, Physical Education, and Recreation, 1971.
21. Novich, Max M., and Buddy Taylor. *Training and Conditioning of Athletes*. Philadelphia: Lea & Febiger, 1970.
22. Oates, Bob. "Big Men Keep Getting Bigger." *Los Angeles Times*, CC 3 (July 19, 1971), 1, 56.
23. "Owens' Seminar on Pedagogical Evaluation." In *The International Olympic Academy Ninth Session at Olympia Greece*. Athens, Greece: M. Pechivanidis, 1970, 185–205.
24. Paul, W. D. "Crash Diet and Wrestling." *Journal of the Iowa Medical Society* (August 1966).
25. Pitts, G. C., R. E. Johnson, and F. C. Consolayir. "Work in the Heat as Affected by Intake of Water, Salt and Glucose." *American Journal of Physiology*, 142 (1944), 253–259.
26. Start, K. B., and James Hines. "The Effect of Warm-Up on the Incidence of Muscle Injury During Activities Involving Maximum Strength, Speed, and Endurance." *Journal of Sports Medicine and Physical Fitness*, 3 (December 1963), 208–217.
27. Stone, W. J., and W. A. Kroll. *Sports Conditioning and Weight Training—Programs for Athletic Competition*. Boston: Allyn and Bacon, 1978.
28. Tipton, C. M., D. J. Zambraski, and T. K. Tching. "Iowa Wrestling Study: Lessons for Physicians." *Rx Sports and Travel* (January–February 1974), 19–22.
29. Van Itallie, Theodore B., and Leonardo Sinisterra. "Nutrition and Athletic Performance." *Journal of American Medical Association*, 162 (November 1956), 1120–1125.
30. Wimore, J. *Athletic Training and Physical Fitness*. Boston: Allyn and Bacon, 1976.

Methods of   **5**
Conditioning

'01 Coach Publications © 1966 by Ray Franks Publishing Ranch

"I'm looking for something more stable. My last job I got the key to the city in September and the gate in November."

To design an effective athletic conditioning program, it is essential for a high school coach to understand various training methods that contribute to the development of physical fitness and improved strength. Isometric, isotonic, and isokinetic principles make separate contributions to conditioning. Each has proved in itself to be totally inadequate, but in combination they can provide maximum development. The coach, the trainer, and the athlete

95

need to understand the purpose and functions of the methods so that a suitable program can be developed for a particular sport.

Objectives

This chapter describes the following techniques:

1. Isometric exercises
2. Isotonic exercises
3. Isokinetic exercises
4. Plyometrics
5. Cardiorespiratory (C.R.) fitness
6. Circuit training
7. Combinations of methods

Isometric Exercises

Isometric exercises are based on the principle of static muscle contraction. There is little motion involved, and maximum contraction takes place in the muscle without the muscle changing position. When a person makes various pushing, pulling, pressing, and flexing movements, certain muscles work against other muscles or against the force of a stationary object.

Although isometric exercises have become popular only recently for athletic training programs, they have existed in other spheres of activity for a long time. In the 1930s, when Charles Atlas publicized his "dynamic tensions" body-building program, which was based on isometric principles, many people who were concerned with excellence in a particular athletic event rejected isometrics as inappropriate for physical conditioning. There was a fear that an athlete using the dynamic tensions program could become muscle bound. However, people interested in building body proportions or symmetry found the program to be very useful.

In 1953, the German scientists Hettinger and Müller published the startling results of their studies of isometric exercise. They claimed that the use of static contractions of two-thirds maximal force for a period of six seconds would improve a person's strength factor at the rate of 5 percent a week. This meant a 100 percent improvement in a twenty-week period (14). Because of these findings, many coaches and athletic trainers began to develop conditioning programs using isometric exercises.

Problems of Isometric Exercises

Isometric exercises, as a conditioning method, were found to create some problems. Many professional athletes who engaged in an isometric exercise program found that their gain in strength could not be sustained or that it was not so extensive as it was supposed to be according to the study. One factor that has been debated is how long a contraction must be held before a gain in strength is effected. Some people believe that six seconds is long enough, but others feel that maximum benefit is derived only after a twelve-second contraction. The consensus of opinion among researchers today indicates that a ten-second contraction of maximal magnitude once a day is sufficient for total strength development of the specific muscles, say the abdominal wall muscles, involved (11).

Although muscle strength is increased through the use of isometric exercises, this method may have questionable value for an athlete who wants to perform a skill that involves motion. It has been shown that if isometric work is done when a muscle is in a certain position, strength of the muscle in that position will be improved; but it is still not known whether strength and endurance of the muscle in other positions, say during the performance of a skill, is increased.

Another problem in the use of isometric exercises is that individuals are unable to measure the amount of force they are exerting during the static contraction. An athlete may think he or she is doing more work than actually is done and therefore reduces his or her efforts. Isometric exercises are effective only if they involve 100 percent exertion.

Also, isometric exercises seem not to improve cardiorespiratory endurance, which is essential for athletic performance. They contribute only to the strength factor of fitness.

Benefits of Isometric Exercises

Isometric exercises are beneficial in building muscle strength for particular skills. In many athletic skills, violent explosions of muscle strength are necessary and desirable. Just before taking off for a jump, a high jumper needs this extra strength; a football player who blocks from a line position needs explosive power. Coaches should study their sports to determine where and when explosive power is needed. Then they can use isometric exercises to supplement the general conditioning program in developing this extra strength.

Isometric exercise may be valuable for someone who is being rehabilitated after an injury or surgery. Since this form of exercise does not use motion, it is especially beneficial in developing muscle strength around knee or hip joints, where movement might have a harmful effect. A person in a cast may prevent muscle atrophy through the use of isometric contractions. Isometric exercises during recuperation may reduce the time needed for complete recovery.

Isometric exercise thus has proved to be a valuable part of a complete training program, since it improves strength of particular muscles. Because of its simplicity, this conditioning method involves neither long periods of time nor a great deal of energy, and equipment needs for a program of isometric exercise are minimal: a wall, a doorway, or a chinning bar.

Isotonic Exercises

Isotonic exercises involve movement produced by a dynamic contraction of the muscles. This contraction is referred to as *concentric.* During an isotonic exercise, muscles work against gravity so that the object of resistance—a weight of some sort—cannot return passively to its original position. Another contraction, referred to as *eccentric,* is needed for this return action. Isotonic exercises use resistive devices, such as dumbbells or barbells, that allow for progressive weight adjustment. It has been established that isotonic exercises help in the development of strength, flexibility and endurance.

Methods of Resistance Training

Isotonic exercises can be used effectively in a well-planned resistance training program.

High school coaches and athletes have been relatively slow to recognize the values of resistance training, partly because they associate it with the sport of weight lifting and the abnormally large muscles that can result from this sport. The two activities, however, involve entirely different concepts: The goal of the sport is to lift a given maximum poundage; resistance training, on the other hand, is based on a series of exercises that progress sequentially and increase total fitness and strength. Though resistance training generally has not been used in a year-round program of preparation for different sports activities, it is being used more and more frequently in off-season training programs.

Most modern resistance training methods are variations of the program developed in 1945 by Dr. Thomas L. De Lorme, who was involved in the rehabilitation of World War II veterans. At first Dr. De Lorme advocated that an individual repeat a given exercise from seventy to one hundred times, stopping for rest between each group or set of ten. The amount of resistance initially used was determined by a system of trial-and-error, testing how much resistance the individual could handle when performing ten successive repetitions of an exercise. Eventually, the number of times the exercise was repeated was reduced to thirty, or three sets. In the first set, the resistance used approximated one-half the individual's maximum lifting ability, the second set involved three-fourths maximum resistance, and the final set was performed at maximum resistance. De Lorme's program, or a variation of it, has been advocated by coaches as an excellent method of progressive resistance training.

Much research has been done to discover the efficiency of different numbers of sets and repetitions, and of the frequency of exercise. Richard Berger, who studied the problem extensively, concluded that three sets of six repetitions is the best combination for strength development (1). But many resistance training instructors who are actually working with athletes advocate three sets of ten repetitions. This seems to be the most popular program in the country today. Most instructors want their athletes to work at least three alternate days a week; for example, Monday, Wednesday, and Friday. Some coaches suggest more than three days a week, using reduced weights or perhaps a variation of the method on the extra days.

Coaches should be familiar with the most common resistance training methods:

De Lorme method   Involves three sets of ten repetitions. The first set is performed with one-half maximum lifting ability, the second set with three-fourths, and final set with maximum resistance.

Oxford method   Uses the same poundage and number of sets (and repetitions) as in the De Lorme method, but applies them in reverse order.

Power method   Uses more than one set of repetitions with each exercise. The poundage is increased with each set, but the number of repetitions is decreased.

Superset method   Provides two different exercises for the same body segment and may involve the antagonistic muscles. There is little or no rest between exercises.

Cheating method   Brings in additional muscle groups to assist with an exercise to permit the handling of greater weights.

Bulk method   Involves several sets for each exercise, with the same number of repetitions and amount of weight for each set.

Triset method   Provides three exercises for a particular part of the body and may involve different muscles. There is little or no rest between exercises.

Double-progressive method   Increases the number of repetitions in a set until a specified number has been reached. The weight used then is increased, and the number of repetitions is reduced to that of the starting point. Then, the number of repetitions is increased as before and the process repeated.

Isotonic Conditioning Program

In designing an isotonic conditioning program, a high school coach should analyze the specific movements used in a sport and develop exercises to improve strength, flexibility, and endurance in the muscles involved in that activity. Conditioning exercises should simulate the actual muscle requirements of the sport and include increased resistance features. (See Figure 5.1.)

Isotonic exercises should be used with specific goals in mind: Athletes who are interested in leg development should be provided with exercises that strengthen that area of the body, and athletes who want to improve their arms and backs should be taught techniques to attain that particular strength. Of course, specialized isotonic exercises designed for a particular activity should be undertaken only if the athlete is in general good condition.

A good example of this approach is shown in the work of Rowland and Button, who worked with swimmers. They analyzed the "eggbeater kick" and then developed a training program that employed the same basic movements used in the kick. Also, the exercises the swimmers were required to do included the principle of increased resistance, with weights applied for certain muscles to work against. This conditioning resulted in greater strength, endurance, and, consequently, in better performances by the swimmers during the season (24).

Discus throwing is another sport that lends itself well to an exercise program devised from analysis of the activity. The lateral fly movement used in throwing the discus can be practiced by using a dumbbell with no release. The weight of the dumbbell can be increased as the athlete's strength increases. This method seems to develop strength more effectively than a resistance training program using the traditional bench press; although the bench press does increase strength and endurance of specific muscles, the dumbell technique actually simulates the movement of throwing the discus.

Leg Development

Perhaps the most important part of the body to develop for athletic participation is the legs, and the importance of leg strength is emphasized by the following comments by professionals. After a lay-off of a year, Paul Hornung, former professional football player with the Green Bay Packers, said:

> I was coming out of the service when I reported to training camp, and I thought I was in pretty good shape. I hadn't worked out much in the Army, but my weight was around 220, pretty close to my playing weight. The only trouble was that I hadn't been running and my legs weren't in any shape at all. They were so heavy, it was unbelievable (19).

After his first game as head coach of the Los Angeles Rams, former coach Tommy Prothro noted that performances early in the season were difficult to assess because the players were heavy-legged from extensive practice sessions. Extensive work on legs should be done early in training so that players have time to regain strength before they must perform. During the season and in off-season sessions, the coach should provide athletes with exercises to maintain leg strength.

A recent controversy among coaches involves the use of deep knee bends, and many claim that this exercise causes a weakening of the knee joints and thus increases the possibility of injury. It should be noted that the isotonic squat exercise is not so extensive as knee bends; if the exercise is done properly, the knee does not bend beyond a 90-degree angle, and the knee therefore does not have so much stress placed on it as in deep knee bends.

Isotonic exercises should not be looked upon as a wonder method, but if they are used properly in conditioning, they can contribute to all aspects of physical fitness and strength development. In developing an isotonic exercise program, the high school coach must remember that he or she is dealing with teenagers, who, in their enthusiasm, are inclined to expend too much energy. The coach should give them the opportunity to rest and rebuild their bodies between workouts. Too much work in one day can tear down muscles faster than the body can restore them, and a young athlete can suffer permanent physical damage.

Because individual athletes have different basic abilities, an isotonic exercise program should allow each person to progress at his or her own speed. There is no set formula to establish the amount of weight an athlete should begin with, so the best method of determining this amount is by supervised trial and error. In this way, the athlete will find the resistance that can be handled satisfactorily in the exercise and can add to it to reach maximum resistance. It is not wise to allow athletes to use excessive resistance when they are learning the techniques of an exercise, because they will become fatigued rapidly and may develop bad conditioning habits.

Once the starting resistance is determined, the key to success in doing isotonic exercises depends a great deal on the self-discipline and determination of the athlete. Generally, it takes approximately two months before one can see significant changes in strength, and during this period the athlete can experience a retrogression in strength before realizing specific improvement. The coach should make certain that athletes understand what is taking place so that they will not despair over temporary setbacks.

The Off-season Isotonic Exercise Program

The usual off-season isotonic exercise program should be conducted at least three days a week. It is not advisable to have athletes lift their maximum

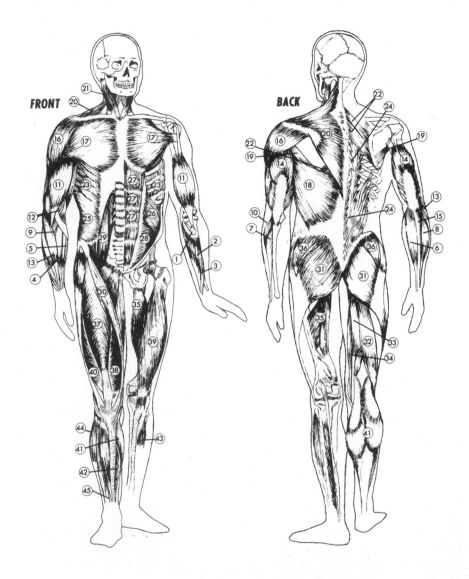

Figure 5.1 *Methods of coordinating muscles, exercises, and sports.*

Figure 5.1 (*Continued*)

Muscle	Action Numbers in ( ) indicate muscles which assist in action.	Exercise Resisting direction of muscle pull.	Sport In which greatest resistance is encountered.
1. Flexor digitorum profundus 2. Flexor digitorum sublimus	Closes fingers.	Squeeze rubber ball; roll up weight on a cord tied to a broomstick with palms down.	Any sport in which one grasps an opponent, partner or equipment, such as wrestling, hand to hand balancing, tennis, horizontal bar, ball bat, etc.
3. Flexor policis longus	Flexes thumb.		
4. Palmaris longus 5. Flexor carpi radialis 6. Flexor carpi ulnaris	Flex wrist palmward and to both sides. (1, 2, 3, 7, 8)	Wrist curls with barbells with palms up and wrist wrestling.	Tennis; throwing baseball, passing a football; handball; ring work; two handed pass in basketball; batting; golf swing.
7. Extensor carpi radialis longus and brevis 8. Extensor carpi ulnaris	Extends wrist.	Wrist curls with barbell with palms down.	Backhand stroke in tennis and badminton; Olympic weight lifting; bait and fly casting.
9. Pronator teres	Pronates forearm.	Slow rotation of forearm holding dumbbell with weights on one end only.	Tennis forehand; shot put; throwing a punch; throwing a baseball; passing a football.
10. Supinator	Supination of forearm. (11)	Slow rotation of forearm holding dumbbell with weights on one end only.	Throwing a curve ball; batting; fencing thrust.
11. Biceps brachii 12. Brachialis	Flexion of elbow. (9)	Chin-ups with fingers toward the body; curls with the barbells—palms up.	Ring work; rope climb; archery; pole vaulting; wrestling; back stroke in swimming.
13. Brachicradialis	Strong elbow flexor with forearm pronated or partially pronated.	Curls with barbells, palms down; chin-ups with fingers away from body.	Rowing; cleaning a barbell; rope climbing.

Figure 5.1. *(Continued).*

Muscle	Action — Numbers in ( ) indicate muscles which assist in action.	Exercise — Resisting direction of muscle pull.	Sport — In which greatest resistance is encountered.
14. Triceps brachii 15. Anconeus	Extends the elbow.	Push-ups; dips on parallel bars; presses with barbells; alternate dumbbell press; triceps extension with barbell (French press).	Breast stroke; shot put; parallel bar work; vaulting; hand shivers in football; hand balancing; batting; pole vaulting; fencing thrust; passing both football or basketball; boxing.
16. Deltoid. (For simplicity this muscle is divided into anterior and posterior fibers only.)	Anterior fibers—adduction, elevation, inward rotation of humerus. Posterior fibers–abduction, depression, outward rotation of humerus.	Pull springs apart in front of chest; standing straight arm lateral raises with dumbbells; press barbell; upright rowing motion with barbell; alternate presses with dumbbells.	Hand balancing; canoeing; shot put; pole vaulting; tennis; archery; batting; fencing thrust; passing a football; tackling; breast stroke; back and crawl strokes; golf swing; handball.
17. Pectoralis major	(A) Forward elevation of humerus. (16) (B) Adduction of humerus. (16, 19) (C) Depression of humerus. (16, 18, 19) Inward rotation of humerus. (18, 19)	A. & C. Prone straight arm pull-overs. B. Wide arm push-ups; bench press with wide grip. C. & B. Prone lateral raises with dumbbells, turning humerus inward.	Tackling; crawl and back strokes; tennis; passing football; throwing a baseball; javelin; pole vaulting; wrestling; shot put; discus throw; straight arm lever position in gymnastics; punching.
18. Latissimus dorsi 19. Teres major	Draws humerus down and backward. (16) Inward rotation of humerus. (16, 17)	Wide arm chin-ups behind the neck; bent-over rowing motion; straight arm pullover in prone position.	Rope climb; canoe racing; ring work; rowing; batting; crawl, back, breast, and butterfly strokes; pole vaulting; golf swing.

Figure 5.1 *(Continued)*

	Action	Exercise	Sports Application
20. Trapezius	A. Tilts head back. (23) B. Elevates shoulder point. C. Adducts scapula. (21)	A. Resist raising of head with weight on headstrap. B. Shoulder shrugs with arms holding weights. C. Pull springs apart in front of chest.	A. Wrestlers' bridge. B. Passing a football; cleaning a barbell; breast stroke. C. Archery; batting; breast stroke.
21. Sternomastoid	Tucking of chin. Rotation of head. Raises sternum in deep breathing.	Lie on back, raise and rotate the head, lower head.	Crawl stroke; tucking chin in wrestling; football; boxing; distance running (breathing).
22. Rhomboids, Major & Minor	Adducts scapula. (20)	Pull springs apart; using wall weights, face wall with arms at front horizontal position, draw arms down to side; wide arm chin-ups behind neck.	Tennis backhand; batting; back and breast strokes.
23. Serratus anterior	Abduction of scapula.	Push-ups; move shoulders upward in prone position holding weights.	Shot put; discus throw; tennis; archery; tackling; crawl stroke; passing a basketball; passing a football; punching.
24. Spinea erector. (Also includes a number of smaller groups.)	A. Extension of spine. (20) B. Lateral flexion of spine. (20, 26, 27) C. Rotation of spine.	A. Dead lifts with barbell. B. & C. Side bends; trunk twisting with barbell across shoulders.	Discus and hammer throw; batting; golf swing; racing start in swimming; diving and tumbling; rowing; blocking in football.
25. External oblique 26. Internal oblique 27. Hectus abdominus 28. Transversalis	Flexion of spine. Lateral flexion of spine. (23) Rotation of the spine. (23) Compression of abdomen.	Sit-ups with bent knees, keeping hands behind the head, touching left knee with right elbow and vice versa; hanging leg raises.	The importance of this group of muscles in all sports, posture and general fitness and appearance cannot be overstated.
29. Illiopsoas	Flexion of trunk. (27) Flexion of thigh. (36)	Sit-ups with knees straight; hanging leg raises; leg lifts.	Running; hurdling; pole vaulting; kicking a football; line play; flutter kick; pike and tuck positions in tumbling and diving.

Figure 5.1 *(Continued)*

Muscle	Action Numbers in ( ) indicate muscles which assist in action.	Exercise Resisting direction of muscle pull.	Sport In which greatest resistance is encountered.
30. Sartorius	Flexion of femur. (35) Flexion of knee. Rotates femur outward.	Sit up with knees straight.	Tumbling and diving.
31. Gluteus maximus	Extends femur. (31, 32, 33) Outward rotation of femur. (31)	Deep knee bends with barbell across shoulders; ride bicycle exercise using iron boots; any running, hopping, or jumping.	Skiing; shot put; running; quick starts in track; all jumping and skipping; line play; skating; swimming start; changing direction while running.
32. Biceps femoris	Extension of femur. (30) Flexion of knee. (40) Outward rotation of femur. (30)	Leg curls using iron boots; ride bicycle exercise using iron boots; leg presses with weights; deep knee bends.	Skiing; skating; quick starts in track and swimming; hurdling; line play; all jumping.
33. Semitendenosus	Flexion of knee. (40) Flexion of femur. (30)		
34. Semimembranosus	Inward rotation of femur.		
35. Adductor magnus	Adduction of femur and outward rotation during adduction.	Adduct leg using resistance of wall pulleys or iron boots.	Skiing; skating; frog kick; broken field running; bareback horseback riding.
36. Gluteus medius	Adduction of femur. (Essential for spring.)	Hopping on one foot.	Hurdling; fencing; frog kick; shot put; running; line play; skating.
37. Rectus femoris	Flexion of femur. (28) Extension of knee.	Deep knee bends; leg presses; leg extension with iron boots.	Skiing; skating; quick starts; all jumping; kick in football or soccer; flutter kick; frog kick; water skiing; diving; trampoline and tumbling; bicycling; catching in baseball.
38. Vastus internus 39. Vastus intermedius 40. Vastus externus	Extension of knee.		

Figure 5.1 *(Continued)*

41. Gastrocnemius	Extension of foot (when knee is almost straight). (44)	Raise on toes with weights on shoulders; running; jumping; hopping.	Quick starts in track; swimming; basketball; football; skating; all jumping; skiing.
42. Soleus	Extension of foot (when knee is bent).		
43. Tibialis anterior	Flexes foot and inverts it.	Sit with feet dangling weights while flexing and inverting foot and recover slowly.	Changing direction while running; skating; skiing.
44. Peroneus longus	Extension of foot. (40, 41, 44) Eversion of foot.	Twist foot using iron boot.	Skating turns; changing direction while running.
45. Flexor hallucis longus	Flexion of big toe. Extension of ankle.	Toe raises standing on edge of board.	Running; all jumping; racing starts.

SOURCE: V. F. Krumdick, "Cramer Muscle Action Chart, No. 10." Courtesy of Cramer Products, Inc., Gardner, Kansas.

NOTE: *Flexion* means bending at a joint, decreasing the angle. (It does not apply to the shoulder in this chart.) *Extension* means straightening at a joint; it is the opposite of flexion. (It does not apply to the shoulder in this chart.) *Adduction* means movement of a part toward the plane which splits the body into halves, left and right. *Abduction* is the opposite of adduction. *Rotation* means movement of a part around an axis. *Pronation* means rotation of the forearm and hand to a palms-down position. *Supination* means rotation of the forearm and hand to a palms-up position; it is the opposite of pronation. *Inversion* means twisting the foot inward at the ankle. *Eversion* means twisting the foot outward at the ankle. *Elevation* means raising a part against gravity. *Depression* means lowering a part, that is, yielding to gravity.

weights each day of the workouts. Rather, the following schedule is suggested: Monday may involve maximum lifts with few repetitions; Wednesday may be spent lifting to approximately 50 percent of maximum ability, increasing the number of repetitions in order to develop endurance; the resistance lifted on Friday should be about 75 percent of maximum. This program seems to provide for the maximum development of the large muscle groups. Some coaches and athletes with more experience prefer to exercise four days a week, concentrating on the upper body and arm strength for two days and spending the other two days on the lower body and leg strength. This alternation of emphasis allows for adequate rest and rebuilding between sessions.

A high school coach may feel reluctant to propose an off-season isotonic conditioning program because of limited equipment, used in the off season by teams whose sports are in season. However, substitute equipment, though perhaps not so adaptable as regular gear, can be used. Also, if the school shop is looking for a meaningful project for students, the coach can suggest that they improvise dumbbells and barbells. The local cement company also is a good source of materials: Excellent makeshift dumbbells or barbells can be made from pipes inserted in cans of different sizes filled with cement. If the coach and athletes use a little imagination, initiative in devising equipment, and the necessary safety precautions, the off-season isotonic exercise program can be successful.

Recommended Isotonic Exercise Routine

There are many isotonic exercise programs that produce good results. One of the basic principles to follow in designing a routine is to arrange the exercises so that the large muscle groups (such as the triceps, biceps, and brachial of the upper arm) are worked first. When the small muscle groups (such as brachioradial, flexor ulnaris, superficial extensors, and flexors of the lower arm) are in a state of fatigue, related large-muscle exercises cannot be executed properly, and the total desired result may not be achieved It is also a wise policy not to use exercises like wrist curls that fatigue the forearms (grip strength) in the beginning of the workout, because in subsequent drills involving the arms, effort will be diminished.

It is important for these exercises to be done in the proper sequence. Generally, three sets should be performed, with repetitions in each set. This suggested routine can be varied by changing the amount of weight used. Regardless of the program, the coach should see that there is a short rest period of two or three minutes between each set, and that breathing is done properly during the exercise.

When doing isotonic exercises, a person initially may have a tendency to hold his or her breath during a lift. Holding the breath stabilizes the muscles of the chest, placing them in a position of static contraction and allowing greater force to be exerted on the weight which is being lifted. But this is a disadvantage because it reduces the use of the muscles to be exercised. Generally, the proper technique is to inhale on the first motion and exhale on the second. The most important rule to remember about breathing is that no matter where one starts in an exercise, breathing should be as close to normal as possible. Normal breathing ensures that the muscles will receive the proper amount of oxygen, and it serves to keep the acid-loss balance of the blood constant within narrow limits.

A recommended routine that provides for total development involves the following exercises:

Standing press   (See Figure 5.2.) Clear the barbell or weight from the floor to a position in front of the chest. Inhale and press the weight straight upward over the head until the arms are extended. Exhale and, with caution, return the weight to the chest position. Raising and lowering actions constitute one repetition. The exercise is designed for deltoid (arm and shoulder) muscles development.

Bench press   (See Figure 5.3) Lie flat on your back on a bench or on the floor, making certain there is no arch in the back. Take the weight from an upright or have two exercise partners hand it to you. This exercise starts with the arms extended over the chest. Lower the weight slowly to the chest and return it to an upright position without stopping. Inhale on the downward action and exhale on the upward movement. This combination constitutes one repetition. The exercise primarily develops the large muscle groups of the chest, shoulders, and triceps of the upper arms.

Bent-over row   (See Figure 5.4, page 112.) Bend forward at the hips until the back is parallel to the floor. The knees may be slightly flexed for balance to relieve stress on the lower back. Lift the weight from the floor and raise it toward the midsection of the body. If the elbows are extended away from the body and the weight raised to the chest, development of the upper back and trapezius muscle and the rear of the deltoid muscle are emphasized as well as the biceps of the arms. If the elbows are kept close to the body and the weight raised to the midsection of the body, emphasis is placed on the latissimus dorsi muscle. The raising and lowering of the weight constitute one repetition. Inhale while raising the weight and exhale while lowering it. The weight should not be allowed to go back to the floor until the repetitions have been completed.

Upright row   (See Figure 5.5, page 113.) Using the overhand grip, raise the weight and stand erect with arms extended down. Spread feet apart to shoulder width for balance, and hands should be placed close together, with the weight resting against the thighs. To begin the exercise, raise the

Figure 5.2   *Standing press.*

weight upward by bending the elbows outward toward the sides. The weight should be brought to the chest level. Inhale on the upward motion. Lower the weight to starting position at the thighs. Exhale on downward motion. Raising and lowering actions constitute one repetition. The exercise affects the muscles of the shoulders, upper back, and upper arms, as well as the gripping muscles of the hands and forearm.

Figure 5.3   *Bench press.*

Curls   (See Figure 5.6, page 114.) Using the underhand grip, lift the weight from the floor and stand erect with it across the thighs in front of the body. Keep upper arms stationary and flex the elbows, which are kept close to the sides. Raise the weight until it is under the chin. Inhale while raising the weight, and exhale while lowering it. These movements constitute one repetition. This exercise is primarily for the development of the biceps and upper arms, but forearms also are strengthened.

Squats   (See Figure 5.7, page 115.) Place the weight back of the shoulders on the spine of the scapulus with the aid of two exercise partners or a squat rack. The feet are placed approximately shoulder width apart and turned slightly outward. Bend the knees and lower the body until the upper thighs are parallel to the floor. For safety of the knee joints it is not advisable to lower the body beyond this point. Balance can be maintained better if the back is kept straight and the eyes are fixed on a point straight ahead. The lowering and raising of the body, which constitute one repetition, should occur without stopping. Inhale while lowering the body, and exhale on the upward action. This exercise is designed primarily for total leg strength.

Figure 5.4 *Bent-over row.*

Sit-ups (See Figure 5.8, page 116.) Sit-ups should be performed on an incline board with a foot strap. If no incline board is available, sit-ups can be done lying flat on the floor with an exercise partner holding the ankles. Knees are bent so that the heels are as close to the buttocks as possible. Hands are placed in front of the shoulders. If weights are used, they should be placed under the chin. Raise forward until chin or elbows, depending on flexibility, touch the knees. Return slowly to the starting position. Inhale on the forward motion, and exhale on the return. Repeat without stopping. The entire motion constitutes one repetition. Care should be taken to avoid a bouncing motion, which will reduce the effectiveness of the exercise. This exercise is designed primarily for strengthening the abdominal muscles, lower back, and upper legs.

It is important for these exercises to be done in the proper sequence. Generally, three sets should be performed, with repetitions in each set. This suggested routine can be varied by changing the amount of resistance used. Regardless of the program, the coach should see that there is a short rest period of two or three minutes between each set, and that breathing is done properly during the exercise.

Figure 5.5 *Upright row.*

A Caution for Women Athletes Doing Sit-Ups

When athletes are asked why they do sit-ups, the usual response is, "I want to strengthen my abdominal muscles." Rarely does an athlete remark, "I want to strengthen my hip flexors." Many exercises today are supposed to strengthen abdominal muscles but place an unnecessary strain on the lower back.

There must be a distinction made between these two basic movements:

Trunk flexion This happens when the vertebral column curves. (For example, when one lifts her shoulders off the floor during the first part of the sit-up.)

Hip flexion This happens when one flexes at the hip joint. For example, when one lifts the lower back off the floor during sit-ups and when doing double leg-lifts (Figure 5.9, page 117).

Why is it important to separate these two movements? There are many individuals who have postural problems as a result of an imbalance between the

Figure 5.6 *Curls.*

hip flexors (iliopsoas and rectus femoris) and trunk flexors (abdominals). When the hip flexors are very strong and the trunk flexors are weak, lordosis (sway back) may result. To help correct this problem, an exercise must strengthen abdominal muscles and not hip flexors. If sit-ups (even bent-knee sit-ups) or double leg-lifts are used to strengthen the abdominals to correct lordosis, one is defeating the purpose of the exercises. Hip flexors work during the second part of the sit-up. Double leg-lifts influence abdominal muscles (isometrically), but it is a strong hip-flexor exercise. Hip-flexion exercises should not be used under these conditions.

Curl-ups (Figure 5.10, page 118) are excellent exercise for trunk flexors because they isolate the abdominals. They should be performed on a padded board (level) with knees bent so that one's feet are close to the buttocks. One should curl up as in the first part of the sit-up and hold for one second and then return to the board. A twist can be added if one wishes to work more of the oblique muscles. If an increase in resistance is desired one should not use an incline. All that is needed is to hold a weight on the chest. Once the lower back leaves the board the hip flexors are beginning to work.

Athletes usually exercise their hip flexors sufficiently during normal running practice. The athletes that should be working them especially are the ones that use them more in competition (gymnasts, runners, hurdlers, divers). These are the athletes who use hip flexion as a basic part of their

Figure 5.7 *Squats.*

competitive movement. The other athletes should spend their training time working abdominal muscles and let the hip flexors strengthen themselves during the running involved in normal workouts.

What happens after the competitive years? Female athletes who have children may do exercises after childbirth to strengthen abdominal muscles. If they choose sit-ups or double leg lifts, they will compound their problems. They will be using hip flexors that should be avoided because of the prenatal pressure they have experienced on the lower back. It is better to do curl-ups and avoid hip-flexion exercises.

A good balance should be kept between trunk flexors and hip flexors. The abdominal muscles should be exercised more. One should treat these two muscle groups independently by working them separately as needed to avoid straining the lower back.

Isokinetic Exercises

Isokinetic exercises involve the use of maximum muscle force throughout a full range of motion. They represent an attempt to combine the best aspects of isometric and isotonic exercises.

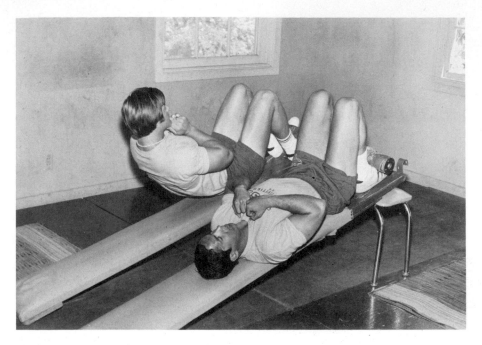

Figure 5.8 *Sit-ups.*

As previously described, isometric exercises involve static muscle contractions and improve muscle strength in a particular position. Isotonic exercises involve dynamic contractions, and muscle strength is developed by utilizing the maximum weight the muscles can accommodate. Both methods are limited in their effects: Isometrics strengthen muscles *only* as they work in particular positions; during isotonics the muscles have to work less hard at certain points of the exercise and thus may not *constantly* be strengthened.

Isokinetics, however, involve muscle action in a full range of motion and require maximum muscle effort during an entire exercise. Mechanical devices such as the Mini Gym and Nautilus are used to control the speed of movement, which varies throughout an entire motion according to skeletal position and muscle tension. The resistance against muscles that the device provides alters with the range of movement and constantly applies maximum manageable force against the muscle. Muscles are taxed to their full capacities regardless of the repetitions or times an exercise is performed. The device accommodates its force to the athlete's immediate, *specific* muscle ability. Consequently, isokinetic exercise should result in maximum muscle development. Although the high cost of isokinetic devices has in the past limited their use at the high school level, recently they have become affordable by most school systems.

Figure 5.9 *Sit-ups showing the hip flexors taking over once the lower back leaves the floor.*

Dr. James Counsilman, coach of both the Olympic and Indiana University swimming teams, has long advocated the use of specificity of exercise and resistance training in the athletic training program. He feels that specificity of exercise is important for transferring from training to the actual activity. One of the real advantages of the isokinetic devices is that they can be used for specific exercises involving movements required by a particular sport. The isokinetic principle is in operation, for example, when a swimmer pulls his or her arms through the water. It is natural, therefore, that Dr. Counsilman would express interest in research supporting the overall superiority of isokinetic exercises to isolated isotonic exercises (5).

Other people concerned with athletic development have commented on the use of isokinetic devices. Tom Fears, professional football coach, said:

> It is an accepted fact that we of the New Orleans Saints work with the law of specificity. We try to exercise our players as much as possible to the approximate movement or actions that each player utilizes within his specific assignment. We know that strength is the most important result we can achieve with our conditioning program and working these same muscles gives us more power and endurance with better coordinated muscles (12).

Figure 5.10 *Curl-ups with hands behind the neck. Head, neck, and shoulder blades off the floor.*

Fears expressed the belief that the isokinetic principle not only allows the players to do fewer repetitions, it is superior to other resistive force exercises used in the past because it provides maximum development of strength.

Dr. Hubert Stephens, who is concerned with rehabilitating patients and is involved in the Wichita Falls, Texas, High School physical education program, expressed the opinion that the isokinetic exercise method holds great promise because, unlike other resistive exercise techniques, it enables individuals to pack maximum exertion into a shorter time period (27).

Plyometrics

Plyometrics is a term that has been used primarily by German and Russian coaches. It describes training that forces muscles engaged in a shortening action to explode into a lengthening action.

Ed Jacoby, head track and field coach at Boise State University, describes the principle of plyometrics as follows: "Plyometric training or indepth training is basically the stopping or breaking of one motion [eccentric] into a forceful movement in the opposite direction [concentric]. This action serves as an immediate stretch reflex which produces extra muscular contraction" (16). Take, for example, an elastic band. Stretch it a little and it will recoil slightly. Stretch it nearly to the maximum, and it will recoil with great force.

The typical athlete, through one method or another, attempts to train for strength or endurance by engaging in exercises that will produce strength by developing either bulk of particular muscles, general strength, power, or muscular endurance. Fred Wilt, a member of the U.S. Olympic teams in 1948 and 1952 and former holder of the indoor two-mile-run world record, describes plyometrics as "Training drills designed to bridge the gap between sheer strength and the power (rate of work or force × velocity) required in producing the explosive-reactive movements so necessary to excellence in jumping, throwing, and sprinting" (31).

Physiologists concerned with strength development have concluded that loaded muscles engaged in concentric contractions are more powerful following an eccentric prestretch phase. A body movement that requires a high velocity, such as jumping or throwing, can best be achieved by starting in the opposite direction. Examples are golf, baseball, and tennis swings. All engage in backward motion prior to the execution of the swing.

Fred Wilt suggests four basic guidelines that should be followed in developing plyometric programs for athletes. These are:

1. Maximum tension develops when the active muscle is stretched quickly (eccentrically).
2. The faster a muscle is forced to lengthen, the greater the tension it exerts.
3. The rate of stretch is more important than the magnitude of stretch.
4. Utilize the overload principle, which specifies that increased strength results only from work at an intensity greater than that to which it is accustomed (31).

Plyometric training differs from other forms of resistance training as to recovery rate. Because of this, beginners should be limited to one session per week and the more advanced individuals should have no more than two sessions. This training tends to slow the nerve-muscle response for a short period of time. Taking all this into consideration, it is desirable to not engage in heavy plyometric workouts for eight to ten days prior to important competition.

Cardiorespiratory (C.R.) Fitness

Chapter 4 discussed the importance of cardiorespiratory fitness—the increased efficiency of the heart to force more blood throughout the body and of the lungs to exchange more oxygen for waste gases.

Figure 5.11 *Running is especially effective in developing cardiorespiratory fitness.*

When the cardiorespiratory system is conditioned, the number of capillaries, which carry blood to and from active muscles, is increased (13). Thus the body develops greater efficiency in exchanging oxygen for lactic acid and other metabolic waste materials, and the muscles can operate longer without becoming fatigued.

Value of Running

All exercise tends to develop C.R. fitness. Running is especially effective.

Sam Adams, coach at the University of California at Santa Barbara, works extensively with decathlon athletes. He estimates that it takes six weeks of smooth, relaxed running—not forced or struggling—an hour a day, with intervals of rest or walking, to develop a high level of cardiorespiratory fitness. When this level is reached, athletes can train for specific skills and spend a minimum amount of time running to maintain C.R. fitness. Because it does take so long to attain C.R. fitness, coaches request that their athletes report for pre-season training in good condition and with a high degree of cardiorespiratory fitness. If an athlete who is not in good condition undergoes a two-week crash program to develop fitness, harm can actually be done. Muscles may be forced to compensate for a weak cardiorespiratory system. Since the muscles cannot obtain the proper exchange of fresh blood and waste materials, fatigue sets in faster and the individual develops patterns of muscle use that actually hinder performance of the skill. These bad habits may be retained by the athlete throughout the season. If a coach can develop a training program that includes relaxed running, he or she will be able to help his athletes achieve cardiorespiratory fitness.

Increase of Stroke Volume

Besides increasing the number of capillaries, another aspect of cardiorespiratory fitness is the increase in stroke volume, or the amount of blood forced through the heart during a single beat. Most athletic conditioning is concerned primarily with an efficient stroke volume by the heart, since athletes are required to perform bursts of speed more often than sustained actions. Following a burst of speed, there generally is a lull in activity and the athlete has a few seconds or minutes to relax and recuperate. Therefore, conditioning programs for sports such as football and baseball should include activities that concentrate on developing this part of the cardiorespiratory system.

Aerobic Point System

Dr. Kenneth H. Cooper has written a book called *Aerobics,* in which he outlines the exercises he believes make the greatest contribution to cardiorespiratory fitness. Active exercises—running, swimming, and walking—are extremely productive, while calisthenics are the least valuable type of activity (3). Dr. Cooper has devised an "aerobic point system," which measures each individual's C.R. fitness. After running for twelve minutes, a person's fitness is determined as follows:

If he or she covers:	He or she is in fitness category:
less than 1.0 miles	1. Very Poor
1.0 to 1.24 miles	2. Poor
1.25 to 1.49 miles	3. Fair
1.50 to 1.74 miles	4. Good
1.75 miles or over	5. Excellent

Dr. Cooper also suggests that an athlete should continue to run during the off-season for several reasons, including a reduction of injuries during the season, greater efficiency in the later stages of a contest, and a long professional career.

Figure 5.12 *When conditioning athletes, the coach should keep in mind the particular demands of the sport.*

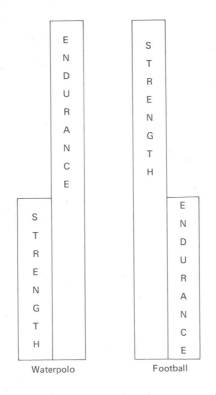

Waterpolo   Football

Figure 5.13 Comparison of the strength and endurance needed to play water polo and football.

Circuit Training

Circuit training is a system of conditioning that involves an athlete's moving, within a limited time schedule, among six or ten places, or "stations," and performing a specific exercise at each station. This system, designed in 1961 by two Englishmen, G. T. Adamson and R. E. Morgan, usually is used when there are many athletes and limited space, equipment, or time.

Circuit training generally should be designed to improve overall conditioning, although it can be used to develop strength or cardiorespiratory endurance. The latter two purposes are not recommended for this training method, however. When circuit training is used during the season, it should follow regular training drills and, because of its strenuous nature, should not be engaged in more than three times a week. In any case, exercises should be chosen that relate closely to the particular sport and that contribute to the specific purpose of the conditioning program.

The usual procedure is for an athlete to move at least three times through the entire circuit of six to ten stations, with minimum rest between stations. The program should take from twenty to thirty minutes, depending on the number of stations and nature of the exercises. A coach should take care not to set up in succession two stations that involve the same muscles. Also, at the start of the session it is advisable to require athletes to perform a limited number of repetitions involving modified resistance and easy for all players. These repetitions should be altered and performed again as the athletes' conditions improve.

Athletes will have to spend more time at certain stations because of the exercises performed there—sit-ups or bench press, for example. The coach should see that these stations have more equipment—slant boards, bench-press stations—so that many athletes can participate simultaneously. If a large number of players is proceeding through the circuit at the same time, the coach can divide them into teams so that they progress as a unit from one station to another. Not only does this method save time, but it can add a safety factor.

Combination of Methods

A coach who wants to achieve maximum development of the athletes through the most efficient training techniques should combine the best features of the different conditioning methods. It is important to keep in mind the demands of the particular sport and the overall condition of each individual athlete.

Also, one must analyze the sport to determine whether strength or endurance is more essential to performance and then devise a training program that gives athletes the required ratio of these qualities. Figure 5.11 shows how the relationship between strength and endurance differs for the sports of waterpolo and football. Waterpolo requires a great deal more endurance for continuous play; football, on the other hand, demands greater strength from participants. A good conditioning program provides the proper proportion of strength and endurance required by the particular sport.

Summary

To develop a successful training program, it is essential for high school coaches—and athletes—to understand the principles of the various conditioning methods that contribute to physical fitness and improved strength.

Isometric exercises build strength in the muscles through static contraction. They can improve muscle strength for particular skills that require force when the muscle is in a particular position.

Isotonic exercises involve the dynamic contraction of muscles. Strength is improved through resistance training exercises based on the principle of increasing the resistance—or amount of weight—muscles can handle.

Modern weight training methods are credited to Dr. Thomas L. De Lorme, and today there are many variations of the De Lorme method: More common methods are Oxford, power, superset, cheating, bulk, triset, and double progressive. A recommended resistance training routine includes the following isotonic exercises in this order: standing press, bench press, bent-over row, upright row, curls, squats, and sit-ups.

Isokinetic exercises involve maximum exertion of muscles throughout a full range of motion and are done with devices that accommodate their force to specific muscle ability. Many coaches feel that isokinetic exercises are more effective than isometric and isotonic methods of conditioning.

Plyometrics is a type of training that forces muscles engaged in eccentric action to lengthen because of the load placed on them even though they are trying to shorten the muscles. It is especially beneficial for skills requiring explosive-reactive movement such as those needed in certain track and field events.

Cardiorespiratory (C.R.) fitness is essential for athletic activities, and it can be attained through all types of exercise. Smooth, relaxed running is generally agreed to be the most efficient method of obtaining C.R. fitness.

Circuit training is a conditioning method that has proved satisfactory for many athletes with limited time, space, or equipment. The system includes six to ten stations where athletes perform a particular series of exercises.

The ideal conditioning program is based on specific demands of the sport and the overall condition of each player. An effective program combines various conditioning methods.

References

1. Berger, Richard A. "Effects of Varied Weight Training Programs on Strength." *Research Quarterly,* 33 (May 1962), 168–181.
2. Burke, Ed. "Specificity Conditioning for Athletes." *United States Sports Academy News,* 2:1 (January– February 1978), 7.
3. Clark, E. Harrison. *Muscular Strength and Endurance in Man.* Englewood Cliffs, N.J.: Prentice-Hall, 1966.
4. Cooper, Kenneth H. *Aerobics.* New York: Bantam Books, 1968.
5. Counsilman, James. "Isokinetic Exercises: A New Concept in Strength Building." *Swimming World and Junior Swimmers,* 10 (November 1969), 4, 5, 15.
6. Crakes, James G. "An Analysis of Some Aspects of an Exercise Training Program Developed by Hettinger and Muller." Master's thesis. University of Oregon, 1957.
7. Dayton, O. William. *Athletic Training and Conditioning.* New York: Ronald Press, 1965.
8. De Lorme, Thomas L. "Restoration of Muscle Power by Heavy-Resistance Exercise." *Journal of Bone Joint Surgery,* 27 (October 1945), 645–667.
9. De Lorme, Thomas L., and Arthur L. Watkins. *Progressive Resistance Exercise.* New York: Appleton-Century-Crofts, 1961.

10. Drinkwater, B. L. "Physiological Responses of Women to Exercise." *Exercise and Sports Sciences Reviews,* 1 (1973), 125–153.
11. Falls, Harold B., *et al. Foundations of Conditioning.* New York: Academic Press, 1970.
12. Fears, Tom. "Build Strength through a Full Range of Motion with the Isokinetic Super Mini-Gym." *Isokinetic Conditioning.* Indpendence, Mo.: Mini-Gym, 1970, 1.
13. Gould, Adrian G., and Joseph A. Dye. *Exercise and Its Physiology.* New York: A. S. Barnes, 1932.
14. Hettinger, T., and E. Z. Muller. "Muskelleistung and Muskeltraining." *Arbeitsphysiologie,* 15 (October 1953), 111–126.
15. Hoffman, Robert L. *Fundamental Isometric Contraction System.* New York: The Bob Hoffman Foundation, 1961.
16. Jacoby, Ed. "Plyometric Strength Training." *Pamphlet,* Boise, Idaho: Boise State University, 1978.
17. Jones, Arthur. *Strength Training—The Present State of the Art.* DeLand, Fla: Nautilus Sports Medical Industries, 1974.
18. Karpovich, Peter V. *Physiology of Muscular Activity.* Philadelphia: W. B. Saunders, 1970.
19. Kramer, Jerry. *Lombardi—Winning Is the Only Thing.* New York: World Publishing, 1970.
20. Moore, James W. *The Psychology of Athletic Coaching.* Minneapolis: Burgess Publishing, 1970.
21. Morehouse, Lawrence E., and A. T. Miller. *Physiology of Exercise.* St. Louis: C. V. Mosby, 1967.
22. Morgan, Ronald E., and G. T. Adamson. *Circuit Training.* New Rochelle, N.Y.: Sportshelf & Soccer Associates, 1961.
23. Peterson, J. A. "Total Conditioning: A Case Study." *Athletic Journal,* 56:1 (September 1975), 40–55.
24. Rowland, Rick, and Sherman G. Button. "Water Polo Weight Training." *Swimming World and Junior Swimmers,* 11 (October 1970), 11, 20.
25. Royce, Joseph. "Re-evaluation of Isometric Training Methods and Results, A Must." *Research Quarterly,* 35 (May 1964), 215–216.
26. Ryan, A. J., and F. L. Allman, Jr., eds. *Sports Medicine.* New York: Academic Press, 1974.
27. Stephens, H., Jr. "The Practicability of Isokinetics." *Isokinetic Conditioning.* Independence, Mo.: Mini-Gym, 1970, 2, 4.
28. Stone, W. J., and W. A. Kroll. *Sports Conditioning and Weight Training— Programs for Athletic Competition.* Boston: Allyn and Bacon, 1978.
29. Wiggin, Paul, Floyd Peters, and Harvey E. Williams. *Off-Season Football Training.* New York: World Publishing, 1967.
30. Wilmore, J. *Athletic Training and Physical Fitness.* Boston: Allyn and Bacon, 1976.
31. Wilt, F. "Plyometrics, What It Is—How It Works." *Athletic Journal,* 55:9 (May 1975), 76, 89–90.

Purchasing and
Caring for Equipment

"Next year we have to get organized!"

Because a high school coach is responsible for the equipment used in athletic activities, he or she should be knowledgeable about methods of purchasing and caring for all types of equipment and supplies. Athletic goods are becoming increasingly expensive, and the coach can reduce spending costs by closely supervising the use and maintenance of equipment. The coach's responsibilities not only require spending athletic budget funds wisely but also protecting players from injury due to ill-fitting or nonprotective gear. Hand-me-down equipment invites problems of legal liability. Sophisticated new equipment and foreign products require increasingly sophisticated knowledge from the coach.

Objectives

This chapter discusses the following aspects of the purchase and care of athletic equipment and supplies:

1. Definitions of equipment, facilities, and supplies
2. Purchasing procedures
3. Purchasing policies
4. Care and maintenance of equipment and supplies
5. Player responsibility caring for equipment and supplies
6. Care and maintenance of artificial surfaces
7. Some suggested sources for sporting goods

Equipment, Facilities, and Supplies

The terms *equipment, facilities,* and *supplies* often are used interchangeably, but their meanings actually are quite different.

Equipment

Equipment refers to such things as football helmets, shoulder pads, uniforms, diving boards, stop watches, trampolines, boxing gloves, and tumbling mats. These items need to be purchased infrequently because they last for a long time.

Facilities

There are indoor facilities such as gymnasiums and outdoor facilities such as tennis courts and stadiums. These areas are sometimes called teaching stations or places where instruction, practice, and play take place.

Supplies

Supplies usually need to be replaced frequently. Included in this category are training room supplies (such as tape, ankle wraps, analgesic balm), socks, balls, T-shirts, and shells for a starting gun.

These definitions apply throughout most of the United States. However, it is important for each high school coach to know if any or all of the terms are interpreted differently in a particular region.

Purchasing Procedures

Purchasing procedures vary among institutions and school districts. As a general rule, small schools or school districts allow the coach or athletic director to do the purchasing, with the superintendent's approval. Larger schools and consolidated school districts usually buy athletic equipment and supplies through a purchasing agent or business office. Coaches must be familiar with both methods.

Direct Purchasing

Direct purchasing has many advantages: A coach is free to choose articles when the need for them arises, to deal directly with salespeople, and to contact dealers personally. If a coach is not well-informed, however, he or she can make poor purchases and thus not receive good value for the money spent. The following is an example of the kind of mistake an inexperienced coach can make with direct purchasing.

A coach needed shoulder pads for the football team. He was approached by an unprincipled salesman who had shoulder pads at "close-out prices." When he checked the budget, the coach found that he had funds to buy twenty shoulder pads; buying at the reduced price, however, he could stretch the available money and purchase forty pads, which he needed. When the shoulder pads were delivered, he discovered that they were flat pads, designed for use only by quarterbacks and wide receivers. They could not be returned or exchanged because the fine print accompanying the bill of sale read, "All sales are final with no exchanges accepted." The coach then had to admit his mistake to the school board and request more funds (21).

Because a coach is responsible for purchasing decisions and consequently for errors, it is essential that he or she be cautious when dealing with salespeople and dealers directly.

When a coach is required by the school to use a direct purchase form, it will probably look like the one in Figure 6.1.

Bid Purchasing

Some schools or school districts require that purchases costing more than a certain sum of money must be sent out for competitive bids. Pertinent information is mailed to various manufacturers and dealers with a request that

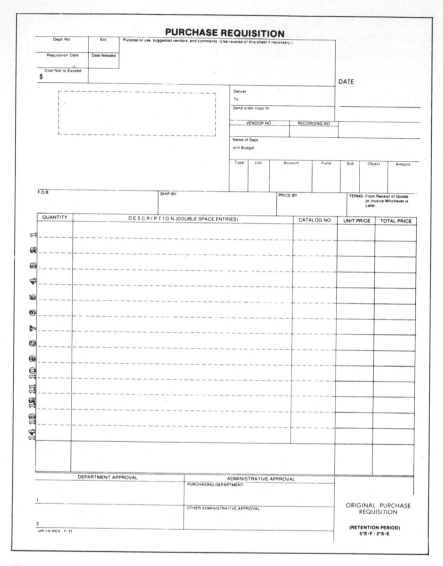

Figure 6.1 *A typical direct purchase form.*

they quote a price for the desired articles within a set time limit. Figure 6.2 shows a typical bid form mailed to the different manufacturers or dealers.

After bids are received, the coach sends a purchase order (Figure 6.3) to the company from whom the material is to be bought.

REQUEST FOR QUOTATION **THIS IS NOT AN ORDER**

RETURN ONE COPY TO

DATE NUMBER

IS YOUR ADDRESS INCLUDING ZIP CODE CORRECT?

TO BE CONSIDERED YOUR QUOTATION MUST BE RECEIVED BY____________________

IF FURTHER INFORMATION IS REQUIRED, PLEASE CONTACT

Please quote your lowest price for the material, and/or services, to be delivered, as specified below. Any deviation from the specifications must be identified and fully described. No charge for package, for drayage, or for any other purpose will be allowed over and above the prices quoted on this sheet. University of California standard purchase order terms and conditions apply. A copy of these conditions will be furnished on request. The right is reserved to accept or reject quotations on each item separately, or as a whole. If unable to quote, please return this form so marked.

ARTICLES SUPPLIED ON THIS FORM SHOULD BE PRODUCED OR MANUFACTURED IN THE UNITED STATES, IF OF FOREIGN MAKE, PLEASE SPECIFY ORIGIN.

UNLESS OTHERWISE SPECIFIED PRICES WILL BE F.O.B. UNIVERSITY OF CALIFORNIA

UNIT PRICE MUST BE EXTENDED

SHOW ANY APPLICABLE TAX SEPARATELY

CASH DISCOUNT__________PER CENT FOR PAYMENT WITHIN__________DAYS FROM RECEIPT OF GOODS OR INVOICE, WHICHEVER IS LATER.

UNIT PRICE	TOTAL PRICE

DELIVERY WILL BE MADE IN ________________DAYS AFTER RECEIPT OF ORDER.

SHIPPING WEIGHT________________LBS. ______METHOD OF SHIPMENT____________________

As a supplier of goods or services to the University of California I/we certify that racially segregated facilities will not be maintained nor provided for employees at any establishment under my/our control, and that I/we adhere to the principles set forth in Executive Orders 11246 and 11375 and undertake specifically _to maintain employment policies and practices that affirmatively promote equality of opportunity for minority group persons and women; to take affirmative steps to hire and promote women and minority group persons at all job levels and in all aspects of employment; to communicate this policy in both English and Spanish to all persons concerned within the company, with outside recruiting services, and the minority community at large; to provide the University on request a breakdown of our total labor force by ethnic group, sex, and job category; and to discuss with the University our policies and practices relating to our affirmative action program.

DATE — TELEPHONE NO (INCLUDING AREA CODE) — SIGNATURE OF FIRM REPRESENTATIVE

UP-9 (REV. 12-71)

Figure 6.2 *A typical bid-request form.*

When the coach suggests items for bid, he or she usually is not allowed to order a particular brand. However, one can include an exact description of the desired article in the specifications for bids. Also, it is wise to state that "no substitute will be acceptable."

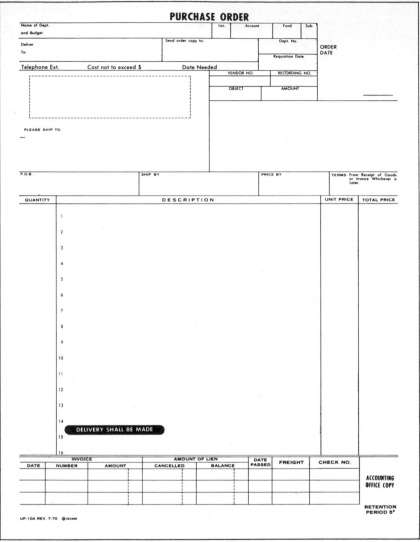

Figure 6.3 *A typical purchase order form.*

The bid-purchasing system has the following disadvantages: failure to secure desired brands; delays in delivery; no direct contact with sales-people; and the inability to take advantage of special-price offers.

Dr. Griffith C. O'Dell, former director of physical education and interscholastic athletics for the Minneapolis, Minnesota, school system, suggests some benefits of bid purchasing (17):

1. It saves the school board substantial amounts of money because of discount prices and lower transportation charges through quantity bidding.
2. It tends to bring about greater uniformity of quality equipment.
3. It reduces the possibility of local school officials' haphazard buying in small amounts from unknown sources.
4. It ensures that supplies and equipment will be on hand when school opens or before the sports season starts.
5. It saves the local school administrators and clerks the trouble and inconvenience of purchasing and delivering supplies and equipment.
6. It relieves the coach of the responsibility of purchasing supplies and equipment and gives him more time for the instruction needed on the athletic field.
7. It omits the possibility of salesmen disrupting school routine by calling upon coaches during the day.

Central Purchasing

Many school districts that purchase supplies and equipment for several schools stock central warehouses with large quantities of standardized materials. Some large districts standardize all sports equipment and supplies: The only difference among the different schools' uniforms is color. After each school makes known its own needs (Figure 6.4), a composite order is drawn up and sent out for bids.

The advantage of centralized purchasing is that materials can be bought well in advance and thus are available when needed. Competitive bidding for large quantities usually results in greater economy. Also, use of a central warehouse ensures that all orders, specifications, contracts, and records are kept in one location and are always accessible.

The disadvantages of the system are that it permits the coach no individual freedom in choosing material and that it fosters waste: Thinking that the central supply well can never run dry, coaches or athletes may become careless about caring for equipment and supplies.

Purchasing Policies

When an athletic department formulates policies for purchasing equipment and supplies, it should follow procedures that make good business sense. The following suggested guidelines can be adapted to any school or school system.

MINNEAPOLIS PUBLIC SCHOOLS
Department of Interschool Athletics

TRACK AND CROSS COUNTRY

On hand inventory	Number needed	Equipment	Check items for pooled buying	Specify make, description, color	Estimated amount
		Pants, sweat			
		Pants			
		Shirts			
		Shirts, sweat			
		Shoes			
		Sox, sweat			

SOURCE: Minneapolis Public Schools.

Figure 6.4 *An athletic request form.*

Keep inventory　No purchases should be made without a complete inventory of what is already in stock. The inventory list should include information about quantity, sizes, and condition of articles. Many schools keep a running inventory, which enables coaches to check at any time on available materials. This system prevents duplication or overpurchase of items. A coach often must initiate purchase requests and so should be involved in taking and keeping inventory records for a special activity. Figure 6.5 shows the necessary information.

Buy according to program needs　Enough equipment should be available so that all interested students can participate. Local interest and enthusiasm often dictate whether a school should increase equipment for a particular sport.

Purchase only quality equipment and supplies　As a general rule, if something is made well it will fit or work well and will last a long time. In buying quality items, a coach should consider the following:

1. Protection. Is the item made well enough to protect a player?
2. Durability. Is the item made of durable material?
3. Cost. Does the length of time a well-made item can last justify the greater initial cost?

CENTRAL UNION HIGH SCHOOL
Department of Athletics

WRESTLING   Equipment Category

Date	Item	New	Used A	Used B	Lost	Dis-card	Total on hand
6-1-72	Shoes—size 7	1	2	1	0	2	4
6-1-72	Shoes—size 10	0	1	5	1	3	6
6-1-72	Shoes—size 11	0	4	1	0	4	5

Used A = practically new. Used B = still usable.

Figure 6.5 *An athletic inventory form.*

4. Appearance. Is the item as attractive as it can be? This characteristic is important for squad morale, although it generally is not as essential as the other three factors.

To judge the quality of equipment and supplies, the coach must be familiar with new materials as well as traditional ones and know whether they have been thoroughly tested.

Deal only with reputable firms   They usually have high standards for the materials they handle and thus assure the purchaser of quality merchandise. The athletic director, coach, or purchasing agent usually is not in a position to know or test merchandise for protection or quality. As a general rule, one can rely on reputable dealers for information and suggestions. These firms usually carry the same brand of materials year after year, so replacements are easy to obtain. Also, reputable manufacturers will stand behind their merchandise and replace faulty goods without hesitation.

Give preference to local dealers   If the local dealer's prices are not out of line and the merchandise quality is good, give preference to that person. He or she generally will provide better service than an out-of-town or national firm. Also, since the dealer is a taxpayer whose money contributes to the athletic program, buying from him or her fosters the coach's public relations.

Standardize uniforms according to color, style, and type   There are many advantages to this system: Replacements from open stock are easily obtained; as the stock builds up, players will be assured of getting uniforms that fit and look exactly alike; the community can recognize and identify a team with a known uniform. Often younger athletes of the community are inspired to become team members by the prestige attached to wearing the uniform.

Plan replacement purchases   Initial purchases, such as of new uniforms or large quantities of shoulder pads, represent a considerable outlay of funds. A coach should state the number of new items needed and how long they are expected to last. In this way, the number of new items needed per year can be established and other needed purchases planned for.

Follow businesslike procedures   Even if a school already has a particular purchasing system, the following procedures should be considered:

1. Put all orders in writing.
2. Make all purchases with order blanks. This practice eliminates bills coming in unexpectedly late in the fiscal year and upsetting careful planning.
3. Use duplicate order blanks (as in Figure 6.1) so that a personal or office record can be kept. Check deliveries for accuracy.
4. Make payment whenever possible to take advantage of discounts. Most firms discount a portion of the cost if they receive payment prior to a given date.

Order in plenty of time to ensure delivery before the material is needed   Sporting goods manufacturers, as a general rule, take at least six months to make their products, and if orders are placed early, the company will be able to plan its production. Also, if they are given enough time, some manufacturers will mark the school's name on certain items.

If an order cannot be paid for until the school's fiscal year begins, the manufacturer can be notified to make an order effective on a certain date. Also, if storage is a problem, delivery can be requested for a particular time.

Conform to regulations set up by the National Federation of High Schools Association   These rules apply particularly to colors of uniforms for home and away, numbers for uniforms, and balls. Just because the word "official" is stamped on a ball or bat, the item is not necessarily qualified for use.

When possible, *purchase in quantity to take advantage of specially reduced prices*.

Take advantage of sales that meet particular needs   Money is not saved if articles bought on sale are not essential to the needs of the sports program. If costs are prohibitive to start a particular program, a coach could buy initial equipment on sale and thus save funds for other necessary items.

Purchase by bid when possible   Regardless of school size, the coach should request bids for all basic equipment. The economics of bid purchasing justify the extra effort involved.

Avoid high-pressure salespeople   Quality merchandise does not need a hard sell; its value speaks for itself.

Avoid gifts or favors   This policy can be difficult to follow when a salesperson or manufacturer offers the coach such tangible and tempting gifts as tennis racquets, shoes, or golf clubs. However, coaches must realize that if they accept such a gift, they are obligated to buy from that source. This limits the coach's freedom of choice, necessary for the best interests of the athletic program.

Purchase with proper fit in mind   The fitting of equipment is very important. Protective items must fit properly to ensure safety. Also, if clothing is the right size, it will last much longer than if it is too small or too large. Most manufacturers provide instructions for fitting procedures, and coaches should follow these recommendations closely. Figure 6.6 shows how to measure for proper fit of athletic equipment.

Purchase clothing that is compatible with weather and playing conditions of the area   Temperature obviously dictates what fabrics are most desirable. Toughness of materials depends on the playing surfaces: Rough, rocky, or frozen areas require materials different from those used for soft grass or synthetic surfaces.

Do not let lack of equipment keep students from participating   Many school districts require that individual athletes provide some of their own equipment, such as shoes. But the opportunity to participate should not be denied to students who are unable to purchase equipment. The coach can canvass other players for equipment no longer needed or that could be lent. Or the coach can help the student find a way to earn money for the necessary equipment.

When participants are expected to purchase personal items, the coach should make arrangements with a local dealer to carry the best brand. Also, the coach can give players' names to the dealer and request that they receive the normal discounts.

Be aware of differences between American-made and foreign-made items   There are those who advocate buying only domestically made goods. This policy should, of course, remain an individual choice. However, coaches should be aware that foreign methods of manufacturing certain

Correct measurement is essential for proper sizing of athletic equipment to insure the comfort of the wearer, the durability of equipment, proper protection, and proper appearance on the field. This is a basic measuring guide for most types of athletic equipment. For perfect fit, it is also recommended that you state height, weight, and any special irregularities of build.

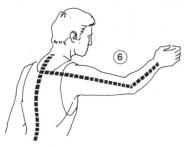

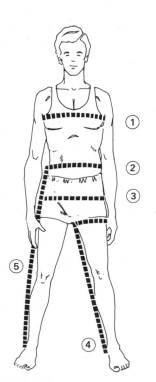

Key to Figures

1. CHEST. Be sure the tape is snug under the arms and over the shoulder blades.

2. WAIST. Place the tape above the hips and around waist like a belt to determine waist measurements.

3. HIPS. Measure hips around the widest part.

4. INSEAM. Measure inseam from the crotch to the top of the heel of the shoe when full-length pants are ordered. For shorter pants, like baseball and football pants, check on the measurement recommendations of the manufacturer.

5. OUTSEAM. Measure from the waistline to top of heel of shoe for full-length pants. For baseball, football, and shorter pants check the measurement recommendations of the particular manufacturer.

6. SLEEVE. Take measurements from center of back over elbow to wrist. Keep elbow bent, straight out from shoulder.

HEAD. (Not shown in diagram). The tape should run across forehead about 1½ inches above eyebrows and back around the large part of the head.

Reprinted by permission of The Athletic Institute and American Association for Health, Physical Education, and Recreation.

Figure 6.6 *How to measure for athletic equipment.*

items differ from American techniques. For instance, many leather shoes made in foreign countries are built on a flat last, which tends to bring on blisters and Achilles' tendon injuries (21). Shoes manufactured in the United States have a bent last, or arch support. Also, coaches should realize that some foreign branches of American companies make items according to American techniques and specifications.

Care and Maintenance
of Equipment and Supplies

Even if a coach is extremely cautious about purchasing only excellent equipment at the lowest possible price, his or her efforts are wasted if the items are not cared for and maintained properly. The following example illustrates how poor management can result in enormous unnecessary cost.

In a football game in Hawaii, a California university team's equipment was soaked by heavy rains. The equipment manager failed to dry everything thoroughly before it was packed in trunks for the return shipment, and when the trunks were eventually unpacked, all the equipment had been ruined. Uniforms were covered with mildew, and the stitching on all the shoes and pads had rotted.

It is important for high school coaches to realize that they are ultimately responsible for equipment used for their particular activities; therefore, they must carefully supervise its maintenance.

Reconditioning Equipment

Reconditioning equipment has become more and more advisable as the athletic dollar has shrunk. Professional reconditioners should be used to restore all articles, especially protective equipment. Some school districts allow the coaches or equipment managers to do it themselves. Too much is at stake to take chances with safety factors. The best policy is to engage only authorized and reputable companies.

Equipment Manager

Many schools include in the athletic staff an equipment manager, who is responsible for keeping all records, issuing equipment and supplies, checking on materials received, making nominal repairs, cleaning clothing, and storing equipment after the season has ended. Because adequate care of athletic materials requires special knowledge, the coach should be prepared to help an untrained equipment manager by offering necessary information about proper maintenance of equipment and supplies.

In the absence of an equipment manager, the coach is responsible for all equipment and supplies used for a sport. He or she can train students, perhaps including the team manager, in proper care and maintenance. A good system involves teaching a few students, who in turn train other interested individuals. Once the system is established, the coach can rely entirely on the students and systematically check from time to time to see that things are being done correctly.

Equipment Room

Ideally, all schools should have an athletic equipment and supplies area to accommodate all materials in daily use as well as in storage. Unfortunately, this situation is not always possible, and the coach must find substitute facilities that have proper conditions. He or she should establish a daily issue room for sports in season and a place for adequate storage.

There are several features that should be included in all equipment and storage rooms:

1. Rooms should be well lighted and airy, with divisions made of wire mesh to allow good circulation. Temperature and dampness should be controlled, and if the room has a cement floor, false flooring of some type should be added. Nothing should be stored on cement.
2. Equipment should be issued from windows so that student traffic is kept out of the room.
3. Table or counter space should be adequate for working with equipment.
4. A security system should be set up so that equipment and supplies cannot be stolen.
5. Open shelving should be adequate for storing bulk items such as shoulder pads.
6. Closed shelving should be available for uniforms and other clothing, and chemicals should be placed in the area to control destructive insects.
7. Bins should be provided for loose items such as socks.
8. High space should be provided for tall items such as vaulting poles.

Drying Room

Because perspiration and moisture cause deterioration of materials, it is desirable to have a room with racks where damp articles can be dried before use the next day. This room ideally should be equipped with forced hot air, but if such an area is not available a coach could use electric heaters and fans in a room to dry wet equipment. In some buildings, the drying rooms and laundry room may be combined.

Issuing Equipment

It is very important to keep careful record of the issuing and receiving of equipment and supplies. Issue cards (Figure 6.7) are one method of control. A player signs the card to acknowledge receiving various items. Once they have been issued, T-shirts, socks, towels, and other supplies that are used every day can be simply exchanged after use for clean, dry supplies.

CENTRAL UNION HIGH SCHOOL

Sport: BASKETBALL   Year:_____

Item	Size	No.	Date issued	Date returned
Towel				
Socks				
Supporter				
Shoes				
Practice pants				
Practice jersey				
Game pants				
Game jersey				
Game warm-up				
Travel bag				

Name_____ Year in School_____

Address_____ Telephone #_____

Athletic Locker #_____ Reg. Room_____

Receipt of the above articles is acknowledged. I promise that the above articles will be used only for regular scheduled school athletics. I also promise to return all articles when requested to do so.

Signature_____

Figure 6.7 *An athletic issue card.*

Markings

All equipment and supplies should be marked clearly so they can be identified easily for school name, player's number, size, and the year the item was purchased. Many manufacturers will premark items if orders are placed early enough. If the coach must do the marking, some suggested methods are:

Cloth. Use a rubber stamp and india ink, or use stencils with lamp black and paint thinner.
Leather. Use electric needles or felt marking pens. If needles are used, care should be taken not to burn identification too deeply.
Plastic. Use felt marking pens or paint.
Wood and metal. Mark with an electric needle.

To facilitate storage and recognition of size, size and number can be combined on cothing. For example, size 32 pants can be numbered from 1–100, size 34 from 101–199, and so on. Also, it is important to include the year of purchase, or perhaps a letter signifying the year. Older items should always be used first; if certain fabrics are left sitting on shelves too long, the strength of the threads can be weakened.

Many coaches feel that if markings are too attractive, the articles become more desirable and thus are more readily stolen. Some schools even include the humorous inscription, "Stolen from the athletic department of . . . ," but that doesn't necessarily decrease their losses. Markings should be primarily for identification and accounting; good management should control losses.

Recommended Procedures for Storage

Although some coaches may need to improvise storage areas, all coaches should follow certain procedures for storing equipment and supplies:

1. Before being stored, all articles should be thoroughly cleaned and repaired.
2. Paired items with laces, such as shoes, should be tied together.
3. Inflated articles, such as balls, should be partially deflated, keeping sufficient pressure to maintain shape.
4. New shoes should be kept in original boxes.
5. Stacking should be avoided unless items are in individual boxes; supplies made of cloth are exceptions to this rule.
6. When possible, articles should be stored according to size.
7. All markings should be checked prior to storage. Those that are not clear should be redone, and new articles should be marked.
8. A coach might find it handy to leave a few articles unmarked so that they can be exchanged for other sizes if necessary.
9. All stored articles should be kept in moisture-free areas and away from contact with cement.
10. All racquets should be stored in presses. Presses require more room, but they help the racquets keep their shape.
11. To prevent warping, items such as bats, javelins, and vaulting poles should be hung vertically on racks or hangers rather than stored flat.
12. Clothing should be stored in insect-proof closets or in cardboard cartons that contain chemicals and can be sealed with masking tape.

General Care of Fabrics

If fabrics are cleaned properly, articles will last longer. It is wise to follow the instructions manufacturers and dealers usually include with new articles. Two sporting goods companies, Wilson and Rawlings, have prepared excellent pamphlets with instructions for care of equipment and supplies. Some good general rules to follow are:

1. If there is any question about whether a fabric is color fast or preshrunk, the article should be dry cleaned. It is a good policy to provide the cleaner with a sample garment and any special cleaning instructions provided by the manufacturer.
2. One little-known fact is that dry cleaning removes dirt and stains, but it generally does not remove perspiration. Washing is the only way to remove perspiration; for some garments it might be necessary both to dry clean and wash to properly clean the article.
3. Cotton articles generally can be laundered without any problems.
4. A good policy is to clean garments as soon after use as possible to ensure maximum wear.
5. Do not clean differently colored articles together. Remember to remove colored laces that might fade and ruin the appearance of garments.
6. In areas where water is hard, a softener will obtain best results.
7. Avoid chlorine bleach because it has a tendency to cause the fabric to fade and weaken. When bleaching is necessary, an oxygen bleach will provide the desired result.
8. Wool should be laundered in cool or lukewarm water (not over 100°) and dried slowly to avoid shrinkage. The product called Woolite, a cold-water wash, has proved to be excellent for wool garments.
9. Knit fabrics shrink slightly. It is helpful to lay these articles flat to dry.
10. To ensure proper cleaning action, avoid overloading washing machines.
11. Elastic materials should be laundered in lukewarm water; high temperatures reduce elasticity.
12. Rayon, nylon, and most synthetics can be cleaned in lukewarm water with detergent or soap, or they can be merely rinsed if they are not too soiled. Synthetics should not be dried with excessive heat.
13. Grass stains are difficult to remove. However, most local laundries have some stain remover and generally will give out the necessary information for handling grass stains.
14. All athletic garments should be completely dry prior to being stored or put back on shelves for reuse.

General Care of Leather Goods

The method of caring for leather goods depends a great deal on locality. Different techniques are required in dry and moist areas. The following are some general hints for the care of leather goods:

1. Excessive moisture or high temperatures cause the most trouble.
2. Damp leather should never be dried on a heater or steam radiator, but rather should be dried slowly with moderate heat.

3. Green mold that occurs in moist areas will rot leather and should be brushed off at once.
4. Leather athletic shoes should be cleaned after every wearing. Dirt and lime from the playing areas should be brushed or scraped off.
5. Leather that has become hardened can be softened with neats-foot oil.
6. Saddle soap can be used to clean soiled leather.
7. Use a good-grade paste for leather that requires shining.
8. Never use excessive oil on leather.

General Hints for Special Items

Some materials require special treatment. Rubber goods can be damaged by direct sunlight, excessive heat, grease, and oil. Plastics can become brittle with excessive heat, but they generally require less care than other materials and normally can be cleaned with mild soap and warm water.

Most helmets are made of plastic alloys, and only the helmet paint and cleaner recommended by the manufacturer should be used on them. Many of the commonly known commercial cleaning products will damage or destroy the helmet shells, and then the helmet will be useless and dangerous to wear. Often, if helmets are painted with paint other than the kind recommended by the manufacturer, the warranty is nullified.

It is a good policy to clean, sanitize, and store helmets according to procedures suggested by the manufacturer. However, when that is not possible, one can clean most helmets by placing them in a whirlpool bath with warm water and a mild detergent for approximately ten minutes and then rinsing them thoroughly.

When each season is over, football shoulder and hip pads should be cleaned and sanitized according to manufacturer's suggestions. The whirlpool treatment is a good method of cleaning these pieces of equipment for storage; they should be dried thoroughly either outdoors or in a room that is not too hot.

Player Responsibility in Caring for Equipment and Supplies

A coach should emphasize to students their obligation to respect and take care of equipment and supplies. He or she must make them realize that the items issued to them are only on loan and that they are expected to return all equipment at the end of the season in good condition.

To impress his football players with the value of equipment and supplies, one high school coach placed everything on a table with large price tags attached. As the athletes were issued their gear, they could see how much each article cost. The coach also spent a good deal of time at the first squad practice explaining correct procedures for caring for equipment. These techniques resulted in player respect for the equipment. (See Figure 6.8.)

A coach may stress the following basic rules:

1. Never throw helmets on the ground: They can crack and lose their protective qualities.
2. Avoid walking with cleated shoes on hard surfaces such as cement.
3. After practice, put all gear in its proper place to prevent it from being walked on in a crowded locker room.
4. Immediately report minor damage such as rips or tears to the equipment manager so that repairs can be made before the defect becomes worse.
5. Avoid sitting on equipment. This rule applies especially to articles stowed in a traveling bag.
6. Wear items issued for athletics only for their intended purposes.
7. Take care of your own equipment and supplies when traveling.
8. Some coaches insist that players pack their own bags after the student manager has placed items in front of the athlete's locker. This practice ensures that all equipment is included and helps teach the players discipline and responsibility.
9. Return *all* equipment at the end of the season so that it can be issued again in the future.

Care and Maintenance of Artificial Surfaces

Artificial playing surfaces are relatively new in athletic facilities. Such surfaces are durable, have multiple uses, and may be used under adverse weather conditions. New improvements are constantly being made to add to their popularity. Manufacturers are quick to point out that care and maintenance are essential to obtain maximum usage and longevity.

The 3M manufacturing company, located in St. Paul, Minnesota, has been one of the leaders in developing both indoor and outdoor artificial surfaces. They claim that their product TARTAN, which was installed on the running track at Macalaster College in St. Paul, Minnesota, in 1963, was the first of its kind in the world. Subsequently, the TARTAN surface was first used for an international track meet at the Pan-American games of 1967 in Winnipeg. Canada, and in the 1968 Olympic games in Mexico City. In 1976 in Montreal, Canada, the Olympics returned to a synthetic running surface. 3M advocates the following system for the care and maintenance of its TARTAN surface:

Specifications

The following guidelines should be used to determine compatibility with TARTAN surfacing. Individual products should be tested on a small area of a surface before treating or coating an entire surface.

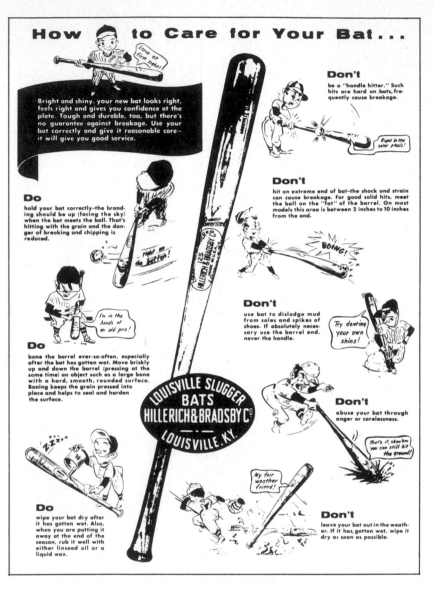

Figure 6.8 *A typical poster about caring for equipment. Such posters are often available from manufacturers.*

Floor Stripper

1. Should be able to remove polymer coatings previously applied.
2. Should be able to remove normal floor stains and traffic marks.
3. Solutions may cause chemical damage to TARTAN surfacing. Ammoniated strippers have been successful in the past.
4. Acid strippers and strong basic cleaners developed to be used on porcelain surfaces will cause damage to the TARTAN surface and are *not* recommended.

Maintenance Finish

1. Should be a metal-interlocking water emulsion system.
2. Should be applied with a mop or lambs-wool applicator.
3. Should have a "slip-resistance" functionality for the desired customer use.
4. Should be removable from the floor by a specified floor stripper.
5. Should not react chemically with the TARTAN surface.

Floor Detergent

1. Should be capable of removing dirt and stains from the synthetic floor surface without removing the finish.
2. Should be capable of removing any floor treatment applied during routine maintenance, for example, mop-treatment material.

Floor Treatment

1. Should be applied to a mop head.
2. Should not be absorbed into the floor, rather perform as a surface treatment.
3. Should not make the floor slippery.
4. Should be capable of removal by a simple detergent solution.

Solvent Cleaner or Mineral Spirits

1. Should be capable of removing difficult stains; black marks, shoe marks, tar, food stains, and other similar stains.
2. Should not react chemically with the TARTAN surface. (Cleaner may damage the surface under prolonged contact.)

Artificial Turf

Despite the allegation from some that artificial turf contributes to injuries, more and more of these surfaces are being installed. One of the leading companies, SuperTurf located in Garland, Texas, has prepared a booklet for the care and maintenance of its product. Although these suggestions are specifically for SuperTurf, their use seems logical for all artificial turfs.

Cleaning

1. Sweeping To maintain the large area, it is necessary to use the proper equipment to remove dust, dirt, and litter. Weekly sweeping of SuperTurf is most important to maintain your installation's original appearance and unique "playability" qualities. This is accomplished by using a machine especially designed to clean

SuperTurf with minimum fiber wear. By using this recommended machine after each game, you will keep your SuperTurf field attractive and clean.

2. Washing   A good rain is the best thing that can happen to maintain SuperTurf. Where there is not enough rain to remove dirt and soil, use of a high pressure water stream will bring loose soil off the surface. In the event that this water-flush procedure does not sufficiently remove imbedded dirt, a shampooing technique is recommended.

3. Stain Removal   Most stains which will occur can quickly be removed with warm water and a regular household detergent. Rinse thoroughly to remove all traces of soap. Chewing gum is a common hazard but can be removed quickly. Wrap an ice cube in a clean cloth and hold it against the gum until it hardens, then scrape with a knife carefully. Any oily substance or grease spot can be removed with cloth and mineral spirits.

Field Striping

To apply field striping many alternate techniques and types of equipment may be used, such as air sprayers, parking-lot line stripers, and airless spray equipment. The following is recommended at this time.

1. Paint   Semi-permanent paint Stadex #15 White Turf-Coat or Sherwin-Williams Metalatex (Also available in all NFL colors).

2. Equipment   GRACO Model President 5 gallon airless sprayer with 28:1 fluid pressure ratio. This unit is available on wheels for ease of handling. This unit also has adequate pump capacity to supply two spray guns. GRACO HYDRA-SPRAY pole gun (3 ft. length) equipped with a GRACO 163-417 Airless tip.

3. Removal of Paint   Water and a stiff brush will work. You may also use a water base ammonia cleaning solution.

Important Do's and Don't's

DO'S

Do remember that dirt is your turf's worst enemy.
Keep your turf clean!
Use "No Smoking" signs as SuperTurf will scorch.

DON'T'S

It is imperative that such activities as the following be prohibited in order to preserve your turf and protect your warranty.

Don't let dirt accumulate. Weekly cleaning is essential.
Prohibit activities that could damage your SuperTurf, such as the shot-put and javelin throw. Prohibit sharp spike track shoes and baseball spikes.
Do not allow linesmen to push pointed markers into turf.
Markers should be blunted and preferably covered.

SuperTurf should not be used as a storage place for materials such as drums, piles of lumber, etc.

Wire brushes, such as is in power or hand sweepers, should not be used.

Your turf should not be used as a work area for construction projects.

Unnecessary vehicle traffic, such as parking cars, and the use of the turf as a road, should be avoided. Vehicles tend to drop grease and will stain the turf.

Any cleaning equipment, method, or material not authorized by SuperTurf Inc. should not be allowed.

Any activities except those that the turf was specifically designed for are prohibited. However, if a need should arise for an unusual use of your turf, SuperTurf Inc. should be contacted prior to this activity.

Some Suggested Sources for Sporting Goods

The number of sporting goods and supplies dealers is too great to include in this chapter; a complete list can be obtained in *The Sporting Goods Directory,* published by The Sporting Goods Dealer, P.O. Box 56, St. Louis, Missouri, 63166. The following sources are given so that coaches will have some idea where to look for equipment for sports normally included in a secondary-school athletic program. The list is not intended as an endorsement of the firms.

General Suppliers

A. M. F. Voit, Inc.
  P.O. Box 958
  Santa Anna, CA 92702
Medalist/Atlas Athletic Co.
  P.O. Box 748
  Sikeston, MO 63801
Rawlings Sporting Goods Co.
  2300 Delmar Boulevard
  St. Louis, MO 63166
A. G. Spalding
  Meadow Street
  Chicopee, MA 01014
Wilson Sporting Goods Co.
  2233 West Street
  River Grove, IL 60171

Archery

American Archery Co.
  P.O. Box 100 Industrial Park
  Oconto Falls, WI 54154
Bear Archery Div. Victor Co.
  Rural Route 1
  Grayling, MI 49738

Ben Pearson, Div. Leisure Group Inc.
  445 S. Figuerra St.
  Los Angeles, CA 90017

Baseball

Everlast Sporting Goods Manufacturing
  Co. Inc.
  750 E. 132nd St.
  Bronx, NY 10454
General Athletic Products Co.
  Riffle Avenue
  Greenville, OH 45331
MacGregor, A. Brunswick Co.
  1 Brunswick Plaza
  Skokie, IL 60076

Basketball

Converse Rubber Co.
  55 Fordham Rd.
  Wilmington, MA 01887
King Co.
  90 University St.
  Box 1110
  Seattle, WA 98111

Sand-Knit, Div. Medalist Industries
  290 Junction Street
  Berlin, WI 54923

Fencing
Castello Fencing Equip. Co., Inc.
  836 Broadway
  New York, NY 10003
Premier Athletic Products
  25 E. Union Ave.
  Rutherford, NJ 07073
Zwickei-Tsa Division
  P.O. Box 309
  Jenkintown, PA 19046

Football
Champion Products Inc.
  314 Monroe Ave.
  Rochester, NY 14618
Jayfro Corp.
  Box 401
  Waterford, CT 06385
Powers Mfg. Co.
  1340 Sycamore St.
  Waterloo, IA 50705

Golf
Cushman Omc-Lincoln
  1401 Cushman Dr.
  Lincoln, NE 68512
Slazenger
  Box 160
  Cornwells Heights, PA 19020
Wittech Golf Supply Co.
  3650 Avondale
  Chicago, IL 60618

Ice Hockey
Bauer Canadian Skate, Inc.
  75 Isabelle St.
  Buffalo, NY 14207
Cooper-Canada Ltd.
  501 Alliance Ave.
  Toronto 9, Ontario, Canada 108

Soccer Sport Supply Co., Inc.
  1745 First Ave.
  New York, NY 10028

Judo
Castello Combative Sports Co.
  836 Broadway
  New York, NY 10003
Ju-Do Mfg., Co.
  P.O. Box 311
  San Gabriel, CA 91778
Judo, Karate Supply and Athletic
Equipment
  6836 S. Mac Dill Ave.
  Tampa, FL 33611

Skiing
Alcock Laight and Westwood Ltd.
  59 Bramelea Rd.
  Bramelea, Ontario, Canada 108
Wigwam Mills, Inc.
  3402 Crocker Ave.
  Sheboygan, WI 53081

Soccer
W.H. Brine Co.
  1450 Highland Ave.
  Needham, MA 02192
Peter Green Co.
  Gay Street
  West Chester, PA 19380
Stall and Dean Manufacturing Co.
  95 Church Street
  Brockton, MA 02401

Swimming
American Playground Device Co.
  1801–33 Jackson St.
  Anderson, IN 46011
Ocean Pool Supply Co.
  17 Stepar Place
  Huntington Station, NY 11746
White Stag Water Sports Div.
  Box 5308
  Carson, CA 90749

Tennis
Golf and Tennis Headgear Co.
  8315 W. 20th Ave.
  Hialeah, FL 33014
Superior Sports Products
  P.O. Box 325
  706 State St.
  Litchfield, IL 62056
Tennis Products, Inc.
  11 Skyview Dr.
  Stamford, CT 06902

Track and Field
Adidas Sport Shoe Vanco.
  5133 W. Grand River Ave.
  Lansing, MI 48901
Cranbarry Inc.
  2 Lincoln Ave.
  Marblehead, MA 01945
Olympic Sports
  745 State Circle
  Ann Arbor, MI 48104

Volleyball
Acme Sporting Goods Mfg. Co.
  2011–11 W. Wabamsia Ave.
  Chicago, IL 60647
Bonham, Inc.
  P.O. Box 487
  Pomona, CA 91769
Mizuno Corp.
  834 South Spring St.
  Los Angeles, CA 90014

Wrestling
General Athletic Products Inc.
  Riffle Ave.
  Greenville, OH 45331
Roderick Wrestling Div.
  Capital Industries Inc.
  332 South Hampton Rd.
  DeSoto, TX 75115
Wilton Manufacturing Co., Inc.
  East Main Street
  Ware, MA 01082

Summary

High school coaches are ultimately responsible for all equipment and supplies used in their sport and should understand various methods of purchasing and maintaining these articles.

Purchases can be made either directly or through competitive bids. The coach or athletic director may be responsible for buying needed equipment, or purchasing may be done by a central business office for the school district.

Regardless of the purchasing method, the coach should be aware of policies that are businesslike and ensure quality materials with the best protection for the players.

The care and efficient management of all equipment and supplies result in considerable savings. Many schools have equipment managers, but the coach should always be able to provide information necessary for maintaining articles used in the sport. Desirable features of a maintenance program include an equipment room and a drying room; special care should be taken in issuing, marking, and storing equipment.

Artificial surfaces require special care and attention.

The coach should emphasize to the players their obligation to respect and care for the equipment and supplies they use for athletics.

References

1. *Athletic Equipment Digest.* St. Louis: Rawlings Sporting Goods Co., 1968. Pamphlet.
2. Bourgaurdez, Virginia, and Charles Heilman. *Sports Equipment: Selection, Care, and Repair.* South Brunswick and New York: A. S. Barnes, 1950.
3. Bucher, Charles A. *Administration of School Health and Physical Education Programs.* 3rd ed. St. Louis: C. V. Mosby, 1963.
4. *Care of Athletic Equipment.* River Grove, Ill.: Wilson Sporting Goods Co. Pamphlet.
5. *Cleaning Athletic Garments.* River Grove, Ill.: Wilson Sporting Goods Co. Pamphlet.
6. *Equipment and Supplies for Athletics, Physical Education and Recreation.* Washington, D.C.: American Association for Health, Physical Education, and Recreation; Chicago: The Athletic Institute, 1960. Pamphlet.
7. Forsythe, Charles E. *The Athletic Director's Handbook.* Englewood Cliffs, N.J.: Prentice-Hall, 1954.
8. Forsythe, Charles E., and I. A. Keller. *Administration of High School Athletics.* 5th ed. Englewood Cliffs, N.J.: Prentice-Hall, 1972.
9. Frost, Reuben B., and Stanley L. Marshall. *Administration of Physical Education and Athletics.* Dubuque, Iowa: William C. Brown, 1977.
10. Fuoss, Donald E., and Robert J. Troppmann. *Creative Management Techniques in Interscholastic Athletics.* New York: John Wiley, 1977.
11. George, Jack F., and Harry A. Lehmann. *School Athletic Administration.* New York: Harper & Row, 1966.
12. *How to Budget, Select, and Order Athletic Equipment.* Chicago: Athletic Goods Manufacturers Association, 1962. Pamphlet.
13. Johnson, M. L. *Functional Administration in Physical and Health Education.* Boston: Houghton Mifflin, 1977.
14. Kacsmarek, John C. "Equipment Care Cardinal Obligation." *The American School Board Journal,* 153 (August 1966), 29.
15. Meyer, Kenneth L. *Purchase, Care and Repair of Athletic Equipment.* St. Louis: Educational Publishers, 1948.
16. Murray, Frank J. "Perpetual Inventory." *Scholastic Coach,* 31 (January 1962), 20, 32.
17. O'Dell, Griffith C. "Proposed Budget for 1971–72 and Annual Report." For the Minneapolis, Minnesota, Public School Department of Interschool Athletics (December 1971).
18. Oosting, Bernard R. "Does Sports Equipment Require a Manager?" *Nations Schools,* 73 (May 1964), 92.
19. Purdy, Robert L. *The Successful High School Athletic Program.* West Nyack, N.Y.: Parker Publishing, 1973.
20. Resick, Matthew C., Beverly L. Seidel, and James G. Mason. *Modern Administrative Practices in Physical Education and Athletics.* Reading, Mass.: Addison-Wesley, 1975.
21. Tropea, Robert. Interview. June 13, 1972.
22. Voltmer, Edward F., and Arthur A. Esslinger. *The Organization and Administration of Physical Education.* New York: Appleton-Century-Crofts, 1967.

Managing a Budget 7

"Federal aid for schools, Hell, How about Federal Aid for Me!"

High school athletic departments handle budgeting in different ways, but in most cases the coach is involved. It is important that the coach be familiar with various budgetary procedures. Some coaches are given complete control of developing and administering the budget for their sports. Others are asked to supply information about their needs to someone in a position of higher authority, who then analyzes it, taking into consideration available funds and the needs of all sports, and informs the coaches of the final budget for their sports. If a coach feels that more money is needed for an activity, adjustments to the budget generally are made.

Because interscholastic athletics have historically been considered extracurricular, high school athletics have traditionally been financed by sources other than taxation, the local school district's normal source of revenue. Funds for the interscholastic athletic program have therefore often been obtained on the principle that one sport, such as football or basketball or hockey, could provide enough income through gate receipts to finance all the sports. In 1954, the Educational Policies Commission of the National Education Association recognized the educational contribution made by athletics and took a position that the total cost of the athletic program should be financed through the general school fund (7). As the educational opportunities offered by sports have been recognized, many school boards have incorporated athletics in the regular curriculum and have included financial support for the athletic program in the school budget. Currently several states, such as New York, have changed their laws so that tax dollars can support interscholastic athletics similar to a department like chemistry or history (22).

Expanding the sports programs throughout the United States has increased demands for additional facilities, equipment, and personnel. Rising costs, also, have made athletic programs extremely expensive, so the school board's financial support for high school sports activities often must be supplemented with income from gate receipts and other fund-raising activities.

Because budgeting procedures vary among school districts and individual schools, it is imperative for a coach to be knowledgeable about how a budget is constructed and administered and what procedures are followed by a particular school. As a member of the athletic staff, the coach contributes to the administration of the budget by using only allocated money and adhering to established policies.

In recent years, high school athletics throughout the nation have felt the pinch of limited funds. Some areas, including Philadelphia, Pennsylvania, and Oakland, California, have had to curtail programs temporarily because they did not have enough funds to meet increased costs. Therefore, it is essential that coaches use wisely the money allowed in the school budget for the athletic department. Fiscal irresponsibility, rather than the number of games won and lost, has caused the dismissals of many coaches.

Objectives

This chapter examines budgeting as it relates to finances involved in high school athletics. The following topics are discussed:

1. Definition and purpose of budgets
2. Budget control and responsibility
3. Criteria for a good budget
4. Methods of budget construction
5. Approval of the budget
6. Periodic appraisals
7. Sources of financial support for high school athletics
8. Athletic guarantees
9. The effects of Title IX on athletic budgeting
10. Data processing techniques

Definition and Purpose of Budgets

There are numerous definitions for the term *budget,* but most include the basic ingredients of expenditure, income, and time. In his book, *The Fundamentals of Public School Administration,* W. G. Reeder defines the term in a manner that seems applicable to athletics: A budget "is a systematized statement which forecasts the probable expenditures and anticipated revenues of an individual, an organization, or an institution during a stated period of time" (21).

Probable expenditures These are expenses essential for conducting the sport. They include salaries, supplies, equipment, travel, and the costs involved in conducting games.

Anticipated income As a general rule, anticipated income comes from two major sources, although funds can be supplied in other ways as well. The principal sources of money are (1) tax revenues, which are used primarily for salaries and construction and maintenance of facilities, and (2) gate receipts, which are used for operating costs. When the athletic department receives funds from other sources, the money usually is applied to general development of the athletic program.

High school budgets usually are devised for a fiscal year that correlates closely with the academic year, running usually from July 1 of one calendar year through June 30 of the next. In only a few instances does the school fiscal year correspond with the calendar year.

The primary purpose of a budget is to establish the most efficient way to spend funds so that the educational goals expected from the various activities can be fulfilled. A secondary purpose of the budget should be to control spending by designating ways in which money can be spent. If the budget is followed, each sport is assured of receiving its allocated share of money for the full term. Without this control, accounts can become garbled, and overexpenditure at the start of the fiscal year results in the reduction of the number of activities normally offered in the spring. Controls should not be too restrictive; they merely should ensure that appropriated funds are used properly.

Budget Control and Responsibility

Regardless of the source of revenue, most school boards are legally responsible for administering all funds provided for the programs under their jurisdiction (6). How these funds are controlled depends on such factors as the size and organization of the school district, the sizes and number of schools in the district, and legal statutes that apply to high school athletics. The school board has the prerogative to establish budgetary control methods; it also can delegate responsibility for the budget. The board may appoint an administrative officer, such as the superintendent of schools or a principal, to administer the budget under its supervision. That person in turn may designate someone else—a member of the purchasing department in the school district's central office, a district athletic director, or a member of the principal's staff—to make certain the budget is followed. But despite the fact that others are directly overseeing expenditure, the school board ultimately is legally responsible for administration of the budget.

The people generally responsible for high school athletic budgets are the school superintendent, central office budget officer, city athletic director, school principal, school athletic director, physical education director, or a faculty member.

School Superintendent

In school districts containing only a few schools, the school superintendent may control all budgeting, including funds for the high school athletic program. In large school districts that include many schools, however, the school superintendent usually does not have time for such details; such responsibility is usually delegated to a staff member.

Central Office Budget Officer

Many school districts include in their organizational structure business officers who are responsible for all purchasing and control of budgets. This position usually is found in larger districts, but some small school districts also have budget officers.

City Athletic Director

Because of the advantages of centralized control, many cities establish a city athletic director to handle all matters concerning high school athletics. This person deals with all fiscal matters, including the control of athletic budgets.

School Principal

Many principals are charged with the responsibility of the athletic budget. The size of the school determines whether the principal actually supervises the budget or whether he or she delegates this task to another person on the staff.

School Athletic Director

As this position gains professional stature, it gains more responsibility— including control of the school athletic budget.

Physical Education Director

In many instances, the physical education director is involved with the athletic program because of the close relationship between physical education and high school athletics. In some areas of the country, only physical education—and not high school athletics—is legally recognized as part of the school curriculum. Therefore, the physical education director is put in charge of controlling the tax money used for the athletic program.

A Faculty Member

In school districts where responsibility for the budget rests within each school, it is not unusual for someone on the faculty to handle funds for high school athletics. Usually this person teaches economics or business, or is the school business manager. This faculty member, the "faculty athletic manager," is concerned primarily with fiscal matters and not with how the athletic program is conducted. Sometimes a coach is given responsibility for administering the budget for his or her own sports program.

Regardless of who is assigned to control the high school athletic budget, sound business and financial procedures are essential to a well-administered program (12). The person responsible should thoroughly understand general fiscal matters and the specific financial procedures of the school district. All activities within each school and district should be regulated by the same financial controls and accounting principles. The accounts of the entire athletic program should be included in an annual audit of school funds, and all relevant information should be made public.

Criteria for a Good Budget

People expect different things from a budget: Some want absolute controls, which dictate policy; some want complete freedom and flexibility and the right to make judgments as a situation dictates. A good athletic budget can be developed that includes the possibility for both extremes. It has certain characteristics:

The athletic program's educational objectives and the money required are identified clearly Too often when an athletic budget is put together, educational aims are ignored, and successful performance or the importance of a particular activity is emphasized. Although these factors should be considered, they should not override the cultural objectives of the total athletic program.

Proposed expenses are based on facts, not hopes Expenditures for equipment and supplies should be estimated according to accurate inventories revealing the exact condition of the materials on hand. If new articles are needed, the budget should project realistic costs for replacements rather than include sums for a great deal of innovative equipment.

If possible, game costs for scheduled events should be included. If, however, there are scheduling problems, the number of home and away games should be established, and the estimates of probable costs should be based on this figure.

Estimated income is derived from accurate accounts The best source of budget information is past records. Also, factors such as traditional rivalry, team records, and the number of contests in the season should be taken into account. If estimates are based on wishful thinking rather than accurate records, the result can be financial loss that can jeopardize the entire athletic program.

Allowance is made for unexpected expenditures A sound budget should primarily offer guidelines. When money is needed for an emergency, there should be enough flexibility within the budget to allow for the transfer of funds designated for another purpose of the use of unallocated money.

Preparation is done well in advance There should be ample time for evaluation and review so that hasty financial decisions need not be made.

The sums included are realistic and can be easily defended as necessary for the program Some people advocate that the amount of money presented in the budget should be larger than actually necessary so that when it is not all used, the department will appear to be saving money. However, budget presentations made in an ethical manner are more justifiable and hence more acceptable to the school board.

Some provision is made for future needs Such provision may take the form of a contingency fund. Although most school districts do not allow unexpended funds to be carried over from one year to the next, the school board may consent to this procedure. In good years, when income exceeds expenses, funds should be set aside to handle the reverse situation. Also, reserve funds are helpful when the department must make an occasional large purchase of new equipment.

Methods of Budget Construction

There are many different methods of constructing a budget, but each technique seems to include four basic steps.

Research into Past, Present, and Future Needs

Previous budgets   To estimate income and expenses, one should consult previous budgets for information. As far as you can tell, were the budgets reasonably accurate? Were the funds they allocated adequate for various aspects of the program? Did they achieve the educational goals of the program?

When the person preparing a budget reviews past information, he or she often finds discrepancies between projected figures and actual income. Unusual circumstances that affected past attendance should be considered, as they can apply to the calculations. One must take into account that unusual weather conditions, a poor team record, or national events may influence attendance and consequently decrease the income for a game.

If no previous budgets are available because the school is new or past records have been destroyed, information usually can be obtained from other schools. Some coaches and administrators often hesitate to discuss financial affairs outside their own schools, but generally they will provide helpful information when they understand its purpose.

Present needs   Fastidious inventories of athletic supplies and equipment are essential for preparing a budget. Actual needs of the department can be established, and unessential expenditures can be avoided. If money is requested for items already on hand, other lower-priority needs of the program may unnecessarily be denied funds.

Future needs   The budget should include funds for possible future needs. Thought must be given to changes in the program, such as the addition of coaches, teams, or different sports. Also, allowance should be made for unexpected scheduling arrangements, such as a long trip or an invitation to a team from another school, an expenditure that requires a large financial guarantee. Sometimes teams outside the home school's league are scheduled on a home-and-home basis, each team paying for its own travel expenses. When it is the home team's turn to play at the other school, the travel costs reflected in the budget will show a considerable increase over the year when the game was played at home.

If an athletic director or fiscal officer is preparing the budget, he or she should consult each person concerned with administering or using funds before estimating a particular program's needs. Each coach should submit a budget for his or her own activity, which then can be compiled into a composite plan for the entire interscholastic athletic program. The coach should list in priority order the needs for the sport. This practice is difficult, but, if cuts must be made, the absolute essentials will be taken care of.

Determining Total Expected Expenses

After past budgets have been reviewed and present and future needs projected, total anticipated expenses can be determined. Some of these expenses are fixed and relatively easy to compute; others are variable and should be computed on a three- to five-year average. Typical items that must be considered are:

supplies
equipment
travel, including transportation, meals, and overnight lodging
awards
health and medical insurance
game production costs, including fees for police protection, ticket sellers,
    ticket takers, officials, and custodians
laundry
incidental repairs
scouting, if allowed
game movies
advertising
guarantees for visiting teams
inflation

Some schools or particular sports may have additional expenditures, such as rental fees for the use of facilities. All possible expenses should be considered and included in the total figure.

Each sport should present an itemized account of anticipated expenses, as shown in Figure 7.1. One of the advantages of this presentation is that previous expenses can be easily compared. Increases or decreases for respective items are pointed out and justified where necessary.

After all coaches have submitted their anticipated expenses, a composite expense budget should be compiled, which includes all anticipated expenses for the athletic department. Figure 7.2 shows how this information can be presented.

CENTRAL UNION HIGH SCHOOL

Year: 1974–75   Sport: BASKETBALL

Items	1973–74 (esti-mated)	1973–74 (actual)	1974–75 (esti-mated)	Increase (+) Decrease (−)
Officials	$400	$400	$350	−50
Ticket takers	100	100	90	−10
Ticket sellers	100	100	90	−10
Custodians	150	150	125	−25
Police	150	150	125	−25
Transportation	350	325	400	+50
Lodging	150	125	200	+50
Meals	150	140	175	+25
Laundry	150	135	150	
Towels	50	50	50	
Awards	200	175	200	
Movies	50	40	40	−10
Insurance	100	100	100	
Balls	150	175	175	+25
Uniforms	400	387	100	−300
Shoes	100	115	125	+25
Guarantees	400	400	200	−200
Clinics	150	150	150	
TOTALS	$3,300	$3,217	$2,845	$−465

NOTE: Reduction due to one less home game and only supplementary uniform purchase.

Figure 7.1   *An itemized account of anticipated expenses for one sport.*

Coaches' salaries or physical plant improvements usually are not listed as athletic expense items, since they generally are considered part of the school's normal expenses and are usually paid for strictly by income from taxes.

Analysis of Income

Income should be estimated through critical analysis. If income is overesti-mated, a deficit can result that embarrasses the school board and some-times causes the dismissal of the budget maker.

As a general rule, the high school athletic program is financed not by reg-ular school revenues but rather by some outside source. However, because

CENTRAL UNION HIGH SCHOOL

Anticipated Athletic Expense Budget 1974–75

Item	1973–74 (esti- mated)	1973–74 (actual)	1974–75 (esti- mated)	Increase (+) Decrease (−)
Baseball	$ 600	$ 615	$ 625	+25
Basketball	2,178	2,346	2,400	+222
Football	3,256	3,175	3,200	−56
Golf	50	40	50	
Hockey	2,861	2,970	3,100	+239
Swimming	300	315	325	+25
Tennis	50	76	75	+25
Track	300	278	300	
Wrestling	150	146	150	
Medical (doctors)	400	400	400	
Training supplies	500	517	500	
League dues	150	150	150	
Miscellaneous	500	471	500	
TOTALS	$11,295	$11,499	$11,775	$+480

Figure 7.2 *A composite budget of anticipated expenses.*

the educational values of athletics are receiving increased recognition, more and more school districts are including high school athletics in the school budget.

In computing the anticipated income for athletics, several sources must be considered, for example, board of education funds, gate receipts, student activity fees, season ticket sales, and money from booster clubs. These and other sources will be discussed in detail later in the chapter.

Figure 7.3 presents a form for preparing the budget for a single school. This method can be adapted easily to a school district that has several schools, the only difference being that each school's total estimated income would be stated separately.

Statement of Final Budget

The final statement of the budget includes the estimates of income and expenses that have been calculated as a result of considering all pertinent information. Funds should be broken down separately for each athletic activity.

In some large school districts, a financial officer in the central office prepares the final budget. Though this method has the advantage of avoiding

CENTRAL UNION HIGH SCHOOL
Estimated Athletic Income 1974–75

Item	1973–74 (esti- mated)	1973–74 (actual)	1974–75 (esti- mated)	Increase (+) Decrease (−)
Football				
gate receipts	$2,100	$1,976	$2,000	−100
Basketball				
gate receipts	4,000	3,870	4,000	
Hockey				
gate receipts	2,250	2,746	2,500	+250
Guarantees	1,000	1,000	1,500	+500
Student				
activity cards	550	600	600	+50
Radio &				
T.V. Rights	250	250	300	+50
District &				
tournament play	1,000		1,000	
Booster Club support	1,000	1,500	1,250	+250
TOTALS	$12,150	$11,942	$13,150	$+1,000

Figure 7.3 *Budget form for a single school.*

duplication, it has the disadvantage of the person's unfamiliarity with particular schools and insensitivity to differences that might exist among them. When the final budget is prepared in the school itself and involves the individuals most concerned with actually spending the money, these people become more aware of their fiscal responsibilities.

The final budget should conform to the budgetary style and practice of the school or school district, so that the people who are responsible for administering funds understand clearly how all figures have been computed and presented.

Approval of the Budget

In most school districts, the school principal accepts the athletic budget as it is presented by the athletic director or the school's business manager. If the budget is acceptable, the principal forwards it to the district business manager or the person serving in that capacity. That person then submits it to the superintendent of schools and finally to the school board, which is legally responsible for school finances (15). At each step of the way, adjustments can be made so that the athletic budget conforms to the fiscal policy of the school district.

Periodic Appraisals

During the school year it is customary for the person administering the budget to make periodic checks to see that funds are being used properly. These appraisals are extremely helpful to the coach, because they specify the amount of money still available for the activity. They also ensure that one sport does not overspend at the expense of another.

In large school systems, the central accounting office generally provides each activity with a monthly balance sheet, which includes monies spent and the balance of funds remaining.

When budget control and accounting are done by the school, a central card for each sport should be established (22). This card usually contains the name of the sport, account number, and the amount of money allocated, and it has provision for a record of purchase orders and venders. As money is spent, that amount is subtracted from the total so that the balance left in the account is known.

Sources of Financial
Support for High School Athletics

As mentioned previously, income for the support of high school athletics comes from many different sources. Ways of obtaining money are especially important for school districts requiring the athletic program to be self-sufficient. There are numerous techniques for acquiring funds, and the methods followed generally depend on the community and the views of its citizens regarding the importance of the athletic program.

Although many educators question the validity of financing school programs with funds not allocated by the school board, if people feel that the high school athletic program is important, then money must be raised to make activities possible. The Wilson Sporting Goods Company has published a booklet entitled *Successful Financial Plans for School Athletics Departments,* with helpful suggestions provided by "superintendents, principals, athletic directors, coaches, and administrators" (26). Some of the ideas that have proved successful in reducing debts and making up deficits are advertisements in sports programs, homecoming queen contests, shares of merchants' profits, Christmas tree sales, "give-a-book" days (donating books for resale), Sadie Hawkins Day dances, vaudeville nights, faculty basketball games, car washes, and student work days.

Following are brief summaries of some commonly used methods of raising money to support the high school athletic program.

Gate Receipts

Tickets can be sold for admission to games. Student tickets always should be offered at a reduced rate, whereas adults should pay a higher price. When ticket prices are set, it is important to remember that they should not compare with the cost of tickets to professional games. The fee charged for high school games should be afforded easily by all students.

Season Tickets

Season tickets can be sold in advance at a reduced rate to encourage attendance at games and ensure a certain amount of income regardless of the team's success or failure. Season tickets should be offered to both students and adults. Many schools provide these tickets in the form of a booklet or punch card, but a season pass also works satisfactorily.

Booster Club Support

Booster clubs can raise money for the athletic program in many ways. They usually have membership fees, and they also provide workers to carry on a wide variety of fund-raising activities outside the school. Enthusiastic management of rummage sales, Las Vegas nights, bingo parties, auctions, suppers, cake sales, and carnivals can result in a good deal of income to support different sports.

Concessions

Because concessions involve food, the coach or athletic director can enlist the help of the home economics instructor or the cafeteria manager to run concessions with student assistants. Some of the income should go to projects in which these people have special interest. If they cannot help, the coach usually can find a civic group such as a veterans' organization or civic club that is willing to handle the concession and share in the profits.

Student Activity Card

The activity card is probably the most widely used student ticket. It is somewhat like the season ticket sold to adults, but it usually can be used for all student events where fees are charged. One advantage of the student activity card is that money from sales is put into a general fund that serves all school programs. Naturally, with the number of students interested in various activities buying cards, the total sales are large, and there is an assured financial base for the operation of all programs.

Radio and TV Rights

Most radio and TV stations are willing to pay a fee for the right to broadcast all home games. This matter must be negotiated with the managers of the stations, and although they pay only a nominal amount of money for high school games, this sum does contribute to the athletic program's total income.

School Carnivals

This method of fund raising requires a great deal of planning and many enthusiastic student workers. Games, sideshows, strength contests, fortune tellers, wheels of fortune, and other "attractions" can be set up either in the gym or in the campus stadium. Prizes can be bought at low cost from carnival supply houses, and local merchants often are willing to donate merchandise to be given away as door prizes. The school carnival usually becomes a traditional social and entertainment event on the calendar of student affairs.

Mineral or Oil Rights

This is an unusual method of financing high school athletics and obviously depends on geographic locality. In states like Texas and California, where oil is found, part of the district's income to carry on the high school athletic program is supplied by oil rights.

Candy Sales

Several candy companies promote advertising by sponsoring groups to sell candies on consignment, with the seller's right to return all unused merchandise. These sales are more profitable when they involve a large group of students, like the freshman class or the lettermen's club. Class or club participation in candy sales also can be developed as a school tradition.

Automated Dispensers

Some schools find it profitable to use automated dispensers for pencils or for different foods such as fruit, candy, pastry, and nuts. A student group— perhaps the lettermen's club—can be assigned to make sure that the machines are filled. Supplies are easily obtained and profits high. In fact, one candy machine placed at a strategic location on the campus of a university has made enough profit to pay the yearly tuition of the athlete who manages the machine.

Gifts and Endowments

Some school districts or schools make special appeals for financial gifts and endowments for athletics. This money usually is set up in a trust fund, and the income earned through interest or premiums is used for athletic program needs. The fund should be managed by a trusted fiscal officer in the school district and should be subject to auditing.

The "Thons"

The "thons," such as, jog-a-thon, swim-a-thon, bike-a-thon, walk-a-thon, have in recent years become a popular way to raise funds for a variety of reasons. In essence, it involves an individual who secures sponsors willing to contribute a given sum of money for a lap or distance negotiated by the participant. When the event is concluded, the donation is computed and the sponsor contributes the amount for the cause. The "thons" have the advantage of involving a large segment of the student body and the school community. There usually is a carnival atmosphere around the event that makes it fun for the participants.

There are unlimited possibilities for supplementing the financial suppor. provided for athletics by the school board. Business professionals, students, and interested citizens are good sources for ideas of fund-raising projects. The success of these projects depends on the enthusiasm of the workers who carry them out, and individual coaches can contribute a great deal by generating the needed spirit.

Athletic Guarantees

An aspect of athletic expenditure that must be considered in figuring the budget is the financial guarantee often made to a visiting team. There are four customary methods of arranging these guarantees.

The most common type of scheduling involves a home-and-home arrangement, with each team handling its own traveling expenses and no money guaranteed. The home team keeps any money that is taken in at the gate. The games may be scheduled for the same year or alternate years.

Also, home-and-home games can be arranged with a set amount of money guaranteed to the visiting team. Each school pays the same amount of money, which usually is established according to each school's ability to pay.

Another method is a flat one-game guarantee, in which one school pays a specific sum of money for another team to travel and play a game. The amount guaranteed depends on the attractiveness of the opponent and the ability of the host school to generate gate appeal. Schools usually work around funds that have been fixed in the budget for this arrangement.

Finally, the traveling team may be given the option of a flat guarantee or a percentage of the gate receipts, whichever sum is greater. In this method, the amount of money set usually is lower than that guaranteed for the flat one-game arrangement. The advantages of this method are that the home team does not have to guarantee so much money, and the visiting team may receive more if the game has great gate appeal. This arrangement is fairly common, especially among schools that can afford financial risks.

The Effects of Title IX on Athletic Budgeting

The cost of conducting interscholastic athletics has not escaped the inflationary spiral influencing budgetary problems for school administrators. Added to that was the passage on July 1, 1972, of the Education Amendments Act, known to most individuals concerned with athletics as Title IX. (See Chapter 11.) This legislation is very controversial and is undergoing changes in interpretation. The final answers will only come about as the outcome of several lawsuits is made known.

The passage of Title IX immediately initiated controversy from many male coaches and athletic administrators. They viewed this law as a force that would take away financial aid for men's programs and give it to women's. Also, a common misconception was that the total financial aid for women and men must be equal. However, this was not the intent of the law and for the most part these fears were unfounded.

Title IX does influence the athletic budget. Equal opportunity implies equal supplies and equipment, travel and daily allowances, medical and training services, coaching, practice and competitive facilities, publicity, and so on. All these items require equal funding. With the dramatic 460 percent increase of girls' participation in interscholastic athletics from 1971–1977, financing had to be found. The National Federation of State High School Associations conducted a survey that revealed that, in 1970–1971, 3,660,000 boys and 294,000 girls participated in interscholastic sports. During 1976–1977, the boys increased to over 4,000,000 while the girls increased to 1,645,000, for a total of 5,754,000 participants (14). The implementation of Title IX has positively influenced girls' participation in interscholastic athletics, and these programs require additional funding.

Data Processing Techniques

Data processing techniques have proved to be very successful in business ventures that look for accuracy, simplicity, and economy. It is logical, then, that school systems should use data processing as an efficient method of computing expenses and income.

Edwin Long, athletic director for the Phoenix, Arizona, school system, has successfully used data processing and is a great advocate of this method. He contributed a section to the book *Secondary School Athletic Administration* explaining how data processing can be used for athletic budgets. His entire article is included here.

Preparing Athletic Budgets through Data Processing[1]

Edwin Long

Director of Athletics
Phoenix (Arizona) Union High School System

Several years ago I became fascinated with the possibility of the use of data processing equipment in the construction of athletic budgets. Not only was I fascinated, I was over my head with work assignments and felt some method had to be devised to construct the athletic budget which could reflect a saving of time and a greater degree of accuracy than we had experienced in the past, when we had used the old-fashioned method of typing athletic budgets, then adding the columns reflecting the sub-totals and eventually a grand total, and finally proofreading and double-checking each of these for accuracy, because it is almost impossible to go through an athletic budget without making an occasional error or two in the cross-multiplying of unit costs versus quantity costs.

Furthermore, the fourth, fifth, and sixth carbons of the athletic budgets were frequently illegible, and the item that appeared on line one of the first copy would appear on about line three of the fifth or sixth carbon. When it came time to read and discuss budgets, it was a serious problem. Consequently, the Phoenix Union High School System embarked upon a method to construct the athletic budgets for its ten high schools through the use of data processing primarily to provide a saving of time and to achieve a greater degree of accuracy in the final product.

Reviewing some of the advantages of data processing budget construction which evolved from our experience, the first, which is one of the things we were looking for, is accuracy. Once the bugs have been worked out on trial runs in the use of this type of budgeting, achievement of accuracy becomes almost foolproof. Along with accuracy comes the point that, if an error is made, it is repeated consistently at all ten schools and usually shows up immediately in the budget reviewing stages.

The second advantage is simplicity. The forms we use in the budget-making process are simple; they are easy to fill out; they reflect a great amount of information; and they are easily understood by the many people involved in the construction of athletic budgets when you have ten high schools and some 13 different sports, including four girls' sports and the pom-pom and cheerleading activities.

The third advantage we have discovered is that budget making through the use of data processing equipment is economical. It saves time and I can think of no more important commodity these days. Very little time is spent by those who initiate the budgets and much less time is spent at my level in reviewing and recommending

[1]Report of the Second National Conference on Secondary School Athletic Administration, *Secondary School Athletic Administration* (Washington, D.C.: American Association for Health, Physical Education, and Recreation, 1969), pp. 57–69. Used by permission.

approval of the budgets. Even more important, much less time is spent in implementing the budgets once they have been prepared and approved by the board of education.

A fourth advantage [is] the by-products which result from having budgets set up on data processing equipment. Two of these by-products we have already implemented and use all the time. Two more bear serious investigation as, in my opinion, they can realistically be used in the future. The first by-product which we use in our district is typing of warehouse requisitions from the original budget. I will go into this in more detail later.

The second by-product is a vendor requisition which is produced in a seven-part copy all filled in and typed out by the machine, ready for the coach who initiated the budget to now initiate the requisition when he sees fit. These requisitions are printed according to code, that is, capital outlay items, supplies, transportation, repairs, and items purchased from gate receipt funds.

A third by-product I can foresee in the future is a purchase order for a vendor which can, I believe, be made from the budget in the same way the requisitions are made. I think this can be easily handled; all that would have to be identified or added to the purchase order or an extra copy of the requisition would be the purchase order number, the vendor's name and address, the unit, and the total price, and it would be ready to mail to the vendor, thus saving retyping of all the other information which goes on a purchase order.

Another by-product I can visualize is the inventory. This is important to all of us and easily adapted to this type of budget making. We could carry a running inventory at a particular school of a particular item to be identified on the budget form at the same time the coach initiates his budget requests for the coming year, by merely adding a second quantity column to reflect the present inventory. Certainly all of us respect the importance and use of inventories, and they can become useful and helpful in screening the athletic budget.

A fifth advantage is speed, which somewhat relates to economy. We can actually make the athletic budgets for ten high schools for 13 different sports—a budget which totals approximately $270,000—in a matter of a very few days. If it had to be done and you had access to the key punch operators and the running time on the data processing equipment, this could very easily be constructed in ten days. Our biggest hold up is the key punch time and the machine running time.

A sixth advantage is control of the requisitioning of items from the athletic budget once it has been approved and placed in the hands of the many coaches in a large multischool district. Whenever you have ten high schools and a large, comprehensive athletic program, if you can control the flow of the requisitions, it is really important to your buyers and your warehouse personnel as well as to you as the athletic director in reviewing the requisitions once more as they are processed. By having all the requisitions printed off the machine at the end of the school year and then separating them by sports, you are able to release a certain sport at a certain time with the instructions that these requisitions be processed immediately. Therefore, you are able to control their flow through the different business offices which may have to be used in your particular school district. In our case, it is budget control first, my office second, and the purchasing division third. By following this procedure, if I have had a change of mind or there is a change of specifications, I am able to adjust the requisitions before they go to purchasing for issuing of a purchase order or a warehouse stock requisition.

The seventh advantage is that of making what I call a "composite" budget of all ten of our high schools, item by item, so I can get a quick bird's eye view of any one item on a district-wide basis. For example, the first item on the football budget might be athletic socks. By turning to the first page of the composite football budget, I can compare and see quantities requested from all ten schools for this particular item. Each item reflects a total quantity for the entire district of ten schools along with the dollars and cents amount budgeted.

Many things can be related immediately and errors can be detected easily. For example, it you know that ten local charter buses will be needed for [a] varsity football team during the season and a school has only budgeted for five, it becomes immediately and easily obvious that a mistake was made in the budgeting. This can be pointed out to the school and corrected in time to avoid an embarrassing situation September first.

In the next few pages, I present the step-by-step process we use in the construction of our athletic budgets.

The first year of using this particular method of budgeting for athletics almost cost me and some of my colleagues our jobs for being so insistent in carrying it out. Our budget making was full of errors. We had changed some of the forms being used and people had difficulty in acclimating themselves to some of these changes. Requisition forms were oddly shaped because margins were needed on the sides for the machines to feed them through for printing purposes; therefore, they came out a little larger than the conventional requisitions. I pleaded that everyone who was upset and disturbed over this type of budget making should please be patient and give us one year to work out the kinks and bugs. They did, and we did, and I venture to say that if we turned budget making back to the old method of a more manual nature, I probably would be fired!

Exhibit A is page one of the athletic budget for one of our high schools in Phoenix. The first column on the left, identified by the heading ID#, refers to the identification number given each item on the budget. We use this number in discussing budget items from time to time over the phone with the buyers or with people at the schools so we can refer to a number rather than a description of an item or a name. Some numbers are prefixed with the letter "S" which indicates that this is a warehouse stock item. When requisitions are printed, the stock items are printed on separate requisitions from the nonstock items. We are very fortunate in Phoenix in that we have a tremendous warehouse system and are able to warehouse about 80 percent of our athletic equipment. As an example, last year we had all of our football jerseys in warehouse stock by the first of February.

The second column, QTY, is the only column left blank in the first step of our budget-making procedure. This item is filled in by the coach and is the key item in the first step of budget construction.

The next column is headed by the letters UN, which means "unit" or "school." Any time that I see Unit 1, I immediately associate this with Camelback High School; Unit 2 is Carl Hayden High School; Unit 3, Central High School; etc.

The fourth column has a heading of DP, which represents "department," or the particular sport involved. For example, the number 73 appearing on this example

Exhibit A. *Athletic budget.*

ATHLETIC BUDGET 1965–1966   FOOTBALL

ID#	QTY	UN	DP	CODE	DESCRIPTION	UN COST	UNIT DESC	AMT
100050	1		73	2130	BELTS WEB CHAMP SIZES:...MED...LG...XLG WIDTH:...1 IN...1¼ INCH	$ .40 EA	24 REP	
S00075	1		73	2130	CHIN STRAPS, ADAMS PRO WHITE	$ .75 EA	40 REP	
S00125	1		73	2130	FACE BARS WILSON F2182	$ 1.75 EA	40 REP	
S00150	1		73	2130	FACE GUARDS RAWL 14NG	$ 6.75 EA	3 REP	
S00175	1		73	2130	FOOTBALLS PENNSYLVANIA PF6S	$12.00 EA	10 REP	
100200	1		73	2130	GAME JERSEYS CHAMP FB26 ...STYLE...SLEEVE ...BODY COLOR...TRIM STYLE ...TRIM COLOR. EXTRAS.... X CUT...SDS...OTHER PUT SIZE BEFORE NUMBER...10...11 ...12...13...14...15...16 ...17...18...19...20...21 ...22...23...24...25...26	$ 4.00 EA	40 REP	

immediately tells me this is a football budget; 74 represents cheerleaders, 75 baseball, and so on down the line with all of athletics being assigned the 70 and 80 series of any of our data processing work. Once acquainted with these numbers, you can read them as if they actually said "football," "baseball," "basketball," etc.

The next column is given the heading CODE. This merely reflects the state code that relates to that particular item, whether it is a capital item or an instructional item, a medical item or repair item, etc. Some items reflect the abbreviation ACT instead of a code number. This indicates that the item is purchased from athletic gate receipts. Each of the different codes can be given a subtotal which also gives a chance to compare different prices in different categories of one budget to another or one school to another and also separates tax budget funds from activity or gate receipt budget funds. When the many codes are added together into a grand total, the result is the total budget for that particular sport; and the sum of these figures gives a particular school's budget. The individual school budgets added together give a grand grand total for the entire district's athletic budget. Having all these things in the machine on a code basis, a department basis, a unit basis, and a quantity basis, makes possible many different studies or breakdowns for comparing the athletic budget.

The next column, DESCRIPTION, describes the particular item presented on that particular line. Included is a complete description, and provision is made for the coach to insert on the requisition all vital information necessary to complete the requisition and sent it to the buyer for purchasing purposes. I am referring to such things as sizes, colors, widths, trim styles, sleeve styles, and other information necessary to give a complete description of all pieces of athletic equipment. In some cases a single line description is all that is needed; sizes, etc., are not vitally important. Other items, such as football game jerseys, require several lines to reflect the size relationship to the jersey number, etc., to have the available information for the buyers or purchasing division.

This column is probably the key to the entire athletic budget because the description of the items must be completely accurate, and must be predetermined or the requisition part of the budget is of no value. Options can be offered here so that the coach can check one or the other of a certain description or style. We established our descriptions, or specifications, through a joint process of working in group meetings with the different coaching departments. We review these annually to meet our latest needs insofar as specification changes are concerned, so few changes have to be made each year.

The next column reflects the UNIT COST of each item. In some cases the unit cost may be a dollar and cent denomination which must be multiplied by the quantity required to come up with the total amount of money to be put in the budget for that particular line for that particular item. For example, to cover football laundry, the unit cost may be $25, and the quantity might be ten. The machine would then multiply ten times $25 to come up with a total of $250 as the amount the coach requests for laundry for football. Our previous year's buying experience dictates the unit costs used for the coming year.

The next column, UNIT DESCRIPTION, is a unit maximum purchase or the most that can be requested of any single item. In no case, however, is enough money provided for a school to purchase a maximum of all items in one budget. We have tried to place a control here by requesting that most of these are purchased only on replacement basis (REP means replacement). If a coach requests a dozen of a certain item, he must come up with the old ones to be discarded or turned in for replacement.

The last column provides space for the insertion of the amount put into the budget for a particular item. This amount doesn't come out even when multiplying the quantity times the unit cost. Instead, the machine automatically adds 4 percent into each line to cover the Arizona sales tax or for payroll items where we have to add 4 percent matching funds.

Exhibit B.   *Budget information memorandum.*

Date: December 13, 1967
To: Coaches, Administrative Assistants
From: Ed Long
Subject: Instructions for preparing the 1968–1969 Athletic Budget

The athletic budget procedure for 1968–1969 is basically the same as it was for 1967–1968. The data processing equipment of the System will be utilized to its fullest extent in assisting you in this process. The step-by-step procedure and timetable follow:

1.   December 12: A printed, tabulated listing of the athletic budgets of each athletic department of each unit was distributed to each unit (through it Administrative Assistant). Duplicate sets of these budgets have been produced for unit distribution as follows:

   a.   One (1) broken copy is for the coaches. This copy is to be filled in by the coach and *returned to me through his Administrative Assistant.*
   b.   One (1) broken copy is to be retained at the unit in the office of the Administrative Assistant for reference.

Coaches are to insert the *number* of items they desire within the framework of the limitation that has been set forth under the heading "Unit Description." Please insert the quantities needed on the dotted line under the heading "QTY."

2.   January 9: The Administrative Assistant is responsible for returning all athletic budgets to me on this date. Quantities needed should have been inserted on all budgets.
3.   February 6: The *priced* budgets (quantities listed times price listed plus 3½% for applicable sales tax) will be returned to the Administrative Assistant. You will be asked to revise your budget if necessary to conform to the total dollar allocation given your unit from Tax Budget and Student Activity Budget funds.
4.   February 13: *All* athletic budgets *completed in final form* are returned to me by this date. If any returned budget is not within the limit of the dollar allocation, I will make the necessary final cuts.
5.   February 20: I will submit the athletic budgets to Mr. Burress, Director of Budgeting.
6.   After the Board of Education has adopted the 1968–1969 budget for the System, four (4) copies of your final athletic budget will be forwarded to each unit. These copies will reflect all changes made while being processed. The Board of Education will formally adopt the budget at its first meeting after July 1, 1968.

Each page of the 1968–1969 athletic budgets has a "header" line. This identifies the school, the athletic budget date, the department of athletics, and the appropriate page number of the department's budget. A second "header" line follows, which contains the following descriptive information:

1. ID#—(item identification number) The numbers assigned to each item are printed immediately below this head. ID#'s preceded by the letter "S" are warehouse stock items.
2. QYT = (quantity) Dotted lines have been created immediately below this heading for the insertion of the quantity of items you wish to budget.
3. UN—(unit) The number appearing below this line is a code identification of the school.
4. DP—(department) Number appearing below this line is a code identification of the department.
5. CODE—Four digit numbers appearing below this line identify designated state code for budgetary purposes.
6. DESCRIPTION—The budget item is properly described below to include vendor's catalog numbers, sizes, colors, widths, etc. PLEASE DO NOT FILL IN THE BLANKS IN THIS SECTION. They will be used at the time the "tabulated requisition" is forwarded to you for completion.
7. UN COST—(unit cost) The expected cost to be incurred for the purchase of the unit(s) described is set forth in the column immediately below this heading. This cost will be used in all cases in extending the *budget amount.* Any substitutes in price or item will not be made unless it is deemed advisable for all units.
8. UNIT DESCRIPTION—In the column immediately below this heading, *maximum* quantities or dollar amounts are set forth. In no case should there be a time when the quantities you set forth as your budget needs exceed the maximums found in this column. If they do, they will be reduced to the maximums stipulated.
9. Allocations for each unit:

   a. From tax budget funds: $15,500
   b. From activity budget funds (by sports)   7,500
   *(district level):   3,150

   Total: all departments $26,150 × 10 = $261,500
   *car purchase and maintenance, post-season activities, awards, equipment man overtime, bleacher rental

1968–1969 Athletic Budget Guidelines

Tax budget funds (by sports):	$15,500	
Activity budget funds (by sports):	7,500	$23,000

District level

Activity budget funds:

Car purchase and maintenance	$1,000	
Post-season activities	500	
Awards	1,000	
Equipment man overtime	200	
Bleachers	450	3,150
		$26,150 × 10 = $261,500

RECAP:
Total tax budget funds	= $15,500 × 10 =	$155,000
Total activity budget funds	= $10,650 × 10 =	$106,500
TOTAL BUDGET	=	$261,500

The first step in budget preparation is to issue a budget information memorandum (Exhibit B), which goes out to each coach. This includes, of course, the date the memo is initiated and to whom it is addressed and reflects basically (1) the procedure to be followed, (2) a calendar schedule to be followed, (3) the inclusion of budget allocations for that particular school and (4) a breakdown of these budget allocations as to how much money is appropriated from tax budget funds and how much from student activity or gate receipt funds.

We also carry a portion of the budget at the district level, which merely means that the amount of money is kept in a lump sum for all ten schools to draw upon as needed. Some of the items purchased from this district-level fund are the annual purchase of previously allocated items such as station wagons and their maintenance, postseason activities (which is an item that can't always be foreseen), awards, some of the athletic equipment men's overtime, and bleacher rental.

For the benefit of new coaches, we also give a brief one- or two-sentence description of the several columns that are reflected in the budget worksheets.

The second step is to give each coach who will be filling out a budget request a complete budget which includes all the things mentioned in Exhibit A. He merely goes through the budget and marks the quantities of items he wishes for a particular sport, line by line, omitting those he does not want. At the end of the budget the coach may write in additional items not already listed but which he thinks he wants so I can review them and give consideration to approval or disapproval of them. Exhibit C shows the first page of the budget form completed by a coach.

Once this rough draft is finished, which doesn't take much time or effort on the part of the coach, it is forwarded to my office. We collect all ten budgets and turn them over to data processing where the recommended quantities are key punched, cross-multiplied by the unit cost to reach the many subtotals and eventual grand total for each individual school. These figures are then added together to reach the grand grand total for the district.

If, at this point, the total requested for a particular school exceeds their allocation, the budget is returned to the school with instructions to cut the budget to stay within the allocated figure. The coaches then go over it again with their own needs in mind, give and take one sport against another, until they cut the budget down to the figure we have allocated in the beginning. Then the budget is resubmitted to me. I check each one over once more before submitting them all to data processing for a second print-out.

The third run (Exhibit D) is our final print-out of athletic budgets for that particular school. At this step, we run multiple copies of the budgets in two formats. First they are run as in Exhibits A and C; then as in Exhibit D, which is called a short form, which merely means that instead of including all the information under the DESCRIPTION column, we have used only the first line which describes the basic item. In other words, game pants, Southland SP67, is all that would appear on that budget, not reflecting the color, body stripe, size, etc., which might be necessary to prepare the

Exhibit C. **Completed budget.**

ALHAMBRA					ATHLETIC BUDGET 1965–1966		FOOTBALL	
ID#	QTY	UN	DP	CODE	DESCRIPTION	UN COST	UNIT DESC	AMT
100025	12	14	73	2130	ATHLETIC SOCKS, CHAMPION 198	$ 8.00 DOZ	24 DOZ	99.36
100050		14	73	2130	BELTS WEB CHAMP	$ .40 EA	24 REP	.00
					SIZES:...MED...LG...XLG			
					WIDTH:...1 IN...1¼ INCH			
S00075	404014	14	73	2130	CHIN STRAPS, ADAMS PRO WHITE	$ .75 EA	40 REP	31.05
S00125	6	14	73	2130	FACE BARS, WILSON F2182	$ 1.75 EA	40 REP	10.86
S00150	3	14	73	2130	FACE GUARDS, RAWL 14 NG	$ 6.75 EA	3 REP	20.90
S00175	10	14	73	2130	FOOTBALLS, PENNSYLVANIA PF6S	$12.00 EA	10 REP	124.20
100200	40	14	73	2130	GAME JERSEYS, CHAMP FB26	$ 4.00 EA	40 REP	165.60
					...STYLE...SLEEVE			
					...BODY COLOR...TRIM STYLE			
					...TRIM COLOR...EXTRAS...			
					X CUT...SDS...OTHER			
					PUT SIZE BEFORE NUMBER...10...11			
					...12...13...14...15...16			
					...17...18...19...20...21			
					...22...23...24...25...26			

Exhibit D. *Final print-out of athletic budget.*

	CAMELBACK				ATHLETIC BUDGET 1965–1966			FOOTBALL
ID#	QTY	UN	DP	CODE	DESCRIPTION	UN COST	UNIT DESC	AMT
S00025	24	01	73	2130	ATHLETIC SOCKS, CHAMPION 198	$ 8.00 DOZ	24 DOZ	198.72
S00075	40	01	73	2130	CHIN STRAPS, ADAMS PRO WHITE	$ .75 EA	40 REP	31.05
S00125	15	01	73	2130	FACE BARS, WILSON F2182	$ 1.75 EA	40 REP	27.11
S00175	10	01	73	2130	FOOTBALLS, PENNSYLVANIA PF6S	$12.00 EA	10 REP	124.20
100200	40	01	73	2130	GAME JERSEYS, CHAMP FB26	$ 4.00 EA	40 REP	165.60
100225	6	01	73	2130	GAME PANTS, SOUTHLAND SP67	$13.50 PR	6 REP	83.83
100250	40	01	73	2130	GAME STOCKINGS, CHAMPION	$ 2.65 PR	40 PR REP	109.71
S00275	24	01	73	2130	GRID PADS, WILSON 9420	$ 1.50 PR	24 PR REP	37.26
100300	15	01	73	2130	HEADGEAR PLASTIC...STYLE.	$18.95 EA	40 REP	294.14
100325	2	01	73	2130	HELMET TAPE.....COLOR.	$ 3.95 ROLL	36 YDS	8.17
S00350	12	01	73	2130	HIP PADS, RAWLINGS 17KP	$ 9.00 PR	12 PR REP	111.78
S00475	48	01	73	2130	INNER SOLES ASSORTED SIZES	$ .25 PR	48 PR REP	12.42
S00500	2	01	73	2140	JAW PADS HELMET, ADAMS	$14.00 DOZ	24 DOZ PR REP	28.98
S00525	4	01	73	2130	KICKING TEE, VOIT	$ 2.10 EA	4 REP	8.69
S00550	40	01	73	2130	KNEE PADS P100	$ 4.00 PR	40 REP	165.60
S00575	2	01	73	2130	OFFICIALS SHIRTS, RAWLINGS 20KRS	$ 6.50 EA	4 EA	13.45
100625	108	01	73	2130	PRACTICE JERSEYS, CHAMPION NY56	$ 3.00 EA	108 REP	335.34

requisition. This shortens the length of the entire budget for each sport to a matter of two or three pages, making them easier to handle. The detailed information isn't really vital after this point, anyway.

Exhibit E shows page one of the composite print-out which I spoke of earlier. This reflects totals in the quantity column and totals in the amount column of each individual item for all ten schools. This is very helpful insofar as putting out the bid and being able to analyze and see how much is being spent on different items on a school-wide basis. This is the only budget I really use in my office. I do not use the ten individual school budgets; I use the composite which is printed out in the short form.

It is easy to read and is the best way to review because all ten budgets can be checked at one time by quick glance, item by item. I can get a quick comparison of what each school asks for and after a time you get to know the schools and the programs and know exactly what to look for in the way of mistakes. You can then make corrections so you don't get caught the following football season budgeted for only half enough money for officials, or transportation, or some fixed charge without which you cannot get by.

We now print out eight budgets for each school, but give only one to each school at this date of our budget season. The others are distributed at the end of the school year after the Board of Education has approved the budget.

At the same time, we also print up the requisitions which are kept in my office until we decide it is the appropriate time to distribute them. For example, in the spring of the year we distribute the football budget, the cross-country portion of the track budget, and the pom-pom and cheerleading budgets. We will process those and get them out of the way before school ends, so we can handle all of our purchasing and delivering to the schools during the summer and have everything ready to go when the coaches come back in the fall at the start of their season.

Our particular method has become so well liked in our school district that we are rapidly moving into it for all of the subject matter areas on a line budget basis, and I know it will become a standard procedure in our school district in Phoenix in the very near future.

Summary

Coaches are involved with budgeting either as users or administrators of funds. Therefore, they must be knowledgeable about how budgets are prepared and what financial procedures the school follows so that they spend the funds wisely.

Budgets are primarily fiscal guidelines that involve income and expenses figured for a certain period of time.

The legal responsibility for the athletic budget remains with the school board. However, control of funds may be delegated to many different individuals, including the school superintendent, central office budget officer, city athletic director, school principal, school athletic director, physical education director, or a faculty member.

Exhibit E. Composite print-out.

ATHLETIC BUDGET 1965–1966 — FOOTBALL

ID#	QTY	UN	DP	CODE	DESCRIPTION	UN COST	UNIT DESC	AMT
S00025	24.00	01	73	5611	ATHLETIC SOCKS, CHAMPION	8.00 DOZ	24 DOZ	199.68
S00025	24.00	02	73	5611	ATHLETIC SOCKS, CHAMPION	8.00 DOZ	24 DOZ	199.68
S00025	12.00	03	73	5611	ATHLETIC SOCKS, CHAMPION	8.00 DOZ	24 DOZ	99.84
S00025	24.00	04	73	5611	ATHLETIC SOCKS, CHAMPION	8.00 DOZ	24 DOZ	199.68
S00025	24.00	05	73	5611	ATHLETIC SOCKS, CHAMPION	8.00 DOZ	24 DOZ	199.68
S00025	24.00	06	73	5611	ATHLETIC SOCKS, CHAMPION	8.00 DOZ	24 DOZ	199.68
S00025	24.00	10	73	5611	ATHLETIC SOCKS, CHAMPION	8.00 DOZ	24 DOZ	199.68
S00025	14.00	14	73	5611	ATHLETIC SOCKS, CHAMPION	8.00 DOZ	24 DOZ	116.48
S00025	24.00	15	73	5611	ATHLETIC SOCKS, CHAMPION	8.00 DOZ	24 DOZ	199.68
S00025	24.00	16	73	5611	ATHLETIC SOCKS, CHAMPION	8.00 DOZ	24 DOZ	199.68
	218.00T							1,813.76T
100050	24.00	01	73	5611	BELTS WEB CHAMP	.40 EA	24 REP	9.98
100050		02	73	5611	BELTS WEB CHAMP	.40 EA	24 REP	
100050		03	73	5611	BELTS WEB CHAMP	.40 EA	24 REP	
100050		04	73	5611	BELTS WEB CHAMP	.40 EA	24 REP	
100050		05	73	5611	BELTS WEB CHAMP	.40 EA	24 REP	
100050		06	73	5611	BELTS WEB CHAMP	.40 EA	24 REP	
100050		10	73	5611	BELTS WEB CHAMP	.40 EA	24 REP	
100050		14	73	5611	BELTS WEB CHAMP	.40 EA	24 REP	
S00050		15	73	5611	BELTS WEB CHAMP	.40 EA	24 REP	
100050		16	73	5611	BELTS WEB CHAMP	.40 EA	24 REP	
	24.00T							9.98T

Exhibit E. *(Continued)*

ATHLETIC BUDGET 1965–1966

FOOTBALL

ID#	QTY	UN	DP	CODE	DESCRIPTION	UN COST	UNIT DESC	AMT
S00075	40.00	01	73	5613	CHIN STRAPS, ADAMS PRO WHITE	.70 EA	40 REP	29.12
S00075	40.00	02	73	5613	CHIN STRAPS, ADAMS PRO WHITE	.70 EA	40 REP	29.12
S00075	20.00	03	73	5613	CHIN STRAPS, ADAMS PRO WHITE	.70 EA	40 REP	14.56
S00075	20.00	04	73	5613	CHIN STRAPS, ADAMS PRO WHITE	.70 EA	40 REP	14.56
S00075	20.00	05	73	5613	CHIN STRAPS, ADAMS PRO WHITE	.70 EA	40 REP	14.56
S00075		06	73	5613	CHIN STRAPS, ADAMS PRO WHITE	.70 EA	40 REP	
S00075	40.00	10	73	5613	CHIN STRAPS, ADAMS PRO WHITE	.70 EA	40 REP	29.12
S00075	40.00	14	73	5613	CHIN STRAPS, ADAMS PRO WHITE	.70 EA	40 REP	29.12
S00075	40.00	15	73	5613	CHIN STRAPS, ADAMS PRO WHITE	.70 EA	40 REP	29.12
S00075		16	73	5613	CHIN STRAPS, ADAMS PRO WHITE	.70 EA	40 REP	
	260.00T							189.28T

Criteria for a good athletic budget include identification of educational objectives and related financial needs, proposal of expenses based on facts, accurate estimates of income, adequate flexibility, realistic and defensible figures, advance preparation, and provision for future needs.

Budgets are constructed by researching past, present, and future needs, estimating total expected expenses, analyzing anticipated income; the final draft is prepared from all pertinent information.

Approval of the budget normally progresses from the coach to the athletic director. Then the school principal, district business manager, superintendent of schools, and, finally, the school board all review the budget.

Periodic appraisals provide the opportunity for better fiscal management.

There are numerous methods of obtaining funds for athletics. The success of fund-raising projects depends on enthusiastic leadership and workers. The coach can contribute by generating spirit.

Financial guarantees often are made to visiting teams. Types of guarantees include home-and-home arrangements either with or without funds, flat one-game amounts, and either a flat sum or a percentage of gate receipts, whichever amount is greater.

Title IX has had a dramatic effect on the increased numbers of girls participating in interscholastic athletics. This change has necessitated a careful review of funding for both boys' and girls' programs.

Data processing techniques have proved successful for athletic budgeting and control and are rapidly being adapted for management of high school athletic finances.

References

1. Athletic Institute. *Equipment and Supplies for Athletics, Physical Education, and Recreation.* Chicago: The Athletic Institute, 1960.
2. Bucher, Charles A. *Administration of School Health and Physical Education Programs.* 3rd ed. St. Louis: C. V. Mosby, 1963.
3. Bucher, Charles A., and Ralph K. Dupee, Jr. *Athletics in Schools and Colleges.* New York: The Center for Applied Research in Education, 1965.
4. Bucher, Charles A., and Linda M. Joseph. *Administrative Dimensions of Health and Physical Education Programs, Including Athletics.* St. Louis: C. V. Mosby, 1971.
5. *Coaches Handbook—A Practical Guide for High School Coaches.* Reprint. Washington, D.C.: American Association for Health, Physical Education, and Recreation, 1965.
6. De Young, Chris A. *Budgeting in Public Schools.* Garden City, N.Y.: Doubleday, 1936.
7. Educational Policies Commission. *School Athletics.* Washington, D.C.: National Education Association, 1954.
8. Fagan, C. B. *Interscholastic Athletic Administration,* 1:2 (Spring 1975), 5.

9. Forsythe, Charles. *The Athletic Director's Handbook.* Englewood Cliffs, N.J.: Prentice-Hall, 1956.
10. Frost, Reuben B., and Stanley L. Marshall. *Administration of Physical Education and Athletics.* Dubuque, Iowa: Wm. C. Brown, 1977.
11. Fuoss, Donald E., and Robert J. Troppmann. *Creative Management Techniques in Interscholastic Athletics.* New York: John Wiley, 1977.
12. George, Jack F., and Harry A. Lehmann. *School Athletic Administration.* New York: Harper & Row, 1966.
13. Hixon, C. G. *The Administration of Interscholastic Athletics.* New York: J. Lowell Pratt, 1967.
14. Hogan, C. L. "From Here to Equality—Title IX." *Women's Sports,* 4:9 (September 1977), 16–24, 60–61.
15. Hughes, William L., Esther French, and Nelson G. Lehstein. *Administration of Physical Education for Schools and Colleges.* New York: Ronald Press, 1962.
16. Johnson, M. L. *Functional Administration in Physical and Health Education.* Boston: Houghton Mifflin, 1977.
17. Linn, Henry H. *School Business Administration.* New York: Ronald Press, 1956.
18. Massie, J. L., and J. Douglas. *Managing: A Contemporary Introduction.* Englewood Cliffs, N.J.: Prentice-Hall, 1973.
19. Morphet, Edgar L., Rae L. Johns, and Theodore C. Reller. *Educational Administration.* Englewood Cliffs, N.J.: Prentice-Hall, 1959.
20. Purdy, Robert L. *The Successful High School Athletic Program.* West Nyack, N.Y.: Parker, 1973.
21. Reeder, Ward G. *The Fundamentals of Public School Administration.* 4th ed. New York: Macmillan, 1958.
22. Resick, Matthew C., Beverly L. Seidel, and James G. Mason. *Modern Administrative Practices in Physical Education and Athletics.* Reading, Mass.: Addison-Wesley, 1970.
23. Ritterskamp, James J., Jr., Forrest L. Abbott, and Bert C. Ahrens. *Purchasing for Educational Institutions.* New York: Bureau of Publications, Teachers College, Columbia University, 1961.
24. *Secondary School Athletic Administration: A New Look.* Washington, D.C.: American Association for Health, Physical Education, and Recreation, 1969.
25. Shea, Edward J., and Elton E. Wieman. *Administrative Policies for Intercollegiate Athletics.* Springfield, Ill.: Charles C. Thomas, 1967.
26. *Successful Financial Plans for School Athletic Departments.* River Grove, Ill.: Wilson Sporting Goods, 1961. Pamphlet.
27. "Title IX: Myth and Fact," *Women Scene,* 2:6 (January 1978), 107, 135.
28. Voltmer, Edward F., and Arthur A. Esslinger. *The Organization and Administration of Physical Education.* 4th ed. New York: Appleton-Century-Crofts, 1967.

Drug Use and Abuse 8

"I have discontinued long talks on account of my throat. Several people have threatened to cut it."

Drug abuse in many areas of North American society has reached a distressing level. Contributing to this dilemma is the fact that the mass media, including radio, newspapers, billboards, magazines, and television, bombard us with advertisements urging us to use all manner of drugs from lotions to tonics. People are led to believe that they can cure any ailment be it physical, mental, or social by taking a pill. As a result, aspirins are taken for headaches and colds, antibiotics for infection, opiates for coughs, Xylocaine for pain in the dentist's chair, caffeine, sedatives and tranquilizers, pep pills, and sex pills. Children are praised for taking medicine without a fuss; it is no wonder, then, that as teenagers and adults they have few inhibitions, when holding a pill in their hands, about popping the tablet into their mouths and swallowing it with ease. Unfortunately, many users do not understand fully the implications, side effects, or addictive qualities of the "ordinary" drugs they take.

Although athletes generally are considered to be healthy, young, and active people who have no need for drugs, they are not immune to the problems of drug use and abuse. In the 1960s, drug use by athletes increased at an alarming rate. In *Sports Illustrated,* Bil Gilbert wrote (19)

> They take them for dubious purposes, they take them in a situation of debatable morality, they take them under conditions that range from dangerously experimental to hazardous to fatal. The use of drugs—legal drugs—by athletes is far from new, but the increase in drug usage in the last 10 years is startling. It could, indeed, menace the tradition and structure of sport itself.

The win-at-all-costs philosophy that sometimes dominates professional and college athletics has also permeated the thinking of many high school coaches. Because they mistakenly believe that drugs can make competitors run faster, throw farther, and jump higher, some coaches advocate the use of drugs by teenage athletes without realizing the potential dangers of this practice.

It is essential for both coaches and athletes to consider the physical, psychological, and ethical aspects of drug use. High school coaches have a responsibility to safeguard the health of the young people under their direction. Because athletes and their peers experiment with alcohol and drugs and because coaches partly in the role of counselor deal with these young people and their parents, they must be aware of the functions and effects—both beneficial and damaging—of different drugs.

Objectives

The purpose of this chapter is to inform the high school coach about various aspects of drug use. It discusses:

1. The influence of drug use by professional athletes on high school athletics
2. The high school coach's responsibility to know the effects of drug use
3. Legal and ethical implications of drug use in high school athletics
4. Drugs commonly used in athletics
5. Blood doping
6. Pain and drugs

7. Physical and psychological drug dependence
8. Drugs commonly abused
9. The high school coach's obligation to educate players about drug abuse

The Influence of Drug Use by Professional Athletes on High School Athletics

Professional athletics have a tremendous influence on both high school coaches and athletes, because professionals supposedly are the best in the nation. The techniques professionals use often are emulated on the playground and high school practice field; ironically, these techniques often involve the use of drugs. Many performances viewed by the American public are artificial, because they are the results of drugs rather than pure physical skill. Despite the efforts of the National Football League owners and administrators to erase the use of drugs, it is estimated that on any given Sunday approximately half the professional football players are using some drug (37). More and more, drug use has become part of the lives of professional athletes and coaches.

Sometimes pro players take risks with drugs on the orders of the coach, trainer, or team physician. Paul Lowe, San Diego Charger football player, in an interview revealed that the team members were provided with steroids at the noon meal on orders from the coach (36). Though the side effects of steroids have been proved to be detrimental, these findings were ignored by team officials; they must have felt that the added weight was necessary "to be competitive." In some instances, peers and managers implicitly press for continued participation with drugs. Bill Walton, all-star center for the Portland Trail Blazers basketball team, requested that he be traded to another team in the spring of 1978. He charged that he could not abide by the drug policy set up for the team. No definite proof was established concerning such a policy and charges with countercharges prevailed.

It is not uncommon for professional teams to participate on the East coast one night and on the West coast the next. Constant change of this type affects most players with a loss of energy and becomes another cause for drugs. Many players resort to some pep pill so they can play with vigor and enthusiasm. Such false energy masks fatigue, sometimes allowing superhuman efforts, but its cost is harm to the basic chemistry of the body.

Professional athletes also use drugs so they can continue to play with injuries. The climb to the top—becoming a regular member of a professional team—is often long and arduous. Having reached this position, professional athletes are reluctant to give someone else a chance to replace them. Joe O'Donnell, a starting guard for Buffalo during the 1971 season, received a severe back injury. He continued to practice and hold his position with the

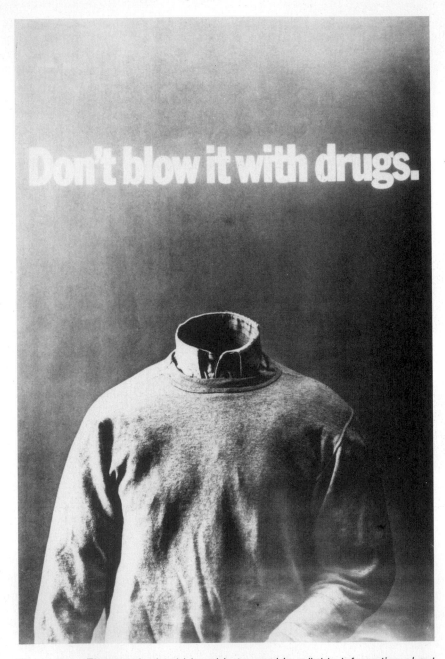

Figure 8.1 *The coach should be able to provide reliable information about the effects of drugs.*

aid of a back brace and pain-killing drugs. He never missed a day of practice until the young player who was contending for his position was injured and out for the rest of the season. When the threat of replacement was removed, Joe O'Donnell took a five-day break from daily practice to allow his back to recover.

In an interview in 1974, Charlie Cowan of the Los Angeles Rams football team said:

> I agree with what our center, Kenny Iman, says. You let a guy come in and play your position while you're getting well and you look up and you don't have a job.
>
> You don't want anyone to take your place because you never know when they'll decide to leave the replacement, then he can't get a veteran's job. It makes a lot of sense. A lot of athletes have lost their jobs because of injury (10).

Thurman Munson, former catcher on the New York Yankee baseball team played with a bad shoulder in the 1978 World Series against the Los Angeles Dodgers. The television commentators did not attempt to hide the fact that Munson played with pain-killing injections and frequently mentioned it during the series as the Dodger baserunners tried to exploit his weakness. Bill Sharman, former coach of the Los Angeles Lakers basketball team, summed up such performances when he said, "It's a great test of character. If a man can play hurt. It shows what kind of competitor he is. A good, hard nosed competitor does it" (10). Interscholastic and intercollegiate athletes should not try to emulate such a performance, but unfortunately some coaches expect their athletes to follow this professional model.

Professional athletes sometimes take drugs to compensate for aging. As individuals become older, they sometimes lose some of the drive and enthusiasm they possessed as young players. They feel they must keep pace with the rookies both in effort and spirit if they are to retain their positions.

Dave Meggysey, former linebacker of the St. Louis Cardinals, admitted to a subcommittee of the California Assembly that was investigating drug abuse in professional athletics that he had on occasion popped pep pills (36). He claimed that he then had the feeling that everybody else was moving at half his speed. Afterward depression and the inability to sleep affected him in such a manner that it took days to overcome the effects of the drugs. Unfortunately, exceptional performances by professional athletes are sometimes followed by rumors (true or not) that the athlete had used a particular drug. This puts pressure on other athletes to look for a crutch in drugs in order to keep up. Arnold J. Mandell, psychiatrist for the San Diego Chargers football team in searching for an answer to drug use, heard one of the players say, "I'm not about to go out there one-on-one against a guy who is grunting and drooling and coming at me with big dilated pupils unless I'm in the same condition" (37).

Most of these motives and circumstances do not exist in interscholastic athletics and should, therefore, lessen the appeal of using drugs. Unfortunately, many high school coaches and athletes have become caught up in the emphasis on winning that pervades professional athletics and consequently use drugs to improve or sustain playing ability. They apparently feel that if a course of action is good for the professionals, they are justified in following it too.

It is essential for a high school coach to keep a proper perspective on success and realize that the health and educational development of the athletes is a primary responsibility, not their winning. Although professional athletes may use drugs to add weight, restore energy, or alleviate pain from an injury, they are playing to earn a living and therefore may feel they must take chances to increase their earning power. Also, their bodies are more mature than those of high school students, and a drug might affect them less adversely than it would a teenager.

The high school coach must avoid the use of drugs. He or she also should be able to provide information about drugs to students who might be tempted to take them because professional athletes do. The AMA committee on the use of drugs in athletics said, "None of the fads, fallacies, and quackery associated with ergogenic aids [pep pills and the like] is of any more assistance to athletic success than the superstition of never changing your underwear during a winning streak" (26).

The High School Coach's
Responsibility to Know the Effects of Drug Use

An athlete's physical and mental condition is the basis for good performance. The athlete is called on to react quickly in a variety of situations, and must be able to think clearly and make instant decisions with confidence. Alertness, determination, and the ability to sustain activity can make the difference between victory and defeat. Drugs can magnify these qualities, but they can also produce negative effects. It is a high school coach's responsibility to teach athletes the effects of different drugs, to correct misinformation, to help students combat peer pressure to take drugs. Because drugs *are* used for therapeutic purposes, the coach has an obligation to research and understand the purposes and functions of drugs commonly used in athletics (27). The coach will then be able to provide logical explanations for students and parents who do not realize the dangers involved.

Willie Johnston, a star player on the soccer team representing Scotland in the World Games in 1978, was sent home from Argentina in disgrace and banned for life from further athletic participation because he took the stimulant *feneanfamin* prior to the game against Peru. Johnston commented, "The Scottish doctor warned us about drugs but I didn't think they were a drug" (48). This situation can be avoided if the coach properly informs the athletes about drug dangers.

The drugs most often used in athletics are basically either restorative or additive. Restorative drugs combat injury, pain, tension, or illness and are given to restore a player's normal prowess. Additive drugs, which are more controversial, are used primarily to improve performance. They influence the nervous system, affect muscle tissue, and sometimes alter a player's personality. The use of additive drugs in athletics is ethically more questionable than the use of restorative drugs.

Legal and Ethical Implications of Drug Use in High School Athletics

Legally, the administration of drugs for relief of pain or alteration of bodily functions is not the prerogative of a high school coach; it is the responsibility of the team physician. Because the team physician is often an interested doctor, who does not know a great deal about athletic injuries, voluntarily offering services to the school, the coach may feel that he or she is more capable of making decisions about treating the players. The coach may very well have more specialized training and experience in athletics, but still not have the right to prescribe the use of drugs. When coaches do recommend drugs, they place themselves in a legally vulnerable position should the drugs cause adverse reactions.

Some high school coaches believe that a chemical compound can convert a short, skinny youngster into a physical giant. When they use "wonder" drugs for other than therapeutic reasons, they give little consideration to possible damaging side effects. Then, ethics and morality become an issue. Does a coach have the right to tamper with another person's body chemistry? The obvious answer is no. Though coaches may be trained in developing individual skills and performances, they do not have the basic medical knowledge necessary to diagnose deficiencies and prescribe treatment for overcoming them. These decisions can be made only by a reliable physician.

Drugs Commonly Used in Athletics

Following is a brief discussion of some of the drugs commonly used in athletics.

Amphetamines

Amphetamines, or pep pills, are synthetic compounds whose effect is similar to that of adrenalin, a natural glandular secretion (2). They affect the central nervous system and, being metabolic stimulants, speed the respiratory and circulatory systems so that a user can remain active and suppress the feeling of fatigue. These drugs also affect the brain, creating a sense of euphoria and relieving mild mental depression. Amphetamines are used for various reasons. Athletes, musicians, and actors take them to increase work capacity; truck drivers take them to stay alert; students cramming for exams take them to stay awake; business professionals take them to increase energy; dieters take them to curb hunger.

Bill Russell, former star center for the Boston Celtics basketball team, admitted using dexadrine while performing but said he quit when he found that he was not making as many rebounds as he imagined. In discussing drug use with a college audience, Russell said that "legal drugs are a bigger problem in the United States than illegal drugs. . . . We've got too much to do in too short a time in this country and we can't do it while we're high. . . . If you can't do your thing without being high, your thing can't amount to very much" (40).

Dr. Robert Kerlan, one of the nations most noted team physicians and an individual who has done a great deal to promote the growth of sports medicine, has said about amphetamines, "There is absolutely no benefit to be derived from such pills and any player who feels he needs a drug to improve performance is uneducated" (41).

Use of amphetamines in athletics accelerated after a 1959 Harvard study by Smith and Beecher, which concluded that performance of about 75 percent of the athletes could be improved through the use of amphetamines (51). The report received widespread publicity, and many coaches, professional athletes, physicians, and trainers consequently advocated use of the drug. Even though conflicting research (22, 30) and subsequent evidence conclusively disproved (36) the claim of the Harvard report and revealed that amphetamines actually produce few—if any—actual benefits or improvements in athletic performance, the myth of the "magic pill" still exists.

Use of amphetamines can impair judgment and create false impressions. (Heavy abuse can cause psychosis characterized by hallucinations.) Also, continued use can cause the body to develop a tolerance for the drugs. When this occurs, increased dosage is required to produce the desired stimulation, and the user can experience nervousness, restlessness, and sleeplessness. Overexertion due to false stimulation can result in death by exhaustion. Abuse of the drugs also can cause death through heart damage and circulatory collapse (42).

Users of amphetamines frequently become addicted, either physically or psychologically. There is some medical dispute about physical addiction (20); however, psychological dependence has been proved and requires psychotherapy to correct. Often, someone who uses amphetamines to stimulate mental and bodily functions resorts to sedatives—or "downers"— to overcome the resulting nervous tension. This alternate use of "uppers" and "downers" can have extremely harmful psychological and physical effects.

Figure 8.2 *"If you can't do your thing without being high, your thing can't amount to very much." (Bill Russell)*

Overdoses or too frequent use of amphetamines can cause complete physical exhaustion, irritability, panic, convulsions, coma, shock, violent or aggressive behavior, malnutrition, cardiac collapse, or death. Typical outward symptoms of amphetamine use are extreme excitability and talkativeness; tremors of the hands; enlarged pupils and heavy perspiration; unpredictability; a need to be busy all the time; abdominal pain and backaches.

Common names for amphetamines are "pep pills," "wake-up," "eye-openers," "copilots," "truck drivers," "bennies," and "speed." Some specific amphetamines and their slang names are: benzedrine—rose-colored, heart-shaped tablets called "peaches," "roses," "hearts," "bennies"; dexamil—round, white double-scored tablets called "cartwheels," "whites," "bennies"; dexadrine or dextroamphetamine sulfate—orange-colored, heart-shaped tablets called "hearts," "oranges," "dexies"; injectable amphetamines—clear liquid called "bombico," "jugs," "bottles"; long-acting amphetamine sulfate capsules—a wide variety of colors called "coast to coast," "L.A. turnabouts," "copilots," "browns"; metamphetamine—injectable liquid called "speed," "meth."

Legally, amphetamines are available only through a physician's prescription. The Drug Abuse Control Amendment of 1965 requires manufacturers to keep detailed records of production, shipment, and distribution (2). Despite these regulations, large quantities of amphetamines of questionable purity are available on the black market.

Androgenic-Anabolic Steroids

Androgenic-anabolic steroids are synthetic male hormone (testosterone) derivatives that originally were developed as a therapeutic aid for patients who had been debilitated as a result of surgery, accident, or age. The purpose of the drug was to increase weight and muscle mass. Athletes, especially those involved in sports in which bulk and strength are important for performance, turned to the drug in anticipation that it would make them bigger and stronger. Steroids do increase bulk, because they reportedly improve the assimilation of protein, but most of the weight increase is due to fluid retention. No increase in strength has resulted from steroid use (17). Although steroids can have detrimental side effects and can cause sterility, many athletes who are driven by a desire to become national or world competitors take the drug in spite of the risk.

Some of the therapeutic benefits attributed to androgenic-anabolic steroids are correction of deficient endocrine function of testes (hypogonadism, hypopituitarism); correction of osteoporosis (decrease in bone substance); correction of menstrual disorders in females; correction of anemia related to impaired utilization of iron (refractory anemia); correction of malnutrition; and addition of weight lost because of surgery, accident, or age. Possible detrimental effects of androgenic-anabolic steroids are:

edema (swelling caused by collection of serous fluid in tissues); sterilization (testical shrinkage and suppression of spermatogenesis); cholestatic hepatitis (liver damage); hirsutism (excessive growth of hair); atrophy of breasts; gynecomastia (overdevelopment of mammary glands in the male); jaundice (yellowish pigmentation of skin caused by bile malfunction); priapism (abnormal, persistent, and painful erection of the penis not caused by sexual drive); acceleration of the growth of long bones with early epiphyseal closure. Some of the most commonly used steroids are anadrol, dianabol, dunabolin, maribolin, nilevar, and winstrol.

Barbiturates

Barbiturates, taken under a physician's direction, have therapeutic value for a wide variety of medical disorders. When used primarily for their intoxicating effects, the drugs can be extremely dangerous.

In the 1930s, barbiturates first significantly appeared on the American drug scene as a replacement for bromides, which had served as a popular sedative since the middle of the nineteenth century (21). Physicians prescribe barbiturates for the treatment of extreme nervousness, high blood pressure, insomnia, and some cases of epilepsy. These drugs artificially relax the central nervous system and induce sleep, aiding the recovery of people who have been injured or have had operations. Many people use barbiturates as "sleeping pills."

There are significant dangers in abuse of barbiturates. Most people who depend on barbiturates have difficulty facing the tensions and anxieties of everyday life. Like alcoholics, they need a crutch to give them a sense of security and well-being. Others indulge in barbituates alone or combine them with other drugs in an attempt to produce a "high": because some drugs can increase the action of others, the effects of some combinations can be fatal. People who combine alcohol and barbiturates can experience enhanced intoxication that can result in mental and emotional confusion, accidental death, or suicide. An overdose of barbiturates can be lethal.

Frequent and daily use exceeding prescribed amounts of barbiturates can produce physical and psychological dependency. The level of body tolerance increases, and more and more of the drug is required to produce desired results. For a person who is physically dependent, sudden withdrawal is extremely dangerous and can cause convulsions, tremors, dizziness, nausea, insomnia, delirium, and severe mental disturbances. All attempts to withdraw from barbiturate dependency should be under the supervision of a physician.

Some typical outward symptoms of excessive barbiturate use are the appearance of drunkenness; slurred speech and loss of coordination; a quick temper and quarrelsome disposition; apparent difficulty in thinking; tremors of hands, lips, and tongue; extreme drowsiness; deterioration of outward physical appearance.

Common names for barbiturates are "barbs," "candy," "goof-balls," "sleeping pills," or "peanuts." Some specific barbiturates and their slang names are : nembutal or phenobarbital sodium, solid yellow capsules called "yellows," "yellow jackets," "nimbies"; seconal, red capsules called "reds," "pinks," "red devils," "seggy," "seccy"; amobarbital sodium, solid blue capsules called "blues," "blue birds," "blue devils," "blue heavens"; tuinal or amobarbital sodium combined with seconal, red and blue capsules called "rainbows," "red and blues," "double trouble"; chlorohydrate, clear liquid called "knock-out drops."

Like amphetamines, barbiturates are legally available only through a physician's prescription, and the Drug Abuse Control Amendment of 1965 requires manufacturers to keep detailed records of production, shipment, and distribution. But also like amphetamines, large quantities of barbiturates of questionable purity are available on the street.

Cortisone

Cortisone normally is prescribed in athletes for relief from pain caused by bursitis or tendonitis. Physicians sometimes prescribe it for rheumatoid arthritis (42). The body produces cortisone naturally in the cortex of the adrenal gland, where steroids also are produced. Activity of the adrenal cortex is controlled by the pituitary gland through an agent designated as ACTH.

Cortisone has three basic natural functions: mineral metabolism, organic metabolism, and tissue reaction. For medical purposes, it is obtained from animal glands or is prepared synthetically from strophanthus or other plants. Its effects are relatively long-lasting, and when taken in moderate doses cortisone seems to have no damaging side effects. However, when taken over a long time or in relatively large doses, the drug can have harmful side effects such as water retention by the cells, bone fragility, and mental disturbance. In addition to these effects, the usual danger of using a pain-killing drug is present. If cortisone is taken continuously over a long period of time, its use should not be stopped abruptly, but withdrawn gradually.

Dimethylsulfoxide (DMSO)

Dimethylsulfoxide, commonly known as DMSO, is a drug manufactured from the resin of fir trees. During the early 1960s, it was widely used as a pain killer through external application to an injured area. It acts as a deterrent against edema and carries other numbing agents through the skin.

This drug has been banned by the Food and Drug Administration as being too dangerous for human use. Because of the manner in which it functions, it can carry through the skin and into the blood stream such things as insecticides from the playing field. Recent experiments have revealed that DMSO can cause blindness (3). Because of the dangers involved, it should not be used, although it is reputed still to be available on the black market.

Ethyl Chloride

Ethyl chloride is a drug administered externally for the relief of pain due to injury. It acts as a pain killer by chilling the area, thus producing a numbing effect. In addition to reducing the pain, ethyl chloride lessens the swelling caused by the injury.

The dangers of using this drug are those characteristic of all pain killers. In addition, the use of ethyl chloride by an inexperienced person can freeze and ultimately destroy tissues.

Local Anesthetics

Although the practice is frowned on by most physicians and coaches, local anesthetics are sometimes used to reduce pain so that an injured athlete can continue playing. These drugs are usually administered by injection and produce a regional nerve block.

The use of local anesthetics does not seem to be common in high school athletics, but some coaches mistakenly advocate it because of pressure to win. They can cause an athlete further damage to the injured area that might be permanent and debilitating.

There are many cases of local anesthetics being used in intercollegiate and professional athletics (19). Unfortunately, the ruined careers that resulted are omitted from the reports.

In the past, the most common local anesthetic used in athletics was Novocain; today, many physicians recommend Xylocaine.

Muscular Relaxants

Muscular relaxants are chemical compounds that, for the most part, are nontoxic and have effectively reduced disorders involving acute muscle spasms. Relaxants function by a selective action on the central nervous system which interrupts abnormal reflex impulses; thus normal muscular activity is allowed with a significant reduction in pain. Athletic injuries for which some physicians commonly prescribe muscle relaxants are bone fractures, joint dislocations, and blows to muscle masses. Use of these drugs normally does not affect the tone, strength, coordination, or voluntary control of muscles. Most muscle relaxants have no psychic or tranquilizing effects.

Some of the best-known muscle relaxants used in athletics are Norflex, Rolaxin, Robarisal, Skelaxin, and Soma.

Oral Enzymes

Oral enzymes are used primarily as adjuncts or supplements to standard therapeutic procedures. How proteolytic enzymes function has not been firmly established, but it is known that they can reduce inflammation and edema, ease pain, speed healing, and accelerate tissue repair. They are especially helpful to combat trauma resulting from athletic injuries such as contusions, lacerations, sprains, dislocations, torn ligaments, and fractures. Physicians occasionally advocate use of oral enzymes following surgery.

Most oral enzymes are obtained naturally from plants, including the pineapple (ananase) and papaya (papase) (29). Other enzymes—such as varidase and buccal-varidase—are obtained through cultivation of a strain of streptococcus under controlled conditions. The enzymes produced in this manner activate a fibrinolytic enzyme in human serum that causes dissolution of blood clots and fibrinous discharge.

Blood Doping

Athletes who engage in activities requiring great endurance, such as distance running, swimming, skating, and cycling, usually have well-developed cardiovascular systems that are able to support strenuous exercise over a long time. Basically, this endurance is due to high oxygen intake. The exchange of oxygen and waste material is normally limited to physiological processes. Some researchers have found that greater concentration of blood hemoglobin or increased cardiac output increases the flow of oxygen (50).

Blood doping means withdrawing a limited amount of an individual's blood at least three weeks prior to an event. Then, just before a contest, the individual is reinjected either with his or her whole blood or with cross-matched blood. The theory behind this procedure is relatively simple: By increasing the blood volume and hemoglobin concentration, an individual might have greater capacity to carry oxygen. *Track & Field News* (7) reported the work of Bjorn Ekblom and associates with the indications that blood doping has been used by international track athletes in an attempt to achieve greater endurance. Many researchers question whether or not blood reinfusion provides the well-conditioned athlete with any additional benefits (59). There are risks involved that medical necessity might justify. However, these justifications vanish when an athlete is trying to gain a competitive edge.

Pain and Drugs

Pain acts as a built-in alarm system to indicate physical injury or malfunction. When you take away the sensation of pain through drugs, you take away the body's defense and the results can be physically damaging. Individuals differ greatly in their pain tolerance—their ability to feel or endure pain. Some have a very low pain threshold and suffer from the slightest discomfort. Normally, these people avoid violent sports such as boxing, wrestling, or football, because they do not enjoy the physical contact. Others have a high pain threshold and can endure a great deal of pain. They usually delight in the hitting and body contact that typically strenuous sports provide. One of the high school coach's obligations is to know the pain tolerance of each athlete so as not to confuse a player's low pain threshold with lack of courage.

Young people are normally endowed with a "do or die" spirit. Because of this tremendous enthusiasm, they may feel that they must keep on participating in a contest and try to shrug off injuries and aches, when they actually are suffering. If an athlete continues to play when injured, he or she can sustain permanent physical damage. A high school coach must be aware of the athletes' spirit and prevent them from becoming badly hurt.

Male athletes falsely assume that continuing to play while hurt displays hypermasculinity. Some believe that not playing when injured is a potential source of humiliation by their peers. Charlie Kreuger, veteran defensive tackle for the San Francisco 49ers football team, when questioned about the wisdom of a fifth knee operation, haughtily replied, "I can't dishonor what I think of myself as a man" (10). Many coaches, at all levels of competition, reflect this same attitude with little or no concern for the athlete's welfare.

Unfortunately, in athletics there does exist the practice of dulling or eliminating pain through drugs. A common television scene in both intercollegiate and professional athletics shows an injured athlete being sprayed on the area of the injury with a pain-killing drug such as ethyl chloride. Too much of the drug can freeze the area and kill the tissue. In the hands of competent people, this method of treatment has many advantages, but improper use of the drug can have extremely detrimental effects. When the athlete no longer feels pain, he or she usually wants to continue to play, but has a false sense of security and easily can reinjure the troubled area without knowing it. Each time the injury occurs, the chances for complete recovery are reduced.

When high school coaches decide to use pain-killing drugs, they must realize that they are risking permanent damage to the players. No victory in high school athletics is worth that risk.

Physical and Psychological Drug Dependence

Physicians, physiologists, psychologists, and most informed individuals are aware that drugs can cause addiction or dependency. Some specialists in drug abuse prefer the term *dependency* to *addiction,* because the latter term originally was used to describe only the physical need for narcotics.

A person who is dependent on drugs is someone who overuses them habitually. Drug dependence involves a compulsive need that the user cannot control. The habit affects not only a user's own physical and mental condition, but also the family's personal, social, and economic lives and society in general.

Psychological dependence usually results from repeated use of drugs that produce euphoria. These drugs may be stimulants such as benzedrine; sedatives such as tranquilizers; hallucinogenics such as LSD; or intoxicants such as alcohol. Tensions and anxieties are forgotten, but return again as soon as the effect of the drug wears off. Then the individual resorts to the drug again to suppress them. A person who is psychologically dependent on drugs feels that he or she is being released from the realities of the world and very often becomes a nonproductive member of society. To break this dependence, the individual must resort to will power and a desire for something stronger than the release achieved through drug use. (Sometimes young people turn to religion to give them inner strength.) Psychological dependence can be overcome, but usually a person needs outside help to solve the problem that initially caused him or her to seek relief in drugs.

Physical drug dependence occurs when the user's body chemistry is altered so radically that to discontinue use of the drug causes withdrawal sickness. Symptoms of this illness are extreme physical discomfort such as chills or fever, severe nausea, violent cramping, convulsions, and periods of delirium. The extent of the symptoms depends on the drug used and the dosage taken. Those attempting to break physical dependence on drugs must be prepared to undergo a period of physical agony and should do so only under medical supervision.

Attempts currently are being made to help withdrawal by substituting other drugs that sustain the body chemistry but do not have the same deleterious effects. Although the substituted drug allows an individual to lead a more normal and productive life, the problem of physical drug dependence remains.

Drugs Commonly Abused

Drug abuse is defined as "the use of legal drugs in a manner or amount contrary to their intended dosage or purpose, and the use of illegal drugs for the purpose of bringing about a change in feeling, mood or behavior" (5). The high school coach, as counselor for both athletes and parents, must be aware of the drugs that high school students most commonly use. A brief explanation of these drugs follows. Additional information can be secured by writing to: Drug Abuse Information, P.O. Box 1701, Washington, D.C., 20015.

Alcohol

Alcohol generally is not recognized by most people as a drug, and yet it is classified as one (27). Its effect may be to produce a sense of euphoria, and continued use can result in both physiological and psychological dependence. Most people regard alcohol as a stimulant because of its initial effect on the central nervous system; actually, it is a depressant and impairs judgment, reduces tensions and inhibitions, and makes the user more accident prone because it affects coordination and reflexes. The amount of alcohol contained in one beer or cocktail is enough to impair the proficiency of a person who weighs between 90 and 120 pounds, whereas two beers or cocktails impair the efficiency of a person weighing between 190 and 210 pounds (27). An individual's physiological condition and psychological state determine the amount that can be consumed without impairment of senses. Also, people have different levels of susceptibility to alcohol.

Continued use of alcohol can impair brain cells and damage organs such as the kidneys and liver. Acute alcoholism refers to a state of mental impairment for an hour or more (27). Chronic alcoholism is a condition in which the individual is more or less under the influence of alcohol all the time and requires continued use of the drug. Most alcoholics cannot quit voluntarily and need help to break their dependence.

Caffeine

Caffeine is a form of drug found in coffee, tea, and cola drinks; it acts as a stimulant to the central nervous system and is used to overcome fatigue and increase alertness. Caffeine can have the dangerous effect of overstimulating a person, who then continues an activity with adverse effects to muscle tissue and organs. Its use by teenagers is not advisable, and the coach should take caution in letting athletes have coffee or tea at a pregame meal or cola drinks as a refreshment before a game. (It is difficult to be more specific because individual metabolic processes differ enough that a sip of coffee for one is the same as a cup for another player.)

Hallucinogenic Drugs

Early anthropological records show that mind-altering substances were found in nuts, herbs, and weeds. Hallucinogenic, or psychedelic, drugs are unique among those that can cause dependence: They have little or no proven medical use, and although they are not known to cause physical dependence they may create a psychological need. These drugs produce hallucinations that can affect the user's mind by causing a distortion of reality. All of the senses—seeing, hearing, tasting, smelling, and touching—may be affected. The user's judgment of time and space is often impaired, and this condition may result in serious accidents.

Many people experiment with hallucinogenic drugs because they have heard stories about the effects produced or simply want acceptance by their peers. Some users are looking for an escape from reality; others are looking for self-improvement. An advocate of psychedelic drugs, Timothy Leary, preached their virtues and disclaimed harmful effects. The publicity drugs consequently received from the news media spread its use among teen-agers, who turned to drugs as a way of discovering personal identities.

One claim made by advocates of hallucinogenic drugs is that they in-crease a person's creative powers. However, this belief seems to be un-founded, and objective observers have noted that increased creativity is only a fantasy in the user's mind (53).

A single use of hallucinogenic drugs may result in tragedy: The risk is too high for casual experimentation. Many people with emotional problems have been pushed past their limits by a single dose of a psychedelic drug.

Typical outward symptoms of hallucinogenic drug use are pupil dilation, which requires the user to wear dark glasses even at night; physical listless-ness and neglect of personal appearance; psychic distortion; suicidal ten-dencies and panic reactions; increase in blood pressure, heart rate, and blood sugar; nausea, chills, flushing, irregular breathing, trembling and sweating hands; lowering of sensory thresholds; expressions of hilarity such as continuous "giggles"; antisocial behavior (15).

Lysergic acid diethylamide (LSD)   The hallucinogenic drug used most by American youth is LSD. Slang names for this drug are "acid," "big D," "cubes," "trips," and "sugar." Dr. Albert Hofmann, a Swiss biochemist, is credited with accidentally having discovered LSD in 1938, while he was working with lysergic acid derived from ergot, a black fungus that some-times develops in place of the seeds on rye grains (35). He did not realize that he had found the most dangerous and potent mind-altering drug known to mankind. It is so powerful that merely by licking the back of a stamp treated with LSD, an individual may experience hallucinations for ten hours or more. Two tablets, each the size of an aspirin, contain enough of the drug for over six thousand doses.

The reactions produced by LSD are usually unpredictable, and because users experience extreme hallucinations, they can lose control of their sense of reality and imagine that they have superhuman qualities, such as an abil-ity to fly. These illusions occasionally result in fatal accidents. An acid trip can be especially hazardous for a person's emotional stability: There is a constant danger of irrational behavior or mental breakdown (suicide is a possibility) and "flashbacks" of the drug's effects may occur weeks or months after the drug is used.

Medical evidence has indicated that LSD can cause serious and damag-ing physical reactions, and recent research (54) also has revealed that LSD may affect the chromosomes of the reproductive system and cause crippling or malformation of a user's children. However, because the evidence to date is inconclusive—though certainly frightening—LSD is regarded as causing only psychological dependence.

LSD use became a problem in 1966, when a great number of people were admitted to psychiatric clinics and emergency wards after trying the drug. LSD can be manufactured in any high school chemistry laboratory. It is colorless and odorless and therefore hard to detect by an unsuspecting user. Fortunately, its hazards have become widely known, less of today's teenagers seem willing to risk the danger it involves.

Legally, LSD comes under the control of the Food and Drug Administration. It is illegal to manufacture and dispense the drug for public consumption. Large quantities of LSD of questionable purity are available on the street (35).

Marijuana

Slang names for marijuana are "pot," "grass," "tea," "gage," "reefers," and "muggles." Marijuana is known as a relaxant and mood elevator, and when taken in large doses it may produce hallucinogenic effects (53). Although it is not known to produce physical dependence, it may cause psychological dependence (32).

Although there is a popular belief that marijuana is not harmful, research evidence indicates that the chemical tetrahydrocannobinol (THC) when used in full strength damages the cells of the cerebral cortex (23). Besides accumulating in the brain, "cannabis" can affect the gonads, produce fetal abnormalities and abortions, weaken the body defenses against diseases, and damage human chromosomes, perhaps resulting in serious genetic damage to future generations (38). There are claims that marijuana use can destroy an athlete's timing, coordination, aggression, and drive (37). THC can remain stored in the nerve endings for as long as a week. The stress of competition may release it, influencing the competitor's behavior.

When used in relatively small doses, marijuana may produce a feeling of well-being and sociability. Many people use the drug in social gatherings as others use alcohol. The initial high may be followed by drowsiness or a short period of depression. The degree of reaction depends on the amount and quality of marijuana used.

An article by Herman W. Land entitled "How a Parent Can Reach His Child about Drugs" lists several possible dangers of marijuana use (34):

1. It loosens inner restraints and inhibitions.
2. It can bring emotional conflicts to the surface.
3. It affects the ability to respond correctly to danger.
4. It is often the first step toward the use of "hard" drugs.
5. It can create psychological dependence.
6. It may lead to withdrawal from the realities of the everyday world.

The United States has attempted to control marijuana since the passage of the Marihuana Tax Act of 1937. According to this act, an individual found guilty of the sale or transfer of marijuana may be sentenced to not less than five or more than twenty years of imprisonment for the first offense. Mere possession may result in a two- to ten-year sentence (58). Although this is the law, today's cultural climate has induced the courts to be more lenient in giving sentences after conviction, and a great many people believe that marijuana should be legalized.

Narcotics

Narcotics are either drugs that come from the opium poppy or those that produce similar effects (14). They are used in athletics as pain killers. When properly administered, narcotics relieve pain and generally induce sleep and thus aid in treatment for injuries and illnesses. The drugs normally affect some cells of the central nervous system that can become dependent on the presence of the drug. When narcotics are taken incorrectly, physiological and psychological dependence results, and the "hooked" narcotic user is usually unaware of the situation until it is too late to do anything about it. Overdoses can produce stupor, coma, convulsions, or death.

Some of the most common narcotics are codeine, cocaine, heroin, methadone, morphine, paregoric, and opium.

Codeine   The slang name for codeine is "schoolboy." It is a weak narcotic that rarely leads to dependence unless taken in large quantities and consumed contrary to directions. Codeine is included in cough syrups to suppress coughing and give relief of pain and can be obtained in many nonprescription cough medicines.

Cocaine   Cocaine is commonly called "snow," "coke," "happy dust," or "sleigh ride." It is manufactured from the coca plant and is a legitimate drug that acts on the central nervous system. Physicians and dentists may use it as a local anesthetic.

When abused, cocaine can serve as a powerful stimulant. It is generally inhaled or snorted through the nose. Authorities claim that cocaine is the most popular narcotic drug abused in America today among the young and affluent (13). It is not known to cause physiological dependence, but psychological dependence can develop. Some users seriously damage the linings of their noses.

Use of cocaine can result in periods of alternate joy and sorrow; continued use causes loss of appetite and weight, and general breakdown of health.

Heroin   Slang names for this drug are "horse," "junk," "scat," "boy," "stuff," and "Harry." Heroin is produced from the opium poppy. It acts as a depressant on the spinal cord and lungs, and for many years was used medically to relieve pain. However, its addictive qualities soon became apparent, and the drug legally was prohibited from further use in America in 1924.

Heroin causes intoxication without the mental confusion and loss of bodily control experienced with excessive use of alcohol. As physiological dependence increases, so do daily dosages; the cost of a heroin habit can exceed $100 a day. The addict loses all sense of conventional morality and sometimes resorts to crime to support the habit.

Withdrawal from heroin is very painful. The first symptoms are a need for sleep and watering eyes and nose. Sweating, dilated pupils, restlessness, extreme twitching of limbs, cramps, thirst, nausea, and vomiting are typical withdrawal symptoms.

Methadone   Methadone—or "dolly"—is one of the synthetic drugs that have been produced as substitutes for narcotics: It produces the same effects but does not cause physiological impairment. Methadone currently is being advocated to relieve the pain of heroin dependence. It can be taken either orally or by injection and can result in both physiological and psychological dependence.

Morphine   Morphine is also called "white stuff" and "M." It has been used medically for many years to relieve pain. When abused, morphine can cause all the usual symptoms of narcotic use. The user suffers primarily from personal neglect, malnutrition, and infections.

Paregoric   Paregoric is a narcotic that is used for medical treatment of intestinal trouble. Like codeine, it is not considered a dangerous narcotic unless abused by individuals who do not follow prescribed treatment.

Opium   This drug is made from the opium poppy and has a medicinal function when used properly. Illegal users ignite a small pill in an opium lamp and then place the pill in an opium pipe, where it gives off a sweet sickening odor. The user inhales the fumes—not the smoke—and becomes intoxicated. Although opium use is not prevalent in America, the drug is used widely in Asia.

Phencyclidine (PCP)   Phencyclidine (PCP) was developed in the 1950s as a surgical anesthetic. It was banned in 1965 because of its erratic side effects. In 1967, PCP became commercially available for veterinary medicine under the trade name, Sernylan. It is used legally as a tranquilizer for large animals.

When PCP was banned in 1965, it surfaced on the black market of San Francisco under the name of "Pea Ce Pill." Some say it was pushed initially by members of the Hell's Angels, thus it obtained one of its common names, "Angel Dust".

PCP is a white powder that can be produced inexpensively at home by pushers. It can be sniffed, injected into the bloodstream, or smoked when mixed with mint, marijuana, or tobacco leaves. Smoking is the most common way it is used.

The effects of the drug are unpredictable. It can act in turn as a depressant, stimulant, or hallucinogen. Large doses can bring on convulsions, psychosis, uncontrollable rage, coma, and death. Irrational or violent actions are typical of chronic users. Even dabblers are not immune to sudden rages. A small dosage can produce a high that resembles drunkenness.

Possession, sale, or intent to manufacture this drug results in a three-year prison term. Many law-enforcement officers are advocating a stiffer prison penalty.

Common names for PCP are "Angel Dust," "goon," "busy bee," "crystal," "hog," "elephant," "tranquilizer," and "superjoint."

The High School Coach's Obligation to Educate Players about Drug Abuse

Every high school coach who is concerned with the welfare of the students has an obligation to educate them about the effects of drug use and abuse. Drug abuse does exist at the high school level; all teenagers—athletes included—are subjected to extreme social pressure to try drugs. The findings released by the National Commission on Marijuana and Drug Abuse in 1972 revealed that approximately 1.5 million teenagers had tried heroin at least once (55). In an earlier report, the same commission revealed that 24 million Americans had tried marijuana at least once and that 8.3 million had continued its use. Represented in this total is 14 percent of all the young people (under twenty-one) in the country.

Richard H. Blum, director of the Program in Drugs, Crime, and Community Studies, Stanford Law School, has reported on studies conducted through 1974 on drug use by students in grades one through twelve (8). Some of the results are startling. For instance, over 80 percent of the second graders studied had used drugs. Included were alcoholic beverages and cigarettes. Marijuana appeared in the third grade, with frequent use by the sixth grade. Drug use expanded substantially between grades two and eleven. Forty-one percent of those studied were using pills, injectables, opiates, or cocaine as well as alcohol, tobacco, and marijuana by the end of grade eleven. Only 15 percent of the students were so low in drug use through high school that they were placed in a no-risk group (19).

A study conducted by the University of Michigan's Institute for Social Research reveals that the number of high school seniors who try marijuana has continued to increase over the years (39). In 1977, 56 percent reported its use with 10 percent saying they used the drug daily or almost daily. No high school coach can ignore the fact that members of the team may be involved in drugs.

It is natural for teenagers to experiment with many different things. If young people are encouraged to make an intelligent decision based on facts about drug abuse, then they may well avoid the temptation to experiment with drugs. Teenagers do not start on drugs or alcohol because of good taste or special appeal: They generally try them to be accepted by their peers or because they are curious. The responsible coach constantly must remind the players about the physiological, emotional, and social dangers of drug abuse. He or she should present this information in such a way that the teenagers realize he or she cares for them and is not merely preaching.

Students should be taught that the way drugs function varies a great deal. Some, like antibiotics, are administered to help augment the body's natural tendency to fight off infection. Basically, however, most drugs are not supportive but influence the nervous and vascular systems. Under normal conditions, nerves give off "neurohumor," which stimulates muscles and organs into action. Some drugs, such as amphetamines, imitate this action and set muscles and organs into motion when they should be at rest. This abnormal use of muscles and organs tears down the tissues and thus can be harmful.

Many drugs like barbiturates have tremendous effects on the vascular system. They can constrict the vascular feeder system, denying blood to the tissues surrounding the main vascular system, and thus destroy cells. Each time cells are killed, scar tissue is formed, and the elasticity of the entire system is reduced. In extreme cases, loss of elasticity can produce death.

The coach also should impress on students the fact that even one indulgence in a drug can result in dependence. They should be made to realize that experimenting with body chemistry is terribly dangerous.

Summary

The increased use of drugs by professional athletes may influence some high school coaches and players who do not realize the dangerous side effects that can result. A high school coach must avoid giving drugs to the athlete.

Pain is a warning signal for physical injury or malfunction. The degree of pain a person can stand is referred to as the pain threshold; pain tolerance varies among individuals. Teenagers, with their do-or-die spirit, are inclined to continue playing when injured because they do not realize the possibility of permanent damage. The coach should know the pain threshold level for each athlete and should avoid use of pain-killing drugs.

Legally, only a physician can administer drugs to a high school player, even though the coach may feel he or she is more capable of making decisions about appropriate treatment for the athletes. Ethically, a coach should not advocate the use of drugs for other than therapeutic reasons.

The high school coach does have a responsibility to be aware of the function and possible side effects of different drugs. And he or she should relay this information to the students.

Blood doping by athletes engaged in sports requiring great endurance is a questionable practice with little evidence to support its use.

Drugs commonly used in athletics are amphetamines, androgenic-anabolic steroids, barbiturates, cortisone, dimethyl sulfoxide, ethyl chloride, local anesthetics, muscle relaxants, and oral enzymes.

Drug dependence can be physiological or psychological. Physiological dependence results from an alteration in the user's body chemistry so that failure to use the drug creates tremendous discomfort. Psychological dependence usually is associated with drugs that create an initial feeling of euphoria. An individual suffering from this dependence usually requires psychiatric help to overcome the habit.

The high school coach must be aware of drugs most commonly used by young people and be alert to drug abuse. Teenagers are prone to experiment with drugs either because they are searching for their own identities or are seeking peer acceptance. The coach should educate the players about the effects of drugs such as alcohol, caffeine, hallucinogens, marijuana, and narcotics.

References

1. Allman, Fred L. "What Medical Services Should We Provide?" Speech given at Western States Conference on Secondary School Athletic Administration. Las Vegas, Nevada (December 14, 1970).
2. *Amphetamines*. Chicago: American Medical Association, 1970. Pamphlet.
3. "Athlete's Use of D.M.S.O., Steroids." *American Medical Association News*. Chicago: American Medical Association, 1970. Pamphlet.
4. *Barbiturates*. Chicago: American Medical Association, 1970. Pamphlet.
5. Bedworth, Albert E., and Joseph A. D'Elia. *Basics of Drug Education*. New York: Baywood, 1973, 271.
6. Benowicz, R. J. *Non-Prescription Drugs and Their Side Effects*. New York: Grosset and Dunlap, 1977, 128.
7. "Blood Doping." *Track & Field News* (November 7, 1971).
8. Blum, R. H., E. Blum, and E. Garfield. *Drug Education: Results and Recommendations*. Lexington, Mass.: D. C. Heath, 1976, 217.
9. Campbell, A. M. G., M. Evans, J. L. G. Thompson, et al. "Cerebral Atrophy in Young Cannabis Smokers." *Lancet*, 2 (December 1971), 1219–1224.
10. Chapin, Dwight. "Athletes Driven by Ego, Pride." *Los Angeles Times*, part 3 (February 11, 1974), 1.

11. Clarke, K. S. "Drugs, Sports and Doping." *Journal of the Maine Medical Association,* 61 (March 1970), 55–58.
12. Curtis, Lindsay R. "Let's Talk About Drugs." Dallas: Tane Press, 1967. Pamphlet.
13. Deutsch, Linda. "Cocaine: In-Crowd Craze." *Santa Barbara Newspress* (October 20, 1978), A–6.
14. *Drug Abuse: A Manual for Law Enforcement Officers.* 2nd ed. Philadelphia: Smith, Kline, and French Laboratories, 1966.
15. Eddy, Nathan B., et al. "Drug Dependence: Its Significance and Characteristics." *Bulletin,* 32:5 Geneva: World Health Organization, (1965), 721–738.
16. Einstein, Stanley. *Beyond Drugs.* New York: Pergamon Press, 1975, 290.
17. Fowler, William, et al. "The Facts about Ergogenic Aids in Athletics." *Journal of Health, Physical Education, and Recreation,* 40 (December 1969), 37–42.
18. ———. "Effect of an Anabolic Steroid on Physical Performance of Young Men." *Journal of Applied Physiology,* 20 (September 1965), 1038–1040.
19. Gilbert, Bil. "Athletes in a Turned On World, Part 1." *Sports Illustrated,* 30 (June 23, 1969), 64–72.
20. ———. "Something Extra On the Ball, Part II." *Sports Illustrated,* 30 (June 30, 1969), 30–42.
21. ———. "High Time to Make Some Rules, Part III." *Sports Illustrated,* 31 (July 7, 1969), 30–35.
22. Golding, Lawrence A., and James R. Bernard. "The Effect of D-amphetamine Sulfate in Physical Performance." *Journal of Sports Medicine, Physical Fitness, 3* (December 1963), 221–224.
23. Grinspoon, L. *Marijuana Reconsidered.* Cambridge, Mass.: Harvard University Press, 1977, 474.
24. ——— and J. B. Baklar. *Cocaine: A Drug and Its Social Evolution.* New York: Basic Books, 1976, 304.
25. ——— and P. Hedblom. *The Speed Culture: Amphetamine Use and Abuse in America.* Cambridge, Mass.: Harvard University Press, 1975, 340.
26. Irwin, Theodore. *Pittsburgh Press Parade* (September 6, 1970), 5.
27. Ivy, Andrew C. "What Everyone Should Know About Alcoholic Beverages." Evanston, Ill.: Signal Press. Pamphlet.
28. Jay, Thelma A. "Death on the Installment Plan." Evanston, Ill.: Signal Press. Pamphlet.
29. Jordan, Edwin P., ed. *Modern Drug Encyclopedia and Therapeutic Index.* 7th ed. New York: R. H. Donnelly, 1958.
30. Karpovich, Peter V. "Effects of Amphetamine Sulphate on Athletic Performance." *Journal of American Association,* 1970 (May 1959), 558–561.
31. Kellor, Richard. "The Realities of Drug Abuse in High School Athletics." *JOHPER,* 4 (April 1972), 43–48.
32. Kolansky, Harold, and William T. Moore. "Effects of Marijuana on Adolescents and Young Adults." *Journal of American Medical Association,* 216 (April 1971), 486–492.
33. ———. "Toxic Effects of Chronic Marijuana Use." *Journal of American Medical Association,* 222 (October 1972), 35–41.
34. Land, Herman W. "How a Parent Can Reach His Child about Drugs." *Today's Health* (August 1971), 43–45.
35. *L.S.D.* Chicago: American Medical Association, 1970. Pamphlet.

36. Maher, Charles. "Artificial Players." *Los Angeles Times,* CC3 (December 18, 1970), 2.
37. Mandell, Arnold J. "Pro Football Fumbles the Drug Scandal." *Psychology Today* (June 9, 1975), 39–41.
38. "Marijuana Found to Hurt Body Defenses." *Los Angeles Times,* part 1 (January 26, 1974), 9.
39. "Marijuana Use Increases While Other Drugs Hold Steady." *Psychology Today* (October 1978), 22, 23.
40. "Morning Briefing." *Los Angeles Times,* CC3 (November 20, 1971), 2.
41. Newham, Ross. "Team Physicians: Do They Have Athletes Interests at Heart." *Los Angeles Times,* part 3 (February 19, 1975), 1, 8.
42. Novich, Max M., and Buddy Taylor. *Training and Conditioning of Athletes.* Philadelphia: Lea & Febiger, 1970.
43. Pierson, William R. "Amphetamine Sulfate and Performance: A Critique." *Journal of American Medical Association,* 177 (August 1961), 345–347.
44. Pinkerton, Peter B. *Toward a Better Understanding of Drugs.* Ventura, Calif.: Ventura Unified School District, 1967.
45. *Proper and Improper Use of Drugs by Athletes.* Investigative Hearings on the Proper and Improper Use of Drugs by Athletes, June 18, July 12, 13, 1973. Washington, D.C.: U.S. Government Printing Office, 1973, 843.
46. Rice, Julius. *Ups and Downs.* New York: Macmillan, 1972, 214.
47. "Runaway Drug Escalation." *Santa Barbara Newspress* (January 6, 1974), A–1.
48. "Scottish Player Banned for Life in Dope Case." *Los Angeles Times,* part 3 (June 6, 1978), 1, 3.
49. Shephard, R. *Frontiers of Fitness.* Springfield, Ill., Charles C. Thomas, 1971, 395.
50. ———. *The Fit Athlete.* Oxford. Oxford University Press, 1978, 214.
51. Smith, D. E., and D. R. Wesson. *Uppers and Downers.* Englewood Cliffs, N.J.: Prentice-Hall, 1973, 152.
52. Smith, Gene M., and Henry K. Beecher. "Amphetamine Sulfate and Athletic Performance—Objective Effects." *Journal of American Medical Association,* 170 (May 1959), 542–557.
53. *The Crutch that Cripples: Drug Dependence.* Chicago: American Medical Association, 1968. Pamphlet.
54. *To Parents about Drugs.* Metropolitan Life Insurance, 1970. Pamphlet.
55. "U.S. Survey, 1.5 Million Teenagers Report Using Heroin." *Santa Barbara Newspress* (May 11, 1972), A–14.
56. Vanek, M., and B. Cratty. *Psychology and the Superior Athlete.* London: Macmillan, 1970, 212.
57. Wesson, D. R., and D. E. Smith. *Barbiturates, Their Use, Misuse, and Abuse.* New York: Human Science Press, 1977, 144.
58. *What We Should Know About Marijuana.* Evanston, Ill.: Signal Press, 1968. Pamphlet.
59. Williams, M. H. *Drugs and Athletic Performance.* Springfield, Ill.: Charles C. Thomas, 1974, 199.
60. Wynn, Victor. "The Anabolic Steroids." *The Practitioner,* 200 (April 1968), 509–518.

Legal Education for High School Coaches 9

'01 Coach Publications ©1966 by Ray Franks Publishing Ranch

"In most communities, they only hang effigies."

The high school coaching and teaching profession includes important legal aspects. Although a school district and its employees, as agents of the state, have traditionally enjoyed "governmental immunity" to lawsuits, courts and state legislatures recently have ruled that school boards and teachers can be judged liable for failure to perform their duty.

There are many different types of cases, including those questioning the individual rights of students who were refused participation because they failed to observe rules; but the majority of legal suits in high school athletics involve negligence on the part of the coach. Every coach has a basic responsibility to protect the students by ensuring a safe playing environment and taking every precaution to prevent accidents. Opening one's eyes to situations that may cause potential legal action against the coach or the institution enables one to avoid many problems.

Objectives

This chapter attempts to acquaint the prospective high school coach with the aspects of this country's legal system that apply to the profession. The following features are discussed:

1. Governmental immunity for school districts and teachers
2. Formation of legal judgments
3. Tort liability and negligence
4. Defense against negligence
5. Contributory negligence
6. Prudence
7. Supervision
8. Equipment and facilities
9. Transportation
10. Medical examinations and waiver forms
11. Medical assistance
12. Dangerous coaching practices
13. Failure of students to conform to rules and regulations

Governmental Immunity for School Districts and Teachers

The doctrine of governmental immunity originated in England, where the king—who was believed to derive his authority from God—enjoyed "sovereign immunity." This concept of the king's divine right was replaced in the eighteenth century by the idea that the ruler's authority was granted by the consent of his subjects. As the representative of the people, the king was conceived to be an extension of them. In 1788, it was established as common law in England that government should be immune to legal action from the people (55). They could not sue themselves.

This doctrine of governmental immunity was brought to the United States in its formative years and also accepted as common law. Citizens drawing up state constitutions deemed it essential to include governmental immunity as a basic tenet of those documents. The first recorded case establishing governmental immunity as law was ruled on in 1812 in Massachusetts. The ruling declared that there could be no action against the public (48). In 1925, the Supreme Court of Appeals in West Virginia ruled that state employees, being agents of the state, should not be liable for negligent acts in the performance of their duties (37).

Because of these rulings, and because the U.S. Constitution assigns each state with the responsibility of providing public education for its citizens, school districts traditionally have claimed that they are agencies of the government and, as such, should be immune to legal action against them. However, in recent years the concept of governmental immunity has been reappraised. In 1959, the Supreme Court of Illinois overruled the common-law rule and held that a board of education could be held liable for all actions of its agents (47). (In this case, it would be teachers and coaches doing their jobs.) In several other states, the courts also have declared governmental immunity for school districts as nonexistent.

State legislatures, too, have passed laws that make it possible for a school district to be declared responsible in a court suit. In 1937, the New York legislature enacted a "save harmless" law, which protects teachers in the event of litigation and holds the school district responsible. California, Minnesota, and Wisconsin have passed similar laws (29). Where such a situation exists, school districts or state educational associations often provide some form of financial protection for their employees. For the most part, however, school districts still enjoy governmental immunity. In his book *The Legal Aspects of Athletics,* Andrew Grieve summarizes each state's legal provisions concerning school districts and school employees (29).

Formation of Legal Judgments

Judgments rendered on legal questions concerning high school athletics are arrived at in one of four ways: they are based on legal statutes, precedent decisions, judicial judgments, or rulings by attorneys general. Coaches should understand how each method functions.

Legal Statutes

Legal statutes are the specific laws that have been enacted by an organized body, such as Congress or the state legislature. These statutes have certain limitations: They must not conflict with the rights state constitutions and the U.S. Constitution guarantee to all citizens. When legal statutes are passed, all citizens are expected to abide by them. Ignorance of a law is not an acceptable reason for failure to comply with it. High school coaches, therefore, have an obligation to know about all state statutes that might relate to athletic activities.

Precedent Decisions

Precedent decisions are judgments that have been made independent of specific statutes and may include judicial judgments of the court. For example, reported appellate court cases are often cited in later decisions and thus become recognized precedents. Such decisions are usually based on social mores or customs and deal with special problems. They are cited as precedents by lawyers and judges who are arguing disputes involving similar circumstances.

Judicial Judgments

Judicial judgments can be made by either a judge or a jury. Because the decision arrived at by a jury involves the opinions of more than one person, this method often is considered to be the fairest. Both a judge and a jury rely heavily on legal statutes and precedent decisions to make judicial judgments. Or, if there is no set course to follow, they make decisions based on related material and establish a precedent for future court action.

Rulings by Attorneys General

Attorneys general often influence laws by interpreting existing statutes or situations in a specific manner. Although these rulings are not necessarily binding because they can be challenged in the courts, they do become accepted as part of the statutes or situation. As such, they become the basis for future legal judgments.

Tort Liability and Negligence

The majority of court cases tried against high school coaches in the United States concern some form of negligence. These cases are commonly referred to as "torts." The word *tort,* which found its way into the American judicial system from English common law, refers to things that are twisted or distorted—contrary to that which is considered right and straight. If a person willfully or negligently causes injury to another, he or she is legally liable and must pay for damages suffered.

A coach's conduct should always ensure the safety of the athletes. Any exposure to danger or risk of bodily harm is considered negligence. Unavoidable accidents are not considered to be caused by negligence and are generally referred to as "fate" or "an act of God." In such cases, the coach is not considered to be at fault.

No specific statutes define negligence, so the courts must consider each case on its own merits. However, commonly accepted guidelines have evolved over the years from judicial judgments involving high school coaches and athletics. They are based on answers to the following questions (8):

1. Did the injured party have a right or obligation to participate? Most high school athletic programs are conducted as extracurricular activities that contribute to a student's education; in this case, a student generally has a right to participate. In some instances, athletics are conducted during the last regularly scheduled class period, and participation is equated to attendance in regular physical education classes. Under such conditions, a student is obligated to be present and to participate.
2. Did the coach have a duty to perform? Coaches are responsible for their students and are considered by law to be acting *in loco parentis*—in the place of the parent. Thus, without question, it is a coach's duty to protect athletes from possible injury.
3. Did an actual breach of duty occur? As a professional, the high school coach is expected to have a high standard of behavior and to possess special knowledge and skills. Regardless of the coach's intentions, an injury resulting from a lack of that knowledge or skill is considered a breach of duty.
4. Did the student athlete suffer bodily injuries? Tort liability based on negligence must involve injury. If a student athlete can prove that he or she was physically harmed, the coach legally can be termed negligent.

If these questions are answered affirmatively, the coach can be proved negligent. It is important for a high school coach to understand that even though a school district may assume the liability of its employees, the coach still is responsible for negligent actions and usually will be included in a court lawsuit.

Defense Against Negligence

Thomas W. Hart, in his article "Elements of Tort Liability as Applied to Athletic Injuries" (31), suggests five basic defenses that can be used against charges of negligence. These are:

1. "Show the accident was unavoidable." This implies that there was nothing the defendant could have done to prevent the injury. Acts of God illustrate this point.

2. "Show the defendant was not the proximate cause of the damage." Proximate cause implies that the defendant was guilty of negligent action, which was the direct cause of injury. The defendant must prove that this was not the case.
3. "Show contributory negligence or comparative negligence." The injured party contributed to the accident through negligent behavior.
4. "Show assumption of risk." The injured party was warned of the dangers involved in the activity and voluntarily participated with full assumption of the risks.
5. "Claim immunity." The defendant claims that as an agent of a governmental body he or she has freedom from legal actions in carrying out governmental responsibilities.

Contributory Negligence

One defense that coaches can use in litigation involving an injury or accident is contributory negligence. Basically, this involves the deliberate action or lack of action by the athlete that led to the accident. Athletes are expected to employ a reasonable standard of behavior or self-protection in performing an act. In determining a standard of conduct to which the athlete must conform, age, maturity, intelligence, training, skill level, and nature of instruction are all taken into account. Essential in the instruction are safety procedures that individuals should follow and information about dangers that may exist in the use of equipment. Failure by athlete to heed warnings, follow an established pattern of behavior, or avoid deliberate actions that result in injury normally would cancel any actionable negligence by the coach.

Prudence

Whether a coach acted with a reasonable amount of prudence has been one of the prevailing factors in legal decisions involving negligence in athletics. Prudence generally is defined by *Webster's Third International Dictionary* as "wisdom shown in the exercise of reason, forethought, and self-control" (30). In conducting athletic activities, a coach should exercise prudence and make every attempt to avoid possible trouble. For instance, if a coach allowed a player to ride back to school after an away game with a friend rather than in the transportation provided for the team, he or she would not only encourage a morale problem among the team but also could be declared negligent if an accident occurred. At the start of the season, the coach should announce team regulations precluding even the possibility of such requests.

The American Association of Health, Physical Education, and Recreation has published a *Coach's Handbook* that lists characteristics of a prudent coach (12):

A reasonably prudent and careful coach

1. Knows the health status of his players
2. Requires medical approval for participation following serious injury or illness
3. Performs services only in those areas in which he is fully qualified
4. Performs the proper act in case of injury
5. Has medical personnel available at all contests and readily available during practice sessions
6. Conducts activities in safe areas
7. Does not diagnose or treat injuries
8. Makes certain that the protective equipment worn by his players is adequate in quality and fits properly
9. Analyzes his coaching methods and procedures for the safety of his players
10. Assigns only qualified personnel to conduct and/or supervise an activity
11. Instructs adequately before permitting performances
12. Keeps an accurate record of serious injuries and his ensuing actions
13. In all his actions or inactions he asks himself, "What would THE reasonably prudent and careful coach do under THESE circumstances?"

In summarizing these characteristics, it is apparent that the high school coach is charged with prudence and care in conducting athletic activities and must consider risks involved for the participants and take steps to reduce the possibility of injuries. Coaches should never gamble on the ability of a young person to bounce back after an injury; they should instead make certain that the student is in the hands of a competent physician and that the student's parents are fully aware of all aspects of the situation.

John Warren Giles, a member of the Bar Association in Washington, D.C., has commented on prudence and liability of coaches, and he advises all people concerned with the administration of high school athletics to procure a personal liability insurance policy for their own protection (27). Such coverage seems advisable regardless of the protection given an individual coach by a particular school district.

The concept of responsibility and prudence is important in almost all areas of interscholastic athletics. The aspects of coaching discussed in the rest of this chapter have been selected because they seem to be the most important for coaches to consider in relation to legal principles. Bear in mind, though, that courts do not always agree in their jurisdictions, and exceptions to many of the generally accepted principles always can be found.

Supervision

Supervision of high school athletic activities is governed by the same laws as that of any other school activity. Coaches should know that these rules are not exhaustive; basically, however, they require that adequate supervision be assigned to an area or activity by the superintendent of schools, school principal, athletic director, department head, or person having such responsibility, and that a reasonable attempt at supervision is made by those so assigned. Most states require that individuals responsible for athletics be members of the high school faculty, and though this regulation generally seems to be observed, the rule is sometimes circumvented through devious methods (29). In the event of an injury, the question of liability under these circumstances is crucial.

Qualifications and Training of Supervisors

One of the most common problems in supervising athletics involves the supervisor's qualifications and training. Generally speaking, a person who has a teaching certificate is trained adequately to handle discipline and to control groups of students. However, this certificate does not necessarily prepare the individual to teach the techniques of a particular sport, so a coach also must be educated to instruct a sport. This requirement can create a problem for school districts that are too small to employ trained instructors for each area of the educational program. In many instances, a school will endeavor to provide sports opportunities for its students by hiring well-meaning but untrained individuals to teach athletics. This is a dangerous practice, because it makes both the instructor and the school district extremely vulnerable to court suits. A school district is considered negligent if it permits a school to use the services of someone who has had previous playing experience but no formal training to help with coaching or supervising a sport (29).

The case of *Stehn* v. *Bernard MacFadden Foundations, Inc.,* is an example of the legal difficulties that can result from inadequate supervision (58). Lowry Stehn was a student who received a paralytic injury in wrestling class. Before he was injured, the school had announced that the wrestling program would be discontinued due to the wrestling instructor's resignation. Another faculty member, who had wrestling experience and had done some coaching in the army, volunteered to continue the program. In his instruction, he taught the boys an agura hold he had learned from his wrestling experience in the army. It is not recorded that he also taught a method of escape from the hold or defense against it. During the class period, students helped supervise and officiate matches. At the time of Stehn's accident, two matches were being held simultaneously, a common practice in such classes, and the instructor was positioned between them. He could supervise only one match at a time, however, and was concentrating on the one in which Stehn was not wrestling.

The plaintiff based the case on inadequate supervision and asked that the jury consider several key questions (3):

1. Was the coach qualified to coach boys of this age in a wrestling program;
2. Was it proper or reasonable to require the plaintiff to wrestle against two different opponents on the same day, particularly when one opponent was more experienced and heavier than the other.
3. Were the school officials negligent for their failure to inform the instructor about the injury caused by [Stehn's opponent] to a boy the year before;
4. Was the supervision furnished by the school officials sufficient for a class of thirty-five wrestlers;
5. Was the agura hold suitable for students of this age;
6. Was it reasonable for a class to practice a hold before they learned how to break it;
7. Was it proper for a classmate of such young age to act as a referee.

After considering all the evidence, the jury decided the case in favor of Lowry Stehn and stated that he should be awarded damages of $385,000. In reviewing the case, it developed that the instructor's experience and training did not prepare him to handle a wrestling class; consequently, the concept of inadequate supervision influenced the court's final judgment.

Number of Supervisors

Another problem in supervising athletics is the number of people needed for adequate direction of an activity. Many states, including California, allow student or cadet teachers to be assigned to work with a high school coach. However, these assistants are not trained thoroughly enough to assume the responsibility of directing a team alone, and they must be supervised by a regularly appointed individual who is always present when the activity is being conducted.

The number of supervisors judged adequate for a certain area or sport is a disputed question. Although the courts have rendered judgments about the number of supervisors needed for playing areas such as playgrounds (11) and swimming pools (15), they have not dealt with the number needed for a particular sport. But there are situations in certain sports that may result in legal action. Sports like baseball, football, and track require large outdoor areas. In many schools whose number of available coaches is limited, it is a normal practice to divide the squads and have different groups of players practicing and using equipment at the same time in different locations. Obviously, one coach cannot cover all areas at once, but supervision by student leaders would, in all likelihood, be considered inadequate. What can coaches do to protect themselves in such a situation and still carry out their assigned duties? There is a course of action open, one that the court would probably consider prudent.

Before an actual practice session, coaches should give players detailed instructions about performance of skills and use of equipment. They should point out apparent dangers and possible risks. Then, when the squad is divided and sent to perform their respective drills, the coach should circulate from one group to another, offering words of advice and suggestions for improving individual techniques. If an accident occurs under these conditions and a liability suit is instigated, the case would be decided on the facts and the situation that prevailed rather than on whether the presence of the coach might have prevented the accident (50).

Necessity for Supervisor's Presence

Under no conditions should a coach leave the practice session area unless a trained supervisor is present. Under normal circumstances, coaches rarely can be faulted for failure to reasonably supervise their activity during games or practice sessions, for they are generally totally engrossed in individual and team development. However, if a coach does leave the playing area because of an injury to one of the players, a phone call, or some outside interference, he or she is guilty of negligence in performing an assigned duty and is subject to a liability suit if an accident occurs during his or her absence. Although coaches have argued that getting medical attention for an injured player is a legitimate reason for leaving the area, the courts have been firm in their contention that absence for any cause is considered failure to perform the duty of supervision.

A New Jersey case that attracted nationwide attention because of the large financial award for damages to the plaintiff applies to most high school athletic situations. When the teacher conducting a gymnastics class left the room to help a student who had received a severe rope burn, he told the students to stop all activity and wait for his return. Some students ignored his warning and proceeded to use the equipment. One boy attempted a stunt off a springboard and injured himself so badly that he became a paraplegic. In the ensuing legal suit, the teacher was charged with negligence for leaving the group unsupervised. The plantiff's argument was based on a previous court decision that stated that children are not responsible for their actions and cannot be assumed to conduct themselves maturely. The jury awarded $1.25 million to the student plus medical expenses to his parents (45). (Later the original award was held to be exorbitant and was reduced to $300,000 plus medical expenses.)

This case points out the risk a coach takes in leaving a group unsupervised. Usually a school district provides rules to follow for such situations, but if there are no regulations, a prudent coach must consider in advance how to handle any situation that might occur. The best procedure to follow

Figure 9.1   *A coach should never leave the practice session area unsupervised.*

when adequate supervision is not available is to cancel the practice session and send the players home. The consequences of a lost day of practice are minimal compared to the possibility of injury and the resulting legal action.

Equipment and Facilities

Equipment

Generally, athletic equipment and facilities represent the greatest expenditure in an athletic budget. If a school lacks adequate funds, it sometimes attempts to stretch the athletic dollar as far as possible by using faulty equipment and facilities. But the safety of the players must take precedence over all other considerations, and no coach should knowingly allow a student to participate with defective or ill-fitting equipment or to use facilities in a state of disrepair. Despite the fact that coaches throughout the country acknowledge this policy, defective equipment and faulty facilities have been the basis for perhaps the greatest number of court cases involving high school athletics.

Because most school districts provide the equipment necessary for a sport, they are liable in the event of an injury that might have been avoided with proper equipment. However, when athletes are required to furnish their own shoes and other items, the coach or school district cannot be responsible for injuries that these items might cause.

The first-string varsity players usually are given the newest and best equipment; used equipment is used to outfit substitutes, junior varsity, and freshman teams. The coach should make certain that the older equipment is in the best possible state of repair and that it has retained its protective qualities. In the absence of trained equipment personnel, the coaches should make it their responsibility to see that all items fit properly. Ill-fitting equipment does not offer a player enough protection. If proper equipment cannot be provided, the player should not be allowed to participate. In the event of an injury even remotely related to unsafe equipment, there is little doubt that the court would judge the coach or school as negligent (56).

Product Liability

Court cases involving product liability have reached such staggering proportions that insurance companies are hesitant to continue handling such policies. Herb Appenzeller, in an article "Sports in the Courts," reported that product-liability suits in 1960 numbered 50,000; in 1970, 500,000; and in 1975 reached an all-time high of 1,000,000. The average award in 1975 amounted to $338,000 (5). A recent judgment of $5.3 million against Riddell, Inc., a Chicago, Illinois, football helmet manufacturer, threatened the manufacture of football helmets in the United States. This judgment was overruled by a higher court, but is still under appeal.

Attorney Gene O'Connor, in a talk at the 1978 annual American Football Coaches Association meeting, warned that "a key issue is the extent of warning given by the manufacturer to the consumer as to the danger of the product" (51). Coaches provided with such information must warn all players of impending and possible danger. All coaches must be concerned with the safety of their players. This new affirmative duty for coaches means that if they want to avoid litigation, they must emphasize dangers and then discipline any player who ignores accepted techniques and rules.

Facilities

Many coaches become so involved in teaching their sport that they overlook unsafe conditions in the practice or playing areas. Even if the facility is the only one available, the coach should realize the obligation to make certain that it is in good repair. If someone else is directly responsible for the upkeep of facilities, the coach should report any hazard at once and keep players away from the area until it is repaired. Some lawyers feel that a coach is well advised to put such information in writing as evidence that he or she reported the faulty condition. This procedure could be awkward when school personnel with different responsibilities have a close social relationship, but it is recognized as a good business practice.

Andrew Grieve, in an article entitled "Physical Education, Athletics, and The Law" (28), deals with safety in facilities and the need for competent supervision. He divides the users of the facilities into three groups. These are:

1. *Invitees.* Those who, without a formal invitation are permitted to use a facility which provides an opportunity for a particular activity. For instance, if the high school coach opens the gymnasium for anyone to play basketball on Saturday morning, they become invitees.
2. *Licensees.* Those who use a facility with the stated or written consent of the owner. In this instance, the high school coach opens the gymnasium on Saturday morning specifically for the ninth-grade junior high school students.
3. *Trespassers.* Those who use a facility without permission and contrary to stated regulations.

Outdoor facilities   Coaches using outdoor facilities should be concerned particularly with protective netting on the backstop or retainer fence, playing surfaces, jumping pits, and bleachers. Protective screen or netting should be maintained so that there are no breaks or holes that balls could pass through; playing surfaces should have no protruding objects such as sprinklers or cement objects (10) like rain drains that are not covered; jumping pits should be constructed in such a way that sides are covered and not harmful to the contestants; bleachers and benches should be inspected periodically to make certain they are in good condition.

Gymnasiums   Gymnasiums present similar problems. There should always be enough mats around equipment, and the walls close to the playing area should have a protective covering. Basketball standards that rest on the floor also should be provided with protection. Mats should be placed under chinning bars (18); basketball backboards must be secure and the hoops intact; shredded basketball nets should be replaced. There are too many different kinds of equipment used in different gymnasiums to point out all potential dangers, but a coach should be aware of each piece of equipment used and make sure that it is in good condition.

Locker rooms   A coach sometimes overlooks the locker and shower rooms, but they also should be carefully checked. Lockers that were not firmly attached and consequently toppled over have been the cause of litigation (21). Benches that are nailed together can fall apart more easily than those

Figure 9.2 *Coaches should realize that they are obligated to ensure that practice and playing areas are safe.*

that are bolted. There should be no sharp edges in the room that could cause a cut. Players should not be allowed to bring soft drinks in glass bottles into the room because of the danger of broken glass.

Supervision of facilities Athletic facilities, both gymnasiums and outdoor areas, are considered by the courts as "attractive nuisances" and potentially dangerous to young people. Those responsible for supervising the facilities should make every attempt to eliminate the chance of injuries. Although outdoor facilities need not be supervised when school is not in session, the school district can be held responsible for negligence if equipment is not maintained. When a gymnasium is in use, it should be supervised at all times, and failure to lock the building when the gym is not being used can cause a liability suit (42). An athlete may want more practice shooting baskets or to work with a particular piece of equipment, and although the coach should encourage players to perform at maximum ability, he or she should never allow them to remain after practice without adequate supervision. If a player happened to be injured in a jump or fall, the coach would have no recourse in the courts when charged with negligence.

Transportation

Interscholastic athletics require transportation more frequently than any other school activity. Coaches must be aware of the legal aspects of transporting team members, so that in the event of an accident they will not be guilty of negligence in carrying out their duties.

An accepted rule to follow is that all transportation should be in either school-owned or certified public-bonded carriers. Contracted school buses are considered certified public carriers. Some rural districts provide buses, and the coach or another school employee has the duty of driving. In this situation, the driver must possess a valid chauffeur's license and know the state laws. For instance, school buses in California must have a first-aid kit aboard when transporting students or the driver is considered negligent.

When private cars are the only source of transportation available, the coach is extremely vulnerable to a liability suit. The coach should take certain precautions by following these rules (44):

1. Check each car to make certain that it is in good condition. In case of an accident, faulty brakes or poor tires are enough evidence to prove negligence on the part of the individual authorizing use of a car.
2. Select drivers carefully. If possible, have only adults drive the cars; avoid anyone who might be considered a reckless driver because of reputation or a bad driving record.
3. Check the driver's insurance to make sure that it is complete and covers the purpose for which the car is being used. At minimum expense, a "rider" can be attached to an ordinary auto policy to protect both driver and passengers.
4. Give each driver complete instructions for the trip, suggesting routs, driving speed, and meeting place. Although the coach may feel awkward instructing parents, they will appreciate this thoroughness and realize that these directions are in everyone's best interest.
5. Be fully aware of the state laws related to motor vehicles. Of particular importance is the legal distinction between "guests" and "passengers" because liability laws for the two categories differ. A "guest" in a car has agreed voluntarily to ride; the driver receives no reimbursement. On the other hand, when the coach assigns players to ride specific cars, or when the driver is paid or reimbursed in some manner, then riders are considered "passengers." This generally recognized difference is not uniformly interpreted by the state statutes. Mere negligence on the part of a driver of guests generally affords the riders little opportunity to recover damages because of an accident; guests must prove willful and wanton negligence against the driver, according to the liability laws of most states. Mere negligence on the part of drivers of passengers is sufficient evidence to allow damages to be awarded by the courts to the passengers.

6. Realize that if a student uses the coach's car for an errand, the student is considered an agent of the coach, and the coach therefore is liable in the event of an accident.

Medical Examinations and Waiver Forms

Medical Examinations

Throughout the nation, athletes generally are required to have medical examinations before they can participate in high school athletic competition. However, the form of these examinations varies greatly among states and sometimes among school districts. In some states or districts, examinations given at the start of the school year clear players for participation in all seasonal sports; in other places, a student is required to have an examination before each season (7). In many cases, these examinations are cursory and seldom reveal physical defects or problems. However, if a defect is discovered, the student usually is given a more comprehensive examination and should not be allowed to participate until he or she has a medical clearance. If the coach does permit the individual to play, and the student sustained an injury related to the problem, the coach is considered guilty of negligence.

A coach legally cannot be considered responsible for injuries that occur when normal physical examinations have not revealed a defect. In the case of *Kerby* v. *Elk Grove High School District,* a student who received a blow on his head by a basketball died as the result of an undiagnosed defective circulatory system (35). The court judged that the coach had carried out his assigned responsibilities and therefore was not negligent in the situation.

Waiver Forms

Many school districts require that parents or guardians sign waiver forms to allow students to participate in high school athletics. Although many of these forms acknowledge that the school district or coach is not liable if a student is injured during sports activities, they actually have little value. It has been established in court that the rights of a minor cannot be signed away by an adult (29). Also, since the coach and the school district are responsible for providing safe practice areas and behaving with prudence, liability suits for negligence can be initiated and won despite the signed waiver forms.

Medical Assistance

Many coaches wonder about the course of action they should take if a player is injured during a practice session or a game. In the first place, no

Figure 9.3 *A coach should understand when injuries can be attributed to negligence.*

practice session or contest should be held unless medical assistance is readily available. During athletic practice, a school nurse should be in the building; during a game, a physician or an athletic trainer who is capable of handling emergencies should be present. If no one with medical training is available to treat an emergency, the coach is responsible for administering first aid. Every high school coach should have a valid first aid certificate and take a yearly refresher course for handling emergency situations.

There is a question of when first aid should be administered, and an excellent answer is given in the *Physical Education Newsletter* (52):

> In general you should not administer first aid unless the injury can be classified as an emergency and there is no doctor or nurse available. In such situations you must administer first aid. If you fail to do so, you can be sued for negligence. When you administer first aid, confine your treatment to alleviating the emergency condition. When an injury cannot be considered as an emergency, send for the school doctor or nurse and do not administer first aid.

Also, in *From the Gym to the Jury,* his book on laws for physical education and athletics, Herb Appenzeller points out that the courts have ruled "that an emergency exists when the situation is such that with immediate medical care 'the pupil might be relieved of his hurt and more serious consequences be avoided' "(3).

The following underlines the importance of following acceptable first aid practices in treating emergencies. A high school student was hurt in a preseason football scrimmage, and the coach realized that the boy had suffered a serious neck injury. The athlete was asked to squeeze the coach's finger, and because he was able to do so, other boys were ordered to pick up the injured player and move him to the sidelines so the scrimmage could continue. There are conflicting reports about whether a doctor was present and who gave the order for the boy to be moved, but the student became a paraplegic because of the injury. Expert testimony at the trial held that because he was able to squeeze the coach's finger after the injury, he should have had normal recovery but that he sustained additional injury when he was moved by the other players. The court upheld this opinion and ruled that the coach was guilty of negligence because he did not have the boy moved on a stretcher, the acceptable practice for moving an injured person (59).

Coaches who have had a comprehensive course of instruction for teaching athletics usually are competent to give medical assistance for cuts, floor and mat burns, and minor contusions. They should deal with preventive measures such as taping to avoid possible injury and let emergencies be handled by specially trained people. Those who cross the boundary from administering first aid to practicing medicine are asking for serious trouble.

Dangerous Coaching Practices ——————————————————————

Inadequately Trained Coaches

Numerous high school coaching practices are not only dangerous for students but also leave the coach open to charges of negligence. Many coaches assume positions they are not adequately prepared for. A coach's teaching load may be too heavy, with responsibility for more than one sport, or the coach may be assigned to handle a sport with which his or her only experience has been as a player in high school or college. Because of student and parent demand to increase the variety of high school sports, specially trained coaches are not always available. (One result of inadequately trained coaching is illustrated by the Stehn case mentioned earlier.) A coach who accepts a position without proper training can be held liable for negligence (58).

Difficult Styles of Play

Television and professional athletics have had a great deal of impact on high school–level styles of play. Although high school athletes today possess a great deal of information about sports, whether they are mature enough to handle certain styles of play is questionable. A coach has the responsibility to analyze players' abilities and not to have them try to master techniques too difficult for their physical development. The courts are filled with case histories in which coaches unwittingly overmatched high school athletes and thus were judged guilty of negligence.

Advocating Violence

Some coaches unwittingly advocate violence by indicating that if the opponent's leading player is put out of action, victory will come much easier. If such talk or inference results in lack of sportsmanship, it can terminate a coaching career. "A new era of tort law has emerged that holds a person responsible for any conduct that endangers the safety of an opponent" (5).

Play with Injury

Some coaches play down injuries. They often remark, "We don't talk about injuries on our team." Such an attitude discourages the athlete from reporting an injury. The injured individual may continue to play, and the injury may result in permanent damage. Other coaches insult or use distorted humor about those who are injured. Such practices can only lead to trouble in the event of serious injury, which results in litigation for the coach.

Athletes Not Physically Ready to Play

A coach should be very careful to ensure that players have received proper physical training and conditioning before they participate in sports, especially those requiring vigorous activity. Most state high school athletic associations have set a limit on the starting date for pre-season practice and in many cases also have established the number of practice sessions a team must have before it can play an actual game. In California, a varsity high school football player must be at least fifteen years old, and each athlete must have ten days of practice before competing in an interschool scrimmage or game (14). If a player is seriously injured because he or she is not in condition or has not practiced sufficiently, the coach is subject to charges of negligence.

Many coaches instruct their athletes to report for the first practice session in top physical condition. Then, without a gradual increase in tempo for the sport, they begin the season with an all-out practice session. This system is dangerous, because some players physically might not be ready for such strenuous activity. An inexperienced coach should be particularly careful not to let enthusiasm cause overextended practice sessions before the players are truly capable of following the directions.

Fighting Between Players

Some sports—and players—are so competitive that occasionally emotions get out of control and a fight erupts. When his happens, the coach has a responsibility to stop the fight rather than encourage it, because physical harm such as a battered eye or loss of a tooth can result. There have been instances where a coach has had the disputers don boxing gloves to settle their differences, but if they have not been trained in the art of boxing, the coach then could be termed negligent in allowing the fight to continue in that way (19).

"Voluntary" Practice Sessions

In recent years, coaches increasingly have avoided practice session regulations, although state athletic associations have actively tried to enforce such rules. Players gather on a supposedly voluntary basis and work out under the direction of a senior player or captain. In some cases, a coach gives the team a syllabus prior to the start of the season, and players are expected to follow this program in informal gatherings. In many cities, high school coaches use public recreation programs as an opportunity to prepare players they will have in class the following year. This practice is used particularly for basketball and other sports requiring a small number of participants. There is little doubt that a coach would be guilty of negligence in such situations if an injury occurred and it was proved that he or she had in-structed individuals to engage in such dangerous and illegal practices.

Failure of Students to Conform to Rules and Regulations

High school athletes traditionally have been barred from further participation if they fail to follow the rules and regulations set forth by the coach. In recent years, students have contested the right of the coach to make such rules (49). The courts have stated that the imposition of reasonable restraints by a coach does not violate a student's constitutional rights (6).

What, then, is a reasonable rule? Rules and regulations should contribute to athletic excellence rather than hinder it, and they must apply equally to all players involved. A good method of establishing reasonable rules is for the coach to meet with team representatives like the captain or senior leaders. Team goals should be decided and then rules and regulations made to help achieve these objectives. When the coach and the players have reached an agreement, they should notify the school board and obtain its approval and support. Then a list of regulations should be distributed to prospective players. Should individuals be required to turn in their uniforms under these conditions, they cannot claim that their rights were violated.

Marshall A. Staunton, legal counsel for the California Teachers' Association, addressed a group of coaches on the "Rights of the Athletic Director and Coaching Staff to Set Grooming and Dress Regulations." He suggested four steps to follow which, he believed, would protect a coach in the event of litigation (57):

> First, the rule should apply solely to athletic teams and not to students generally;
> Second, the rule should contain a statement that restriction on dress and grooming of team members [is] necessary to prevent disruption of team morale which would have a prejudicial effect on team spirit and proper team discipline cannot be maintained in the absences of the rule;
> Third, the rule should be supported by a statement that benefits gained by such a rule are the development of character, initiative, and teamwork which outweigh any impairment of student's rights; and
> Fourth, the rule should be supported by a statement that proper habits of discipline and the development of personality cannot be achieved by any other alternatives.

It has been an accepted right of the school board to establish rules it feels are necessary for control in education that eliminate possible distractions for students (41). High school coaches following reasonable procedures have the same right in attempting to achieve athletic excellence. However, a prudent coach should ask the school board to approve regulations so that a student's freedom is not limited.

Summary

High school coaches are faced with legal problems that involve the everyday operations of coaching. Therefore, they must become aware of the legal aspects of athletics that relate to their coaching duties.

Traditionally, school boards and teachers have enjoyed "governmental immunity," because they are agents of the state. In recent years, this concept has been challenged in some states, and the courts have ruled that school boards can be held liable for their actions.

Legal judgments are based on statutes enacted by an organized body such as the state legislature, on precedent decisions for similar cases, on the decision of a judge or jury, and on rulings by attorneys general.

Tort liability or negligence has been the basis for most cases brought against individual coaches or school boards. Negligence is considered to be behavior that is not prudent and results in injury to another person. Because there are no specific statutes that define negligence, each case must be considered on its own merits.

Some suggested defenses against negligence are:

1. Show the accident was unavoidable
2. Show the defendant's act was not the proximate cause of damage
3. Show contributory negligence or comparative negligence
4. Show assumption of risk
5. Claim immunity

Contributory negligence can be used as a defense by a defendant. It involves actions by the plaintiff that contributed to the injury.

Many cases have been based on prudence. Prudence is defined as "wisdom shown in the exercise of reason, forethought, and self-control." In conducting athletic activities, coaches should exercise prudence and make every attempt to avoid possible problems.

Supervision of high school athletics is governed by the same laws as any other school activity. Adequate supervision must be provided at all times in all areas. Instructors must have proper formal training to teach their sports, because previous participation in an activity is legally considered inadequate preparation.

The school and the coach share responsibility to provide safe equipment and athletic facilities, both outdoors and indoors. Athletes must be warned of potential dangers in using equipment and facilities. Individuals using facilities are classified as invitees, licensees, and trespassers. Use of facilities should always be supervised.

Because interscholastic athletics require a great deal of transportation, the coach should be aware of the responsibility to provide safe transportation. If certified public-bonded carriers cannot be used, private cars and drivers should be selected carefully. The coach also should be familiar with state laws concerning motor vehicles.

Medical examinations at the start of the school year or prior to each sport season usually are required for athletic participation. Coaches cannot be held liable for injuries related to defects not revealed by the examination.

The coach must give first aid if there is an emergency and no person with medical training is available. He or she should follow accepted first aid procedures.

In conducting their sports, many coaches follow dangerous practices, leaving them defenseless in the event of injury to a student. A coach should not accept a position he or she is not properly trained to handle; should not demand overly difficult styles of play; should not push players who are not physically ready; should not encourage fighting between players; should not advocate violence; and should not defy regulations.

In recent years, athletes have contested the coach's right to bar them from participation if they do not conform to training or grooming and dress regulations. However, the courts have upheld the school's—and thus the coach's—right to make such rules as long as they are reasonable. Regulations should contribute to athletic excellence and apply equally to all players.

Glossary

A high school coach should understand the following legal terms:

abrogate   To repeal a former law by legislative act, by constitutional authority, or by usage

accident   An unforeseen event occurring without the will or design of the person whose act causes it

act of commission   Behavior considered unreasonable under the circumstances

act of God   An accident considered due to forces of nature and therefore unavoidable

act of omission   Failure of an individual to perform an act of safety for others

ad litem   Usually used when minors are, in fact, the plaintiffs; because they are minors they must sue by "next friend," referring to the parent or guardian who is plaintiff for the suit

appellant   The party who takes an appeal from one court to another

appellate court   A court that reviews judgments of a lower court to determine the fairness of a trial

assault   The attempt to harm another without actually touching the individual

assumption of risk   A concept implying that individuals who participate voluntarily in an activity assume the risks inherent in that activity

attractive nuisance   A potentially dangerous situation that may attract the attention of individuals

battery   Unlawful beating or other wrongful physical violence inflicted on another individual without consent

certificate   A written statement certifying that an individual has completed the requirements for a particular occupation

common law   A law derived from customary usage; common laws usually are established by judgments that deal with special problems

comparative negligence   Contribution to a negligent act by both the injured party and the person in a position of responsibility

court suit   An action taken to the courts for the recovery of rights or compensation for injury due to infringement of rights

contributory negligence   Factors that contribute to negligence but do not directly cause it

damages   Compensation for injury or loss due to an illegal act

defendant   The party against whom a lawsuit is charged

due process   Individuals have a right to be treated fairly under the law (according to the fifth and fourteenth amendments to the U.S. Constitution)

foreseeability   Liability for negligent conduct when a person could have foreseen the harmful consequences of an act yet disregarded them

governmental immunity   Freedom from legal action due to one's governmental function or responsibility

in loco parentis   In place of the parent injunction, a formal court order issued to stop a specific action

invitees   Individuals using a facility, without formal invitation, which provides an opportunity for a particular activity

judgment   A decision handed down by a judge or jury in concluding a trial

liability   Legal responsibilities that are not fulfilled and therefore are enforceable by court action

license   A legal permit

licensee   An individual who uses a facility with the stated or assumed consent of the owner or responsible person

litigation   A court action in which two or more individuals resolve their differences of opinion

lower court   The court in which a case first is tried by either judge or jury

negligence   The failure to conduct oneself in a reasonably prudent manner to avoid exposing others to dangers or risk of injury

plaintiff   An individual who initiates a court action by filing a complaint

precedent   Previous court judgments used to decide similar court suits involving comparable circumstances

proximate cause   Negligent action by an individual that was the direct and immediate cause of injury

remanded   Sent back (usually for new trail)

statute   A law established by a legal body such as the U.S. Congress or a state legislature

tort   A wrong or injury that does not result from a crime or breach of contract

trespassers   Individuals who have no permission to use a facility

volente non fit injuria   No wrong is done to one who consents

References

1. Alexander, Ruth, and Kern Alexander. *Teachers and Torts*. Middletown, Ky.. Maxwell, 1971.
2. Appenzeller, Herb. *Athletics and the Law*. Charlottesville, Va.: Michie, 1975, 262.
3. ———. *From the Gym to the Jury*. Charlottesville, Va.: Michie, 1970.
4. ———. *Selected Problems in Sports Safety*. Washington, D.C.: AAHPER, 1975, 73–78.
5. ———. "Sports in the Courts." *United States Sports Academy News,* 1:2, 4, 5.
6. *Bagley* v. *Washington Township Hospital District,* 65 2nd 499 (California, 1966).
7. *Bellman* v. *San Francisco High School District 73,* 9 2nd 596 (California, 1937).
8. Bird, Patrick J. "Tort Liability." *Journal of Health, Physical Education, and Recreation,* 41 (January 1970), 38–40.
9. Bolmeier, Edward. *Teachers Legal Rights, Restraints, and Liabilities*. Cincinnati: W. H. Anderson, 1971, 103–115.
10. *Bridge* v. *Board of Education of City of Los Angeles,* 38 Pac. 2nd 199 (California, 1934).
11. *Charonnat* v. *San Francisco Unified School District,* 133 P 2nd 643 (California, 1943).
12. *Coach's Handbook—A Practical Guide for High School Coaches*. Washington, D.C.: American Association for Health, Physical Education, and Recreation, 1960.
13. Condon, Jane. "The Fight for Fit Equipment." *Women's Sports,* 4:9 (September 1977), 64–68.
14. "Constitution and By-Laws of California Interscholastic Federation." C.I.F. Offices: Santa Barbara, Calif., 1970.
15. *Curicio* v. *City of New York,* 275 N.Y. 20, 9 N.E. 2nd (New York, 1937).
16. Drowatzky, J. N. "Liability: You Could Be Sued." *Journal of Physical Education and Recreation,* 49:5 (May 1978), 17, 18.
17. ———. "On the Fixing Line: Negligence in Physical Education." *Journal Law and Education,* 6 (1977), 481–490.
18. *Fein* v. *Board of Education, New York City,* 111 N.E. 2nd 732 (New York, 1953).
19. *Feuerstein* v. *Board of Education,* 202 N.Y. Supp. 2nd 524 (New York, 1960).
20. Frazer, C. "Was the Coach Negligent." *Athletic Journal,* 54 (January 1974), 14, 74–75.
21. *Freund* v. *Oakland Board of Education,* 82 P 2nd 197 (California, 1938).
22. Frost, R. B., and S. L. Marshall. *Administration of Physical Education and Athletics*. Dubuque, Iowa: Wm. C. Brown, 1977, 402.

23. Fuoss, D. E., and R. J. Troppmann. *Creative Management Techniques in Interscholastic Athletics.* New York, N.Y.: John Wiley, 1977, 494.
24. Garber, Lee O., and Newton Edwards. *Tort and Contractual Liability of School Districts and School Boards.* Danville, Ill: The Interstate, 1963.
25. *Gardner* v. *State of New York,* 22 N.E. 2nd 344 (New York, 1939).
26. Gauerke, W. E. *What Educators Should Know About School Law.* Englewood Cliffs, N.J.: Prentice-Hall, 1968, 63.
27. Giles, John Watten. "Liability of Coaches and Athletic Instructors." *Athletic Journal,* 42 (February 1962), 18–19, 49.
28. Grieve, Andrew. "Physical Education, Athletics, and the Law." *Journal of Health, Physical Education, and Recreation,* 45:8 (October 1974), 24–25.
29. ———— . *The Legal Aspects of Athletics.* South Brunswick and New York: A. S. Barnes, 1969.
30. Grove, Philip B., ed. *Webster's Third International Dictionary.* Springfield, Mass.: G. & C. Merriam, 1961.
31. Hart, Thomas W. "Elements of Tort Liability as Applied to Athletic Injuries." *The Journal of School Health,* 46:4 (April 1976), 200–203.
32. Hogan, John C. "Sports in the Courts." *Phi Delta Kappan,* 55 (October 1974), 132–135.
33. Johnson, M. L. *Functional Administration in Physical and Health Education.* Boston: Houghton Mifflin, 1977, 387.
34. Kastle, K. D. "Tort Liability and Educational Personnel." *Educational Horizons,* 54:1 (Fall 1975), 21–23.
35. *Kerby* v. *Elk Grove High School District,* 36 P 2nd 431 (California, 1934).
36. Kidd, T. R. "Afterward Is Too Late." *The Physical Educator,* 28 (October 1971), 120–121.
37. *Krutili* v. *Board of Education,* 99 W. Va. 466, 129 (West Virginia, 1925).
38. Langerman, S., and N. Fidel. "Responsibility Is Also Part of the Game." *Trial,* 13 (1977), 22–25.
39. Leibee, Howard C. *Tort Liability for Injuries to Pupils.* Ann Arbor, Mich.: Campus Publishers, 1965.
40. ———— . *Liability for Accidents in Physical Education, Athletics, and Recreation.* Ann Arbor, Mich.: Campus Publishers, 1965.
41. *Lemard* v. *School Committee of Attleboro,* 212 N.E. 2nd 468 (Massachusetts, 1965).
42. *Longo* v. *New York City Board of Education,* 255 N.Y. 719 (New York, 1932).
43. Mallios, H. C. "Physical Education and The Law." *Physical Educator,* 31–32 (May 1975), 61–63.
44. *McMullen* v. *Ursuline Order of Sisters,* 56 N.M. 570 2nd 1052 (New Mexico, 1952).
45. *Miller et al.* v. *Board of Education of the Borough of Chatham,* Sup. Ct. L. Division, No. L-7241-63 (New Jersey, 1964).
46. Minn. Stat., 3098 (Mason, 1937).
47. *Molitor* v. *Kaneland Community Unit District 18,* Ill. 11 163 N.E. 2nd 89 (Illinois, 1959).
48. *Mower* v. *Leicester,* 9 Mass. 247 (Massachusetts, 1812).

49. *Nehaus* v. *Torrey and Tamalpais High School District.* In "The Coaches and the Courts." *Journal of Health, Physical Education, and Recreation,* 41 (June 1970), 10, 60.

50. North Carolina Code, 5780 (Anno Michie, ed., 1939), 78–83a. Added by Laws of 1935, ch. 245. Amended in part by Laws of 1939, ch. 267.

51. O'Connor, Gene. "The Football Coach and Liability." *The American Football Coaches Association Proceedings.* (January 1978), 41–44.

52. *Physical Education Newsletter,* 7 (March 1963), 4.

53. Resick, M. C., B. L. Seidel, and J. Mason. *Modern Administrative Practices in Physical Education and Athletics.* 2nd ed. Reading, Mass: Addison-Wesley, 1975, 404.

54. Rosenfield, H. N. *Liability for School Accidents.* New York: Harper & Row, 1940.

55. *Russell* v. *Men of Devon,* 2 Term Rep. 671, 100 Eng. Rep. 359 (1788).

56. *Spanel* v. *Mounds View School District 118,* N.W. 2nd 795 (Minnesota, 1962).

57. Staunton, M. A. "The Rights of the Athletic Director and Coaching Staff to Set Grooming and Dress Regulations." Paper presented at State Conference of Athletic Directors in San Francisco, Calif., May 17, 1969.

58. *Stehn* v. *Bernard MacFadden Foundations, Inc.* Civil Action 4398 U.S. District Court for the Middle District of Tenn. Nashville Div. Tennessee, 1969.

59. *Welch* v. *Dunsmuir Joint Union High School District,* 326 2nd 633 (California, 1958).

Public Relations **10**

"It's from the booster club, men—they say
they're behind us 100 percent . . . win or tie."

A major part of the high school coach's job is to establish and maintain good
public relations with the school community. Coaches who have been successful in promoting their programs and thus increasing opportunities their
students have had to master public relations. The position of coach makes
the individual a public figure. As such, the coach represents the school and
the profession. The coach's actions and words can influence the opinions of

members of the school community who are concerned with athletics: players, parents, other coaches, students, fellow teachers and school staff members, booster groups, the news media, and citizens whose taxes pay for the schools. The coach can convey to these people the benefits and educational opportunities high school athletics offer and thus win continued support for the school's athletic program.

Just as successful business professionals realize the value of public relations in developing favorable reputations for their policies and products, high school coaches also can communicate a positive image of their sports, teams, and athletics in general through a well-planned public relations program. Publicity is an important tool for developing public understanding; also, a coach's relationships with individual students and members of the community and the information supplied about his or her goals contribute to good public relations.

Objectives

The following chapter defines public relations and suggests principles and methods for developing a high school athletic public relations program; it also presents aspects of public relations that should help a high school coach deal with the groups forming the school community:

1. Public relations defined
2. Developing a high school athletic public relations program
3. Public relations and the school community
4. Players
5. Parents
6. Other coaches and members of the athletic staff
7. Fellow teachers and school staff members
8. Game officials
9. College recruiters
10. The Parent Teachers Association (P.T.A.)
11. The news media
12. Booster groups
13. The students
14. Crowd and player control

Public Relations Defined

Professional literature in the field of high school athletics is full of definitions of public relations and of the "whys and wherefores" for an excellent public relations program. Underlying all these definitions are such concepts as public opinion, understanding, and goodwill; justification for the activity; participants' attitudes; individual and group involvement; the promotion of good rapport between schools and individual members of the school community. With this in mind, public relations in athletics can be defined here as the development and use of techniques to provide information and influence public opinion so that individuals and groups support athletic activities. Basically public relations attempt to encourage positive involvement, promote a favorable image, and gain active support for athletic programs.

Developing a High School
Athletic Public Relations Program

The costs of building and maintaining sports facilities—arenas, playing fields, and gymnasiums—have become so high that many high school coaches are placed in the position of defending their athletic programs to the people whose taxes pay for these facilities. To communicate the need for athletics and the educational values they can provide, a coach should develop a sound public relations program.

A coach should have an athletic program that is a positive educational experience for all students who participate. If the coach has a "good product," he or she will be able to convince the public of its worth. Also, the coach must be *personally convinced* of the soundness of this program and its benefit for students. A person who is truly enthusiastic about a cause is able to transmit this enthusiasm to others and win their support.

The information a coach provides about the athletic program is essential for public understanding. It should always be truthful, for propaganda designed merely to manipulate opinions will more often than not defeat the coach's purpose and cause a loss of credibility. The coach's approach to public relations should be indirect, because "hard-sell" techniques are often offensive and only temporarily convincing. If a coach presents adequate information about athletics so that people can decide for themselves about the value of the program, he or she will have many more avid supporters.

Cooperative effort by all the coaches of a school is important for effective public relations, because all sports in an athletic program should contribute equally to the development of student participants. A coach must avoid believing that his or her own sport is more important than the others, for dissension within the coaching staff can dilute the value of the entire program.

To determine weak spots, there should be continued evaluation of one's coaching abilities and techniques. This will help strengthen the athletic program presented to the public. Charles H. Moser, Athletic Director for the Abilene, Texas, public schools, has been recognized for his outstanding athletic program. One important element of public relations, he believes, is a coach's self-evaluation, necessary because of the role in counseling and motivating students. Figure 10.2 shows a form Moser devised to help coaches evaluate themselves.

Figure 10.1 *A coach emcees the dedication of a playing field.*

The coach's public relations program must involve continuous effort to convey a lasting impression; all athletic programs seem to operate in cycles, and it is important to have a good public image to get through the low points when the team just can't seem to win. To make certain that the impression they are promoting is positive, coaches should continuously evaluate the effectiveness of their public relations program. In this way, they can determine whether information is reaching all segments of the public and how well it is being received. Then they can spend greater effort on weak spots in their preparation and presentation.

	1	2	3	4	5
1. Character and personal habits					
2. Dedication to the profession					
3. Willingness to work and make personal sacrifices					
4. Ability to inspire students					
5. Initiative and originality					
6. Ability to develop aggressiveness					
7. Ability to finish an assignment					
8. Ability to criticize a student and still not be personal					
9. Ability to carry out details					
10. Knowledge of the game you are teaching					
11. Promptness (to school, on the field, etc.)					
12. Ability to be consistent each day.					
13. Ability to get along with other teachers, principals, and other coaches					
14. Neatness of dress, on and off the field					
15. Philosophy of athletics and education in general					

1 = Poor 2 = Below average 3 = Average 4 = Above average 5 = Excellent
SOURCE: Abilene Public Schools, Abilene, Texas.

Figure 10.2 *Coach's self-evaluation sheet.*

One of the major purposes of the public relations program is to promote a positive professional image. Too often negative aspects of high school athletics are reported simply because they make sensational news stories. To combat the destructive effect of these reports, a coach should have an optimistic attitude and emphasize the benefits of participation in sports. Rather than dwelling on the number of games a team has lost, he or she should talk about its wins and point out especially good performances of the players. Instead of saying that the team has lost seven out of ten games, say that it has *won* three out of ten! Also, his or her own conduct should bring credit to the profession.

Three groups that can help a high school coach strengthen the public relations program are other members of the school community, the news media, and students. If other people in the school system become involved in the athletic program and understand its objectives, they can communicate information to individuals whom the coach might not be able to talk to personally. Through various news media—television, radio, reports, bulletins, magazines, and professional journals such as *The Athletic Journal* and *The Scholastic Coach*—coaches can also reach much of the public who provides educational tax dollars. A coach can discuss the value of high school athletics and present views on current developments.

Enthusiastic young people, however, are one of the best means of communication to the adults of the community. Parents are a vitally interested audience, and their children influence their opinions. If a boy or girl respects the coach and enjoys participating in sports, his or her parents will undoubtedly support the athletic program.

Public Relations and the School Community

The Players

Every group of individuals concerned with athletics is important in a coach's development of good public relations. But if there is one group more significant that the others, it is the players. The way a student reacts to the coach's methods affects the opinions and attitudes of fellow students, parents, and friends. At the dinner table, each athlete is a daily reporter of what takes place on the practice field, and what he or she says reflects either satisfaction or unhappiness with the program or coach. To establish a good relationship with the players, coaches should not pamper them to gain their favor. Rather, they should present a sound program for the athletes to follow and win their respect by setting a strong example. The critical issues in forming a favorable player-coach relationship vary with individuals and situations. But there are some general approaches that can be helpful.

The coach should recognize the individual differences that exist among the players and provide activities and challenges for both the gifted athlete and the average athlete who barely makes the squad. Sportsmanship and the positive values of athletics should prevail among the principles the coach presents.

Coaches should be knowledgeable about their particular sport and be able to teach participants to become good players. Coaching techniques and methods should be personal as well as original. In other words be yourself, don't be a perfect likeness of successful coaches such as Bear Bryant or Billie Moore. Don't be counterfeit. Young people are extremely perceptive; if they see phoniness, they lose respect.

Honesty is a necessary element in the coach's relationship with the players. When an athlete's performance is particularly bad, the coach should evaluate it sincerely and tell the student exactly where to improve.

The coach should treat all players equally and show no favoritism on or off the field. A star athlete should understand that he or she is no more special

Figure 10.3 *Enthusiastic young people are the best channel of communication to the adults of the community.*

than the least skilled player, and the coach will earn respect from all the team members if the rules apply to each of them equally. He or she can also form strong relationships with the students by developing a sincere interest in each player. Since a high school coach's job is to guide young people through their formative years, he or she is able to help individuals better by being genuinely interested. If, for example, a player is injured and either

Figure 10.4 *A coach should be firm in demanding from the players their best performances.*

hospitalized or kept at home, regular visits by the coach will show the player that the coach really cares about him or her as a person, not just a member of the team.

A coach should have certain qualities that will help win respect and affection in dealing with athletes. If one is tactfully aggressive in upholding individual interests as well as team efforts, the entire athletic program benefits. If the players know the coach will support them, they will cooperate to the maximum. Also, by explaining rules, regulations, techniques, and goals, the coach will develop understanding in the players, and they will be convinced that what they are trying to do is correct.

As a leader and often a disciplinarian, a coach should be firm in demanding from the players their best performances. These demands must not exceed a student's ability. In being firm, one should also be kind. If a player is forgiven for a foolish error, rather than being chastised unmercifully, the student will respond gratefully and try to do better. Above all, coaches should be patient. They must remember that athletes learn at different rates, and be willing to spend more time with some players to help them learn certain skills or techniques. Patience is a necessary quality for all coaches to possess.

The Parents

One of the most important segments of the public is the parents of the players. Because parents play such a vital part in supporting the school system and its educational programs, the coach must make an effort to know them and inform them about the nature and values of high school athletics. This phase of the coach's public relations program requires a lot of effort, but the results are gratifying.

The size and nature of the school community will influence the coach's public relations techniques. It is difficult to become acquainted with the parents of a player who lives some distance away. Also, some parents may have job schedules that do not coordinate with the coach's schedule. But an energetic and imaginative coach can work out methods of reaching the parents of the players.

When a new family with a prospective athlete moves into the school district, the coach should make a special effort to visit their home and welcome them. A display of friendship and offer of help does much to ease some fears and establish a good relationship.

Before the season starts the coach can send a letter to the parents of the players outlining goals and objectives of the program, rules and regulations governing team members, practice schedules and demands, suggested training habits, travel procedures, and anything peculiar to the particular sport. By knowing such information in advance, the parents are aware of what is expected of participants during the season. The coach should explain any change in procedures in a follow-up letter.

During the season, some coaches find it helpful to send to parents weekly or monthly newsletters that report on the team's progress, outstanding performances of individual players, and others' improvement and contribution to the team. In this way, the coach helps make the parents feel they are directly involved with the team and stimulates their interest. Because these newsletters require a great deal of time the coach can enlist the assistance of school secretarial help or, if that is unavailable, appeal to the typing instructor for student assistance.

Postgame gatherings also help develop rapport between parents and the coach, as do special functions like an intrasquad football scrimmage followed by a pot-luck luncheon for players and their parents. This personal involvement gives parents the opportunity to get to know the coach and inquire about the progress of their sons and daughters.

A coach may find, too, that a separate parent-seating section at the games adds to a good relationship with parents. The parents enjoy the courtesy afforded them, become better acquainted with each other, and identify more closely with the team.

The impact of high school athletics on a player's home life can be tremendous. Normal family schedules often are turned topsy-turvy because of athletic practice schedules, games, and travel. Consequently, a coach should make an effort to involve parents by developing their understanding of the demands of a sport. Then they will be willing to make adjustments in normal family schedules and support the coach's athletic program.

Other Coaches and Members of the Athletic Staff

A coach's public relations program must reflect the thinking of the entire athletic staff to be effective. The enthusiastic support of other coaches and athletic assistants will strengthen a coach's attempt to tell the public about the benefits of the athletic program. And to ensure this support, a coach must always place his or her own sport in relation to the others, remembering that each activity contributes to the total program. A coach should, of course, be dedicated to a particular sport, but must not feel that it is the most important one offered by the school.

Nor should the coach be tempted to belittle its importance. Although each sport has intrinsic value, some may receive more attention than others. The athletic program may have a limited amount of money, resulting in cutbacks in certain areas. The locality may afford special opportunities for a particular sport, and climate may limit possibilities for another; the community may be especially interested in a particular sport because of past success. All these factors—and others—should be considered by a coach who feels that a certain sport is slighted. He or she should be more concerned with helping the students and conveying to the community the value of the total athletic program.

Good relationships among coaches in a high school help them to present a positive public image. Many departments have one head coach in charge of assistant coaches; each has a responsibility to the others. The head coach should trust his or her assistants and publicly give them credit for their contribution to the success of the team. In turn, assistant coaches should never be guilty of second-guessing the head coach and should be consistently loyal. In working toward common objectives, they can present a strong program that will win public support and high regard by other coaches in the profession.

Fellow Teachers and School Staff Members

High school coaches can be extremely influential members of the faculty. Because they have contact with a great many students, they can do much to promote school morale and help with school discipline. Fellow teachers sometimes do not understand the coach's role and may resent his or her position. The coach must make an effort to maintain good relationships with other teachers and thus reduce possible friction.

As merely a member of the faculty, a coach should not expect special treatment, should attend all faculty meetings, and perform the same duties as other teachers. The primary responsibility—like that of the other members of the faculty—is to the students. All teachers in a high school should be working for the welfare of the total educational program.

By displaying an active interest in the activities of other departments, the coach will show support for the entire school program. There may be times when a coach needs help from another teacher. A good relationship with fellow faculty members can be obtained if there is cooperation. Because coaches have a unique position and close contact with students, they may be able to help with a disciplinary problem or to motivate students who lack interest in academic subjects.

Public criticism of a fellow faculty member is unprofessional and should be avoided. Because of the coach's wide-ranging influence, a derogatory comment made about another teacher can be especially damaging to the person concerned. Good relations with other members of the school staff— secretaries, custodians, equipment room personnel—are also important. Their cooperation and enthusiasm can help the coach's athletic program function smoothly.

Game Officials

A coach also can present a positive public image by maintaining good relationships with game officials. Because he or she has worked hard teaching the players techniques and skills and sees the students performing their best, it often is difficult for the coach to agree with the official when an infraction of the rules is called. It is important for the coach to respect the official's different perspective and to understand various interpretations of rules so that players will not be confused about differences of opinion between their coach and the official. It can be helpful for coaches to attend officials' clinics so they are familiar with all significant explanations of rules.

The one area of officiating that causes the most differences of opinion involves judgment calls. And, unfortunately for the coach and the team, the official has the last word. The coach, naturally, tends to agree with calls made in his or her team's favor and to disapprove of calls against the team. The official views the play from the standpoint of training and bases decisions on this experience. Inevitably, the difference between the two viewpoints will cause disagreements, but the coach must keep composed and remember that a show of anger will be witnessed by both team members and fans. The coach should remember, too, that the official's calls are not *always* against his or her team.

Friendship between a coach and an official is a sensitive issue, and the coach will find that because of their positions it is a good idea to maintain good but not close relationships. One should greet officials in a friendly fashion but avoid overly familiar behavior, which might be questioned by the opposition, spectators, or even the officials themselves. It is unwise, too, for coaches and officials to be seen together in a public place before or after a game. Although such meetings might result totally out of friendship, there is always the possibility witnesses might suspect the possibility of bribery or the official's favoring the coach's team because of their friendship. This would be especially likely in games that were hotly contested and whose final outcome rested on an official's decision. It is easier to avoid situations that might be misinterpreted than to have to explain them.

The coach should not be directly involved in selecting officials for a game, but a master list of efficient officials can be made and presented to the athletic director or person who selects officials. The coach should avoid choosing personal friends or graduates of the school to officiate: They would be placed in a touchy position, and to avoid being accused of favoritism might in fact make calls that give the other team the benefit of any doubt.

When the coach is responsible for paying an official, the check should be presented before game time thus avoiding possible conflict if there is disagreement about the way the game has been called. If the coach has questions about certain interpretations or decisions, it is better to speak to the official during the game with another coach present and not to enter the official's dressing room after the game.

If the coach disagrees strongly with the officials' decisions, complaints can be aired in a postgame evaluation and specific information may be provided on the rating card supplied by the officials' association. Not only does this system help improve officiating practices in general, it also gives the coach an outlet for expressing an opinion so that he or she does not personally confront the official. The coach's position requires professional behavior. Explosive anger and public accusation of officials causes the coach to lose respect from both the team and the spectators.

If the coach blames the team's losses on the officials' decisions, he or she will become preoccupied with winning and will lose sight of the main

Figure 10.5 *A self-indulgent show of anger by the coach over an official's decision is bad public relations.*

objective—teaching high school athletes to perform at their highest levels of ability. In showing good sportsmanship and respect for the game officials, the coach will in turn gain respect from the players.

College Recruiters

In planning their public relations programs, high school coaches also should consider how to deal with college recruiters. Sometimes, in the desire to find talented athletes, a recruiter may become overzealous in pursuing players. The coach has a responsibility for the students and thus should try to ensure that an athlete gets his or her share of college offers without interference in his or her high school experience. The National Collegiate Athletic Association (NCAA), the National Association of Intercollegiate Athletics (NAIA), and the National Federation of State High School Associations have established general guidelines for recruiting practices (11); the coach must see that these regulations are not violated. Before a recruiter can contact a student athlete on the high school grounds, for example, he or she must receive permission from the school principal. The recruiter may go directly to the coach for information, but the coach may not arrange for a player to leave class without the principal's approval.

In protecting the best interests of the students, the coach should be aware of situations that could be detrimental. A recruiter who is unable to see an athlete perform during a scheduled game might request a demonstration of the player's skills. This demonstration could be interpreted as a try-out, which is illegal, and the athlete consequently could be declared ineligible.

The coach also should guard against interference from recruiters in the activities of high school students. If a player is visited by one or more recruiters during the athletic season, his or her concentration on the sport and studies can be disrupted, with the result of poor performance in both areas. If athletes take recruiting joy rides to visit athletic events at several college campuses, they can become so physically and emotionally exhausted that their efforts on the high school playing field suffer. A recruiter's visit to an athlete who is participating in a tournament away from the high school not only interferes with the student's activity but also may violate the regulation that does not allow recruiters to contact a prospective athlete at playing facilities off school grounds unless the athlete is released by his or her school.

The athlete's family life also can be disrupted by constant phone calls, trips away from home, frequent visits by recruiters, and pressure from friends. Although some families thrive on this attention, others find it annoying. The coach should try to prevent recruiters from this interference.

Entertainment of senior athletes is limited to areas near the student's home or to college campuses, and excessive entertainment at either place is prohibited. Also, it is illegal for recruiters to give high school athletes complimentary tickets to professional games.

Recruiters frequently ask high school coaches to send them academic transcripts for student athletes. But because this system has been abused and grades have been altered, the Joint Committee on Standards for Interscholastic Athletics—composed of members of the National Association of Secondary School Principals, the National Federation of State High School Associations, and representatives of the American Alliance for Health, Physical Education, and Recreation—strongly advocates that transcripts be sent only to college and university admissions offices.

The coach may also be asked by a recruiter to intercede on behalf of an athlete whose grades are not good enough for admission to a particular college. It would be very convenient if an instructor changed a grade and made the student eligible, but the coach must not support such deception. It is a disservice to the student, who might not be able to do the academic work at that college.

When a coach deals with college recruiters, he or she receives a great deal of attention and flattery, which can tempt the coach to overlook violations of regulations. The responsibility of a high school coach is paramount, and a positive image depends on a personal image based on integrity.

Following certain procedures will minimize recruiter interference and still provide college admission opportunities for student athletes. The high school coach should not allow a recruiter to contact athletes until after their playing eligibility is over and, during the athletic season, should refuse to make any comments to recruiters about player ability. Also, he or she should avoid personal entertainment and favors that might create an obligation to recruiters.

Students should be discouraged from traveling to colleges during the competition season, and all players should be educated in legal recruiting practices and the extent of aid a player legally may accept in an athletic scholarship.

The Parent Teachers Association (P.T.A.)

The Parent Teachers Association (P.T.A.) is another group the high school coach should consider in a public relations program, because it includes many parents who are not directly involved with the athletic program. One can speak at P.T.A. meetings to explain certain aspects of interscholastic athletics and encourage parental support. Also, the P.T.A. is a fine potential source for help in securing athletic facilities.

An example of how a coach can use the P.T.A. for public relations occurred in a school in California. Because of a series of unfortunate injuries in football, local citizens demanded that the sport be eliminated from the school's athletic program and parents began to refuse to let their sons participate. It was obvious that football was in trouble. The head coach planned to present a program at the P.T.A. meeting to show parents what protective measures are taken and to explain the benefits of participation in the sport. Because of the controversy a very large audience turned out for the meeting.

In the lobby, the coach had set up an exhibit of all the normal equipment so that the parents could examine it closely. During the program, a young man was completely dressed with the equipment, and the coach described each separate piece, explaining how it was made and its protective qualities. Then the coach discussed the objectives of the football program and the educational value of the sport. He also answered questions from the audience. This program made such an impact on the parents, most of whom had never before understood the nature of football equipment, that many enthusiastically supported the team, ending the controversy.

The success of the football coach's presentation encouraged athletic and P.T.A. officials to have coaches of other sports make similar presentations. In sports like swimming, which do not involve a lot of equipment, the coaches combined their efforts to describe the benefits of participation in each activity.

These public presentations resulted in active support from the parents for the athletic program and the coaches directing it.

The News Media

Because much of the information the public receives about interscholastic athletics comes from the newpapers, television, and radio, it is essential for a coach to develop good relations with sports writers, T.V. reporters, and radio commentators. In many ways, they are the most important people in the coach's professional life, because their stories establish the public image of the team.

To form a good working relationship with each reporter, the coach should make an effort to get acquainted by visiting the sports office and giving invitations to visit the school by having lunch or coffee get togethers. The coach can provide information that will help the reporter in describing team performance: the coach's own background and previous experience and other "inside" information about the team and individual players.

If the reporter knows what a player *can* do, he or she will not make an issue of a sub-par performance when the player is injured. Also, if the coach explains before a game about a new technique, the reporter will be able to provide a better account of the result. It is a good idea to "talk shop" with reporters in informal sessions and give them technical information about the theories behind certain playing styles. This knowledge will help them in writing their stories and answering questions for the public.

There are other ways in which a coach can help the reporter publicize team performance. Because news people often run out of inspiration in reporting high school games, the coach can help by supplying an approach for the account of a game. It helps to give some meaningful comments about the team's performance, to point out particularly successful plays, and to give the reporter a lead statement for an article or broadcast. Also, he or she should provide an up-to-date roster of the team, with information about jersey numbers, heights, weights, ages, previous experience, and positions—and names spelled correctly. The coach can give the reporter statistics about a game that analyze the play of both the home team and the opponent. Since the coach needs these figures anyway and can probably enlist student help in taking down the information, it is easy to pass them on to news people. These statistics will be especially helpful to a reporter who was not able to attend the game.

Reporters are eager to obtain postgame comments, and the coach can make both their jobs easier if there is a policy about when he or she will talk to reporters after a game. Some coaches like to have a few minutes by

Figure 10.6 *Because the public receives most of its information about interscholastic athletics through the news media, a coach should develop good working relationships with sports writers.*

themselves after a close contest, and the reporters should understand when they will be welcome in the dressing room. But the coach should not make a reporter wait longer than fifteen minutes, because there are news deadlines to be met.

A coach should be aware of certain problems in sports reporting. Space in newspapers and time on television and radio is limited. Because of these limitations, pre- and postgame athletic stories often are not so complete as the biased coach and team supporters think they should be. The coach should realize that a reporter cannot include everything and should be concerned primarily with the accuracy of the information given.

Another area that requires a coach's tact and understanding is which reporter should get the information about an important interscholastic contest. The sports reporters for morning and evening papers may be in conflict for the "scoop," and a coach can either reach an agreement with both sports editors about who should receive the information or give releases alternately. In the latter case, one should be careful not to leak news that would cause a breakdown of the system.

Because an out-of-town game may be difficult for a reporter to attend, the coach can help by including the reporter in the school travel group or calling in a story about the game. If the information is called in, the coach should make the arrangement with a reporter in advance so that he or she may be assured of having the news appear. Also, quotes can be part of the account and will make it more interesting for readers, viewers, and listeners.

Coaches can maintain good relationships with news people by praising the approach or style in their stories. They can give away complimentary tickets to games with extras for assistants or family. Members of the news media also appreciate invitations to social activities given by booster groups or parents, in order to become acquainted with players.

The coach should remember that reporters will probably ask some fairly provocative questions, which may be poorly stated or asked to start a controversy. It is important that the coach be patient and keep "cool." A good example is former coach John Wooden's performance at the Los Angeles Sports Writers' luncheon in 1971. Wooden, whose basketball teams at U.C.L.A. had won an unprecedented number of N.C.A.A. championships, and who is known for his patience and cooperation, was attacked about his team's schedule and the selection of one of his players as "player of the week." Coach Wooden resented the downgrading of his player and the inference that his schedule was weak. He responded to the insinuations by praising the player, his team, and the team's record. Though he lambasted the reporters, his remarks were polite and his response made headlines the next day. The result was that his team—and the sport—received good promotion by the press.

Many coaches feel that to establish good public relations with members of the news media requires a lot of their time and effort. This is certainly true, but, to benefit the image of the sport, team, and coach, it is essential. Citizens of the community read the newspapers, listen to the radio, and watch television, and the information they receive influences their opinions and often determines the amount of support they give to the athletic program.

Booster Groups

Booster groups for high school athletic programs are becoming more and more important because of the taxpayers' reluctance to support such activities. In many sections of the country, high school athletic programs must be financially self-sufficient. Although athletics contribute a great deal to the education of young people and therefore should be included as an area of education supported by the tax dollar, many educators and citizens unfortunately regard sports as totally separate from formal education and expect athletic programs to generate their own financial support. Coaches then form booster groups.

Some booster groups are made up of a few individuals who give a large initial financial contribution and pay high dues. Although this approach is certainly beneficial to the team, it is also important to have more than just a few fans in the stands at game time. A booster group composed of a large number of supporters is, therefore, most effective, even though organizing activities may require more time and effort.

In forming a booster group, the coach must realize that the success of the group depends on its leadership. The leader of the group obviously must have a sincere interest in the athletic program and, of course, some spare hours. Very oftern, the ideal leader is a merchant or businessman who participated in high school athletics.

The group's success also depends on the coach's role in generating enthusiasm. The coach could have weekly luncheon or dinner meetings during the season for the men and women in the group and show films of the team in action or of college or professional teams. If a coach takes the time to explain the philosophy of the sport, to diagram plays, and to explain different styles of play, members of the booster group become more knowledgeable and livelier in their enthusiasm. The coach also can arrange special seating for the booster group members at games. Having the stands filled, too, does wonders for the players' morale.

A gimmick that helps stimulate booster group involvement is naming a group member as "booster coach of the week." This "coach" attends all practice sessions and meets with the coach when game plans are being made. On the day of the game, he or she keeps the same schedule as the coach, meeting with the team for pregame sessions, taping procedures, and sitting on the bench during the game.

Booster group support can be extended to benefit the entire educational program. The coach therefore should make a strong effort to maintain good public relations with the boosters who are benefactors for the athletic program.

The Students

Because a high school coach can have a great deal of influence on the student body, dedication and enthusiasm are important in creating school spirit. The effect on all the students can be tremendous. Following is an example of a coach's positive influence on the student body.

In a small rural community in California, a new young coach was faced with a difficult situation: The former coach had been dismissed because he was unethical and gave the students a negative example with his complete disrespect for administrators and classroom teachers. The entire student body had become unruly and disrespectful of teachers and staff. There were incidents of students hitting teachers. Among the leaders of the students were some athletes who thought they should have special privileges. Because they were athletes they felt regular rules did not apply to them. They even demanded good grades *gratis* from their teachers.

The new coach decided to tackle the situation. At the first team meeting, the coach informed the players of his philosophy of life and the value he attached to good citizenship. He explained that he would not tolerate disrespect for the faculty and that failure to adhere to his standards would result in dismissal from the squad. A few weeks later, one of the star players shouted obscenities at a teacher, so at the next practice the coach berated the boy in front of his teammates and expelled him from the team. Some of the other players sided with the boy and left, too. The community became concerned because they wanted a winning team, but the coach stood his ground, explained his position, and won the support of many parents.

Eventually, his approach worked. The players who remained on the team played well and exerted a positive influence on fellow students. By the middle of the school year all evidence of general student disrespect had disappeared. The players who had left the squad asked to be reinstated the next year; and the coach granted their request on the condition that their conduct would be under constant scrutiny. The coach had gained the respect of the students, and his influence was felt throughout the entire school community. In remaining true to his convictions, he created a positive public image. Although this situation is extreme, it does illustrate some ways a coach can develop good public relations through the student body.

A coach can generate support from the student body at large in several other ways. First, favoritism should not be shown to athletes in the classroom. If all students in academic classes are treated in the same way, the coach will be popular and will earn a reputation for fairness. One can meet with student leaders who are not athletes to explain the objectives and philosophy of the athletic program and to outline how the school and the players will benefit. These young people will appreciate the coach's interest and effort to involve them in the sport, even though they are not active participants.

An assembly structured around the coach's explanation of the athletic program to new students is helpful for generating student interest and support. A former star athlete who returns to speak on how the coach and participation in athletics helped him or her can also bring about a positive reaction from students and strengthen school spirit. If the coach becomes acquainted with the cheerleaders or pep team and explains the influence they have, they will enthusiastically support the team and transmit this ardor to other students. When the coach convinces all the students that the team is worth yelling for, their parents and other members of the community also will be persuaded to give their support.

These are but a few of the techniques that a coach can practice to generate general student-body support that acts positively in all facets of school life.

Crowd and Player Control

The image the community has of a high school coach, the sport, and the team depends to a large extent on the coach's effect on crowd and player behavior. Controlling the excitement of spectators has become one of the major problems in interscholastic athletics. There have been many incidents of physical attacks on officials, players, coaches, and fans, as well as vandalism in dressing rooms and on school property. The increasing number of incidents has caused some school administrators to consider dropping interscholastic athletic activities; others have eliminated night games and do not announce where a game will be played until shortly before game time. Community and school officials have spent hours discussing ways of solving this serious problem. Every high school coach has a major responsibility in handling this issue.

The coach always must set an example of good sportsmanship, because actions on the sidelines have a tremendous effect on the way players and fans behave. People in the crowd may be inclined to react violently when the officials' decisions or penalties are called against their school's team, but by controlling his or her own emotions the coach positively influences the attitude of the spectators.

The coach's self-conduct has perhaps the most significant effect on the behavior of the players and the crowd, but some other constructive measures will also keep people from getting out of hand. It is important to teach players how to behave with opponents and officials. They must learn to accept the officials' calls without displaying emotion; if a player becomes too upset over a decision, it is the coach's responsibility to remove the athlete from the game until the player has quieted down.

When the game is played at home, students—both athletes and fans—should be encouraged to be good hosts. The notion that one must hate an opponent to win has no place in high school athletics. Players should greet their opponents in a friendly manner and publicly shake hands with them before and after the contest. Spectators can be reminded that unsportsman-like crowd behavior may result in penalties for the team.

The coach can talk with cheerleaders and impress on them their responsibility to generate enthusiastic support for the team, not hostility toward the opposing team. They should realize that disrespectful yells against the opponent can cause trouble and present a bad image of the school.

When selecting game officials, the coach should avoid someone who reacts favorably to home crowds. Although they are supposed to ignore the fans, some officials do react in one way or another to cheers or boos.

Also, a coach can work with spectators to educate them in proper game conduct. He or she might give as assembly speech to point out the positive features of good sportsmanship, or speak at local civic clubs, stressing the necessity for emotional control and ethical conduct. Many people violate rules of conduct because they have never been told what sort of behavior is expected of them.

Summary

Successful public relations programs are essential for high school coaches to communicate to members of the school community the educational opportunities and benefits athletics offer. A coach should have a positive, well-planned approach to win public support for the athletic program.

Public relations are basically techniques designed to provide information and influence public opinion to gain support for the teams, the coaches, and interscholastic athletics in general.

Public relations should be built around a good athletic program, the coach's personal conviction and indirect approach, true information, a positive professional image, and continuous evaluation. It should involve all members of the school community including students, parents, school staff, fellow coaches, and members of the news media.

In dealing with players, the coach should be honest, have a sincere interest in each player and treat them all equally, and be knowledgeable about the sport, firm, tactfully aggressive, kind, and patient. He or she must always be genuine to develop good relationships with students.

Parents are an important segment of the school community, and the coach should make a special effort to inform them about the objectives, values, and nature of interscholastic athletics. Through the P.T.A., a coach can make contact with many parents who are not directly involved in the athletic program.

Each coach should be convinced of the value and importance of the sport, at the same time recognizing the value of other sports in the total program and actively supporting them. The public relations program should reflect the thinking of the entire athletic staff.

Coaches should never forget that their real role is that of a teacher. They should take an interest in the activities of other departments and not expect special treatment as a member of the faculty.

Coaches should always work in cooperation with other members of the school staff—secretaries, janitors, and equipment personnel—who contribute to the success of the athletic program.

Coaches should avoid familiarity with game officials, but maintain good relationships with them. They must respect different perspectives on certain plays and control their anger over controversial situations.

In dealing with college recruiters, the high school coach should try to ensure that students receive opportunities for college without having their high school lives interfered with.

The news media includes radio commentators, television reporters, and newspaper sports writers. A coach should make an attempt to become acquainted with these people in a manner that will foster mutual trust. The coach can help these reporters by giving them information, and should be aware of problems such as time and space limitations. In dealing with reporters, the coach should remember to maintain his or her composure. The information the public receives influences the support it will give to the athletic program.

Booster groups have become more important as funds for high school athletics need to be sought outside the school's financial structure. Large groups of supporters are generally more effective than ones made up of just a few people who give large contributions. The success of a booster group depends on its leadership and the coach's ability to generate enthusiasm.

Coaches should remember that their position enables them to create a positive influence on the student body. By gaining the support of all the students, they will also win support from parents and other members of the community.

The high school coach's self-conduct can have a tremendous effect on crowd and player behavior. The image that he or she conveys of the sport and the team depends on influence in controlling the excitement of spectators.

References

1. American Association of School Administrators. *Public Relations for America's Schools*. Washington, D.C.: American Association for Health, Physical Education, and Recreation, 1950.

2. Bortner, Doyle M. *Public Relations for Teachers.* New York: Simmons-Boardman, 1959.
3. Bright, Sallie E. *Public Relations Programs—How to Plan Them.* New York: National Publicity Council for Health and Welfare Services, 1950.
4. Brownell, Clifford L., Leo Gans, and Tufie Z. Maroon. *Public Relations in Education.* New York: McGraw-Hill, 1955.
5. Bubas, Vic. "Selling Yourself in a New Situation." *Scholastic Coach,* 31:4 (December 1961), 18, 29.
6. Dapper, Gloria. *Public Relations for Educators.* New York: Macmillan, 1964.
7. David, Michael G. "Get Some Public Relations in Your Swimming." *The Athletic Journal,* 48 (October 1967), 2, 37.
8. Duke, Wayne. "Public Relations in Athletics." *Journal of Health, Physical Education, and Recreation,* 30:7 (October 1959), 17.
9. Eilefson, L. "A 'Marketing Approach' to Athletic Fund Raising." *Athletic Administration,* 12:2 (Winter 1977), 18, 19.
10. Forsythe, Charles E. *The Athletic Director's Handbook.* Englewood Cliffs, N.J.: Prentice-Hall, 1956.
11. Forsythe, Charles E., and I. A. Keller. *Administration of High School Athletics.* 5th ed. Englewood Cliffs, N.J.: Prentice-Hall, 1972.
12. Frost, R. B., and S. J. Marshall. *Administration of Physical Education and Athletics,* Dubuque, Iowa: Wm. C. Brown, 1977, 402.
13. Fuoss, D. E., and R. J. Troppmann. *Creative Management Techniques in Interscholastic Athletics.* New York: John Wiley, 1977, 494.
14. George, Jack F., and Harry A. Lehmann. *School Athletic Administration.* New York: Harper & Row, 1966.
15. Gillombardo, Joe. "Public Relations Checklist for Gymnastic Coaches." *Athletic Journal,* 49:4 (December 1968), 36, 43.
16. Harmon, James J. "Public Relations: A Necessity." *School and Community,* 58 (December 1971), 17.
17. Harral, Stewart. *Public Relations for Churches.* New York: Abingdon-Cokesbury Press, 1945.
18. "How Public Relations Can Help You Gain Support for Your Program and Budget." *The Athletic Educator's Report,* 806 (April 1977), 6, 8.
19. Hughes, William L., Esther French, and Nelson C. Lehstein. *Administration of Physical Education for Schools and Colleges.* New York: Ronald Press, 1962.
20. Johnson, M. L. *Functional Administration in Physical and Health Education.* Boston: Houghton Mifflin, 1977, 387.
21. Kagan, Paul. "Do-It-Yourself Publicity." *The Scholastic Coach,* 33 (June 1964), 20, 30.
22. Kindred, L. W., D. Bagin, and D. R. Gallagher. *The School and Community Relations.* Englewood Cliffs, N.J.: Prentice-Hall, 1976, 351.
23. Kobre, S. *Successful Public Relations for Colleges and Universities.* New York: Hastings House, 1974, 444.
24. Lehsten, E. L., and N. G. Lehsten. *Administration of Physical Education for Schools and Colleges.* New York: Ronald Press, 1972, 541.
25. Lesley, Phillip, ed. *Public Relations Handbook.* 2nd ed. Englewood Cliffs, N.J.: Prentice-Hall, 1972.

26. O'Quinn, Mickey. "Booster Club Boosts Team through Films." *The Athletic Journal,* 44 (June 1964), 38–39.
27. Purdy, R. L. *The Successful High School Athletic Program.* West Nyack, N.Y.: Parker, 1973.
28. Sine, R. L. "Fill 'Er Up." *Athletic Journal,* 55 (December 1974), 24.
29. St. John, W. D. "P.R. Dealing with Angry Adults." *Today's Education,* 64 (November 1975).
30. Starr, Edward. *What You Should Know about Public Relations.* Dobbs Ferry, N.Y.: Oceana Publications, 1968.
31. Steinberg, Charles S. *The Mass Communications: Public Relations, Public Opinion, and Mass Media.* New York: Harper & Row, 1958.
32. Stonesifer, Richard J. "Public Relations and Administration." *The Educational Record,* 45 (Summer 1964), 324–327.
33. Thompson, Maria. "For Immediate Release: Getting Your Team in the News." *Women's Sports,* 3:9 (September 1976), 56.
34. Voltmer, Edward F., and Arthur A. Esslinger. *The Organization and Administration of Physical Education.* 4th ed. New York: Appleton-Century-Crofts, 1967.
35. Walch, R. "Sports P.R. and How to Get It." *Coaching Clinic,* 13 (May 1975), 18, 19.

Women's Competition **11**

Ms. Coach

Women's athletic competition and physical activity constitute one of the fastest growing trends in the nation's culture. The rapid growth of women's sports seems to have been brought about by the women's rights movement, judicial decisions, and Title IX. A discussion of girls' participation in interscholastic athletics can be found in Chapter 2. Included in that section is a brief historical sketch of factors that have influenced women's athletic participation in the United States since 1900.

Knowledgeable individuals recognize the tremendous surge in all types of athletic activities for women since 1960. Yet, most current research and literature in the sports world deals with male-dominated activities. Very little research has been conducted on female athletics and competition, though this situation has improved in recent years. Myths and prejudices about women's participation in sports still prevail in some sections of the United States. Fortunately, these are being displaced by more factual information. We cannot underestimate the national significance of women's athletics. To quote a special committee from the AMA reporting on the medical aspects of sports (6):

> There is no medical or scientific rationale for restricting the normal female from participating in vigorous non-contact sports, and many reasons to encourage such participation. Physical activity and sports programs can contribute greatly to personal fulfillment and healthful living of women.

Objectives

This chapter presents the following factors influencing women's athletic participation:

1. Title IX
2. The female image
3. Conditioning for the female athlete
4. Weight training for the female athlete
5. Menstruation and the female athlete
6. Some unique problems of the woman coach and the female athlete
7. Some unique problems of the male coaching the female athlete
8. Mixed competition

Title IX

Title IX has helped increase women's participation in athletics throughout the United States. Title IX is an Educational Amendment Act that is similar to Title VI, the Civil Rights Act of 1964. However, it applies directly to discrimination based on sex and is limited to educational programs and related activities. It also covers employment of educators.

Title IX was introduced in Congress in 1971 as an amendment to Title VI. It passed on June 23, 1972, and is administered by the Department of Health, Education, and Welfare (HEW). Basically, it prohibits sex discrimination in federally assisted educational programs. The following quotation best describes the spirit of the law (14):

No person in the United States shall, on the basis of sex, be excluded from participation in, be denied the benefits of, or be subjected to discrimination under any education program or activity receiving federal financial assistance . . . .

On June 20, 1974, the proposed regulations were published in the Federal Register with an invitation for public comments. Approximately 10,000 statements regarding various phases of the law were received. On May 27, 1975, President Ford signed the Title IX regulations, and they were published on June 4, 1975, with the president's approval. The effective date of the law was July 21, 1975. Institutions were to start a self-evaluation process immediately and to achieve compliance with the laws by July 21, 1976, for elementary schools, and by July 21, 1978, for secondary and post secondary schools. Failure to comply with the law meant the denial of federal funds to institutions or programs receiving such financial aid. Caspar W. Weinberger was secretary of HEW when this law went into effect.

Section 86.41 on athletics is of primary concern to those charged with conducting interscholastic and intercollegiate programs. This section covers not only interscholastic teams, but also club teams and intramurals. It also re-emphasizes the denial of benefits in the event of sexual discrimination. Paramount to the understanding of the law is that it provides for equal opportunity, not equal funding.

The law also allows institutions to sponsor separate teams for men and women where selection is based on competitive skill or the activity involves body contact. The contact sports listed are boxing, wrestling, rugby, ice hockey, football, and basketball. In the event that an institution sponsors an activity, such as tennis, for one sex but not for the other, members of the excluded sex must be allowed to try out for the team.

In determining equal opportunity for the respective teams, directors of such programs are to consider such items as the following (14):

Whether the sports selected reflect the interest and abilities of both sexes
Provision of supplies and equipment
Game and practice schedules
Travel and per diem
Coaching and academic tutoring opportunities and the assignment and pay of the coaches and tutors
Locker rooms, practice and competitive facilities
Medical and training services
Housing and dining facilities and services
Publicity

Athletic scholarships are of particular concern for women athletes, especially at the intercollegiate level, because many institutions did not include them as part of women's benefits. The 1975 regulations provide as follows (14):

> To the extent that a recipient awards athletic scholarships or grants-in-aid, it must provide reasonable opportunities for such awards for members of each sex in proportion to the number of each sex participating in interscholastic or intercollegiate athletics.

One of the basic misconceptions about Title IX is that men and women must be treated identically in all facets of athletics. This misconception has led intercollegiate leaders to proclaim that Title IX will force the discontinuation of many sports programs. The original law did not suggest a duplication of programs but rather stressed that opportunities be equal for both sexes in the total program.

In the fall of 1978, Joseph Califano, secretary of HEW, suggested a new interpretation: per-capita expenditure for men's and women's sports based on the number of participants. This is a radical departure from the original intent of the law; and, many leaders of the intercollegiate programs feel that the original fears of sports elimination will prove accurate if it remains in force. This will hurt the total programs of both men and women.

The Female Image

Queen Victoria's reign over England (1837–1901) had a tremendous impact on the attitudes and role expected of women in the Western world. The feminine role required women to be passive, submissive, gentle, nurturant, dependent, and obedient (10). "Feminine delicacy was considered visible evidence of their superior sensibility, the 'finer clay' of which they were made. Women who were not delicate by nature became so by design" (28). This doctrine of femininity was openly advocated by society; a woman who did not fit the mold was looked on as unwomanly. The ultimate Victorian goal was "attracting a man and bearing a child" (15).

In 1872, Justice Bradley of the U.S. Supreme Court characterized male and female roles by concurring in the case of *Bradley* v. *State* as follows:

> Man is, or should be, woman's protector and defender. The natural and proper timidity and delicacy which belongs to the female sex evidently unfits it for many of the occupations of civil life. The constitution of the family organization, which is founded on the divine ordinance, as well as in the nature of things, indicates the domestic sphere as that which properly belongs to the domain and function of womanhood. . . . The paramount destiny and mission of women is to fulfill the noble and benign offices of wife and mother. This is the law of the Creator (3).

This attitude prevailed for approximately one hundred years, until the Supreme Court justices retreated from it and established a different posture on the role of women in society.

For decades, a woman's role in American society has been housewife and mother, whereas a man's has been protector and provider. Superstition and myths have prevailed relative to women participating in strenuous physical activity. Yet, history depicts women pioneers as toiling beside their men as they fought to survive and settle the West. Despite the many sagas of that period of American development illustrating the ability of a woman to withstand strenuous activity and hardship, the genteel female stereotype persisted. Social barriers were created in athletics, where the activities were dominated by images of masculinity: courage, toughness, strength, and emotional control. Socialization of a young child began soon after birth, with toys and games providing a natural means of communicating role stereotypes. Boys were encouraged to behave as little men, while girls were told to behave like little ladies. Parental and peer pressure on the child to conform to a role was tremendous and became progressively greater as the child matured from adolescence to adulthood.

With the acceptance of sports as a valuable social and healthful pursuit, women began to increase their participation. The accepted wearing apparel of the time restricted the type of activity engaged in (7). The sports considered ladylike were tennis, croquet, golf, field hockey, and cycling. During the first quarter of the twentieth century, "limited sports for women was accepted, provided that it took place under conditions which maximized that which was thought to be good for women (as per the Victorian ideal) and minimized the threat to her womanliness" (15). Sports that taxed one's energies or that required an inordinate amount of strength were considered inappropriate.

Society today is witnessing a redefinition of cultural values and sex roles. This has been brought about by such factors as the following:

1. During World War I, women served as nurses and became part of the war effort.
2. Ratification of the nineteenth amendment to the Constitution granted women's suffrage, which to some symbolized the equality of sexes.
3. The advent of the uninhibited jazz age (1920–1929) tended to relax the restrictiveness of the Victorian female image.
4. The great depression of the thirties provided social and economic pressures that restricted the female's ability to be on her own. Though there were numerous recreational facilities and programs developed during this period, there is little evidence pointing to women's participation (7).
5. World War II saw the expansion of the women's branches of the armed services and greater participation in industry as the nation's manpower was depleted by the male's participation in the armed forces. Women who took wartime positions wanted to continue to be gainfully employed. Thirty percent of the women from ages 18–64 were in the labor force in 1940. By 1970, the number had risen to 50 percent.

6. The new feminism has developed. "The old feminism was a rebellion against conditions that had grown too oppressive to tolerate, the new feminism was a product of inequalities that were too unjust to continue to tolerate" (15). New feminism can be characterized as a revolt against social attitudes. Included in this revolt is the plea for equality in sports opportunities.

The role of women in society has dramatically changed during the past two decades. It will continue to change in the future as the feminist movement gains in popularity. At present, the greatest single social problem facing the woman athlete is the discrimination she must meet because of her sex. The traditional female role in American society is undergoing constant change and redefinition. "The transformation of our society from patriarchal dominance to matriarchal equality will play a major role in freeing the female athlete from prejudices which in the past have denied her equality in the area of athletics" (39). The demand for equality in athletic opportunities is the result of a cry for equality in all spheres of life.

Conditioning for the Female Athlete

The role of physiological conditioning for women cannot be overemphasized. Proper conditioning techniques, if all other factors are adequate, may provide superior performance and reduce the risk of injuries. Some researchers believe that there is little or no reason to advocate different training programs for men and women. These conjectures are based on studies emphasizing the similarities of the sexes (40). Opinions on conditioning programs diverge widely. These views have been set forth in chapters 4 and 5.

Superior performance by athletes normally requires prolonged periods of conditioning. The athlete should carefully plan these programs and fully understand them. Such understanding encourages the dedication necessary to attain maximum performance. All athletes and coaches should realize that no known drug or chemical substance effectively improves the performance of a well-conditioned athlete.

Physiological fitness confers on the athlete the ability to perform consistently, thus fulfilling maximum potential. An important consideration for all coaches to realize is that any conditioning program must be modified according to each player's ability. The daily exercise needed to gain and maintain peak efficiency has been insufficiently researched. Coaches who have provided such guidance have done so through observation and empirical methods. In prescribing conditioning programs, coaches must be aware of a vulnerable point in the amount of time and exertion an athlete can spend in practicing a skill. Mental or physical exhaustion may produce staleness.

R. J. Shepherd, in his book *The Fit Athlete,* points out that there are five biological factors needed for success in athletics (36). They are strength,

Figure 11.1 *Women's participation in all areas of athletics has been increasing steadily since 1960.*

endurance, speed, agility, and flexibility. All these components can be influenced to some degree by a meaningful conditioning program, though some can be affected more than others. Examples of activities requiring these ingredients are:

1. Strength. Activities requiring strength are those activities that need explosive power, such as throwing, jumping, or moving resistive objects.
2. Endurance. This includes both cardiovascular and muscular endurance. Some regard cardiovascular endurance as one of the most important factors for athletic success (see Chapter 5). Muscular endurance allows for repeated performances with a minimal drop in results.
3. Speed. Speed of movement or reaction time is basically a genetic gift. There are conflicting reports on the ability of individuals to influence these innate gifts. Evidence seems to indicate that it is possible to slightly improve speed through a diligent program of exercise and conditioning.
4. Agility. Agility requires great neuromuscular coordination that must be developed for a particular activity such as figure skating. Repeated performance of the same skill seems to develop a reflex condition that allows individuals to respond with a smooth flow of action.
5. Flexibility. Flexibility is obtained through ballistic or static stretching exercises. It is very important in an activity such as gymnastics or any activity requiring elasticity of movement.

Klafs and Lyon, in their book *The Female Athlete* (second edition), provide excellent descriptions of exercises and training programs for women that might be helpful for all who coach women (22).

Weight Training for the Female Athlete

The myths and fears surrounding the use of weights by women are fast being displaced by the concept that they are an indispensable tool for the serious competitor. In the past, women who cherished their femininity feared the social stigma of bulging muscles. This prevented them from using weights in their athletic training programs. At the present time, it is believed that increases in the average woman's basic strength do not necessarily correlate with muscle size. Researchers have indicated that a woman the same size as a man engaged in similar programs will develop only one-tenth the muscle mass (41). This is credited to genetic differences between the sexes.

The male hormone, testosterone, contributes to the masculine image and allows for the development of greater muscle mass and definition. Similarly, the female hormone, estrogen, contributes to the secondary sex features of women. Harmon Brown, M.D., in an article on weight training for women, sums up the effects of weight training on muscle mass as follows:

> . . . heavy weight training for prolonged periods in these (female) athletes pro-
> duced only minimal signs of muscle hypertrophy, and the heavy "bulkiness"
> seen in men who weight train did not develop. We believe that this is because
> muscle hypertrophy is caused by the male hormone testosterone. Since
> women produce only 6–8% as much of this hormone as men, their potential for
> great muscular hypertrophy is limited (4).

Such observations might lead some athletes and coaches to prescribe the use of male hormones in the form of steroids to increase muscle mass. There is no proof that such muscle mass would increase strength over that developed by normal training. No one should advocate the use of male hormones to increase the effectiveness of a female athlete. The possibility of side effects causing permanent damage is tremendous.

Weight training and weight lifting should not be confused. Weight training employs the overload principle (see Chapter 5) and a series of resistance exercises to develop strength and endurance. Weight lifting, on the other hand, is a competitive event employing prescribed lifting techniques in which one participant tries to lift more weight than the opponent. It is an activity necessitating great power and strength.

Many of today's famous women athletes, such as Jane Frederick, pentathlete; Wilma Rudolph, track; Margaret Court, tennis; Diana Nyad, swimmer; Amy Olcott, golf; and Mary Jo Peppler, volleyball, engage in weight training. Most use free weights such as dumbbells or barbells, whereas others use machines such as Universal or Nautilus. Women may employ similar exercises as men (see Chapter 5) with the expectation of attaining desirable results. Coaches and athletes both recognize that properly executed weight training can improve the strength component that is essential for superior athletic performance. Women's apprehensions and fears about weight training are disappearing as knowledge and dissemination of research results increase.

Menstruation and the Female Athlete

Menstruation is a cyclic event for girls and women occurring approximately every twenty-eight days for about thirty-five years of their lives. The rhythm of the cycle varies widely. The length of the menstrual period normally is from three to five days, though two to seven days may be considered normal (5). Most researchers divide the menstrual cycle into four phases: premenstrual, menstrual, postmenstrual, and intermenstrual.

Menarche for many girls occurs between the ages of twelve to fourteen, though a range of nine to sixteen years is common (33). Evidence indicates that the age of menarche for women who participate in athletics may be later than that of the nonathlete. R. M. Malina studied a group of women track athletes and compared them to a group of nonathletes. The average age of menarche for the athletes was 13.58 years. This compared with 12.23 years for the nonathlete. The 1.35 year differential represents a significant statistical difference (23).

Menstruation and other gynecological implications have concerned for several decades those associated with women's participation in athletic competition. Much research has been carried out with a variety of conflicting conclusions. Some research conclusions are as follows:

1. Performance in athletic contests for women seems to be greatest in the immediate postmenstrual period and up to the fifteenth day of the cycle (34).
2. The effect of menstruation on physical performance seems to be relatively small. A study of the women on the 1964 and 1968 U.S. Olympic teams, gold medal winners and world record holders, revealed that these individuals successfully participated in all phases of the menstrual cycle (36).
3. Individual variations including such factors as duration and amount of flow characterizes the menstrual cycle (34).
4. Women athletes may engage in intensive training on the first day after menstruation starts. Such training may continue for a fifteen-day period, after which it seems advisable to taper off until the second day of menstruation when intensive training may begin again (34, 40).
5. Dysmenorrhea characterized by lower abdominal cramps and accompanied by headache, backache, leg ache, abdominal swelling, or nausea occurs just prior to the menstrual flow. The degree of dysmenorrhea in women varies from intense pain to slight difficulty and is neither aggravated nor relieved by active participation in sports (5). Pain tolerance is very personal. It should not be ignored. So although research of this sort has merit, common sense indicates discretion. Pain in a body organ indicates distress. By giving the distressed organs rest, strength can be regained.
6. Sports participation will not significantly change the menstrual cycle for the majority of individuals (5).
7. Abdominal and relative general strength is greater following rather than during menstruation for the average female athlete (5, 42).
8. Injuries to female reproductive organs while participating in athletic competition is rare because of the well-protected position of these organs in the body (34, 40).
9. Some physicians suggest that women athletes avoid torque or jarring forces, such as jumping or twisting with the pelvis during the first two days of menstruation because the womb is heavy and engorged with blood (5).

10. The physical changes that take place during menstruation can affect judgment and produce slow reaction time in some women (9).
11. Cultural taboos and social mores can negatively influence the performance of women athletes during the premenstrual and menstrual cycle (8).
12. Some female athletes are using birth control pills containing various combinations of estrogenic substances and synthetic progestational agents to regulate or delay menstruation. There is no known research as to whether or not these drugs enhance or hinder performances. There may be serious side effects influencing the body chemistry, suggesting that the use of these drugs should be avoided.

Because it is impossible to arrange schedules of competition so that some member of a team is not in her menstrual cycle, coaches must be aware of the complexities of menstruation so that they can alleviate fears thus aiding performance. A summary published in the "Any Questions?" section of the *British Medical Journal* concerns the skill, speed, and endurance of women athletes during menstruation and provides an interesting conclusion.

> For most women athletes, menstruation is not an important factor and has no effect on performance provided that the individual does not expect and anticipate an adverse effect and has been encouraged to ignore it. There is certainly no direct relationship between the days of the cycle and any aspect of performance. Any adverse effect would be expected to occur either premenstrually or on the first day, especially if there is much dysmenorrhea. In a few cases, this is certainly true. On the other hand, it is unlikely that any woman who suffers really severe dysmenorrhea will become a top-class athlete (1).

Some Unique Problems of the Woman Coach and the Female Athlete

Many female athletes discover that they are faced with factors unique to their participation in competitive athletics. Some of these situations, which have existed for many years, are rapidly being obliterated as society accepts the concept that females have athletic ability and can benefit from sports competition. Some of the complexities faced by the female athlete and the female coach are typified by the following:

1. Some coaches refuse to recognize the dedication and seriousness of women athletes. These coaches with tenacious memories of the "play day" and the social atmosphere of women's athletic events in the past need to consign such thoughts to oblivion. Women, receiving such treatment, will do well to preserve their equanimity by making light of the situation. In doing so, they will preserve their athletic prowess as well as their ability to concentrate on their goals.

2. There still are a large number of women who teach physical education that haven't accepted the philosophy of girls participating in highly competitive sports. These teachers prefer to perpetuate the play-day atmosphere. They actively try to dissuade the gifted woman athlete from seriously participating in athletics. The athletic world is very competitive and, though participation should be fun for the athlete, there is little room for a laissez-faire attitude.

3. The masculine image of sports in the United States involves some complexities for the female:

   a. Can she forget the societal plea "be a lady, not a tomboy"?

   b. Can she take a label of "overaggressive" or "woman jock"?

   c. Can she endure being compared to male athletes?

   d. Can she postpone bearing children?

   For a determined young woman striving for quality and a degree of excellence in active competition, the aforementioned difficulties will not be thwarting. Such women, who have the high purpose of fulfilling their desire to compete as an immediate goal, also have the wisdom and foresight to modify any urge for traditional family-life goals.

4. The problem of protective equipment is of great concern to many female athletes. Unfortunately, in the past, makers of protective equipment for athletes have concentrated their efforts on male-oriented sports. As a result, there has been little research to study the needs of women athletes. The rapid increase of women's athletic teams should remedy this lack in the future.

5. Until recently, women athletes have lacked the opportunity to develop their full potential. Lack of facilities, equipment, coaching, publicity, and funding have limited their athletic opportunities. With the advent of Title IX, these limiting factors may be eliminated.

6. The lack of professional training and background in sports activities can create an atmosphere of little respect for the coach by the female athlete. In the past, the traditional physical education preparation program included very little information for coaching. As a result, many women who attempted to coach female athletes were ill prepared. In recent years, athletic coaching programs such as that established at many universities including the University of California, Santa Barbara, in 1968, have offered women an opportunity to obtain coaching expertise that has commanded respect.

7. Some of the enigmas to be solved by women coaches are:

   a. being sensitive to criticism

   b. feeling insecure in a new role

   c. responding to male chauvinists who govern sports

   These enigmas can be very perplexing because they stem simply from being female, not from performance or ability. If the female coach understands this, she can handle all quandaries with creative imagination. Now, as women's sports are beginning to develop, there is an unprecedented opportunity to build new ideas and ideals into exceptional athletic programs. There is definitely the opportunity to de-emphasize or obliterate the "win or else" philosophy and other ills that have infiltrated so much of the men's athletic programs. Many other innovations are within the realm of possibility.

Some Unique Problems of the Male Coaching the Female Athlete

That opportunities for women to participate in competitive athletics have increased is a well-established fact. People generally ignore, though, that without the help of male coaches many programs might not have existed. Some male coaches have failed to recognize that certain differences exist between men and women. These differences cannot be verified except by empirical methods, because there seem to be no criteria for demonstrating an emotion or proving an aspiration. Differences in socialization may cause men and women to bring different attitudes and styles to their athletic endeavors. Traditional stereotypes suggest that these differences manifest themselves in cut-and-dried ways. (One such stereotype holds that women will compete less aggressively than men.) In reality though, these stereotypes are seldom accurate on an individual basis. For the male coaching the female athlete, it is wise to recognize that the competitive attitude of the female may differ from that of her male counterpart. But the coach should also remember that each athlete's individual personality is the ultimate determinant of his or her approach and performance.

Other complexities for the male coaching the female athletes are:

1. Some coaches lack a basic knowledge of anatomy, physiology, and the psychology of women. This lack often results in ignorance concerning female responses to physiological stress in training.
2. The coach must be professional at all times. Problems arise if he develops special relationships with players. Team spirit can easily be ruined because of such relationships.
3. Even though some men coach women because they prefer to do so, they are often looked on as weak, and it is often assumed they couldn't obtain a position coaching a men's team.
4. If a man has previously coached males, he must be careful to adapt his coaching methods to fit female performance.
5. Female athletes start with less strength than males. This discrepancy must be considered when planning programs.

Figure 11.2 *The coach should remember that each athlete's individual personality is the ultimate determinant of his or her approach and performance.*

6. Male coaches cannot enter the locker room following practice or contests to confer with female athletes. However, this should not limit their ability to effectively relate to problems of individual performance.
7. Serving as a personal advisor to the athletes is one of the roles a coach must assume. It can be difficult for a male coach to relate to problems that are uniquely female.
8. Coaches who are ignorant of the rules for female sports must learn a second set of rules as well as adopt game strategies that accommodate the basic abilities of the athletes.
9. Because of the lack of opportunity, female athletes may lack basic sports skills. This requires patience and demonstrating ability from the coach.

Mixed Competition

Mixed competition among the sexes has not been part of sports in the United States. As previously pointed out, sports have been primarily male dominated. Females were expected to take a passive role as spectators.

However, recent judicial rulings have decreed that in the absence of women's teams women must be allowed to try out for traditionally male-oriented activities. Such rulings have affected little leagues, junior and senior high schools, and intercollegiate teams. One may protest that women have always successfully participated in non-contact sports such as tennis and diving. This is true, but competition becomes a complex matter when women compete in contact sports.

Males and females are equal in physical development until the onset of puberty. At this time, secondary sex features become evident. Differences in anatomy and physiology following puberty become pronounced. The average male becomes taller and heavier than the average female who is shorter and lighter. The male takes on masculine characteristics of muscle definition, beard, and deep voice. The female breasts develop and rounded contours in muscle definition appear. In addition, a wide range of development exists within each sex. Some females who possess more male hormones than average become more masculine in appearance than their male counterparts, who are effeminate in appearance and behavior.

Researchers have established that the average female cannot approach the basic strength of the average male. The female is thus at a distinct disadvantage in activities where the frequency and severity of collision force is substantial. Women develop less muscle mass per unit of body weight and bone density than do males. Even if girls and boys are matched according to age, height, and weight, girls are still predisposed to greater possible body injury because the proportion of adipose tissue to lean body weight differs between the sexes (6). The average woman possesses 22–25 percent adipose tissue, as compared to 12–15 percent in males. The inordinate risk of injury to women in contact sports outweighs the potential benefits of participation.

The courts have established that unequal competition is a justifiable cause for a lawsuit to be decided in favor of the plaintiff. In several cases, younger and lighter boys have competed with older and heavier opponents. Injuries that have resulted from such competition have been ruled as negligence by the coach. These cases bring up the legal question of females participating against males and the injuries that may result. It would seem that an easy case could be made for unequal competition, and law suits would decide in favor of the female competitor.

Psychological problems may surface during mixed competition. The masculine image in the United States includes aggression and competitiveness. Males are taught to treat females with courtesy and respect. It is difficult for them to hit a ball forcefully at a woman, such as a spike in volleyball, or to hit a woman directly, as in contact sports. Failure to do so undermines the very nature of some sports, which are supposed to encourage controlled aggressive behavior.

For a woman to maintain a feminine image in mixed competition may be difficult psychologically for both women and men. Some women hesitate to put forth an all-out effort that might result in victory over a male opponent. The male ego often cannot handle defeat by a female. The female faces the dilemma of winning and possibly not being able to maintain normal social relationships with the males. If she loses because she didn't try, she doesn't live up to her own expectations and therefore thinks less of herself. Thus the possible benefits of mixed participation are negated. However, it is evident that there are many women and men who can handle this situation.

Summary

Increased physical activity and athletic competition for women is one of the fastest growing and most significant developments in the nation's culture. Myths about and prejudices against female competition still prevail in some areas of the United States, though factual information is slowly coming to light.

Title IX is an Educational Amendment Act passed by Congress on June 23, 1972. It was signed into law on May 27, 1975, with an effective date of July 21, 1975. Title IX provides for equal opportunity, regardless of sex, in educational programs receiving federal assistance. Athletics is but one part of this act. Educational institutions were instructed to conduct a self-evaluation with compliance as follows: elementary schools, July 21, 1976; secondary and post secondary, July 21, 1978. Failure to comply with the law meant denial of federal funds.

Queen Victoria's reign over England had a tremendous impact on the Western world. It established a feminine image that required women to be passive, submissive, gentle, dependent, nurturant, and obedient. It tended to place women on a pedestal. They were not expected to participate in the occupations of civil life. Their primary roles were as housewives and mothers. Superstition and myths surrounded their ability to endure strenuous activities and hardships.

The role of women in the United States has dramatically changed during the past two decades. The new feminism is a product of inequities and a revolt against social attitudes. The demand for equality in athletic opportunities is the result of a cry for equality in all spheres of life and a redefinition of the female image.

Correct conditioning, if all other factors are adequate, provides superior performance and reduces the risk of injuries. Researchers indicate that the dissimilarities of the sexes suggest no reason to advocate different training programs. Some opinions regarding different methods are provided in chapters 4 and 5.

Biological factors needed for success in athletics are strength, endurance, speed, agility, and flexibility. These components can be influenced to varying degrees by excellent conditioning programs.

The myths and fears surrounding the use of weights to increase strength are fast being displaced by the concept that they are an indispensable tool for the serious competitor. Women do not need to fear bulging muscles when employing weight training because genetic differences between sexes prevent the female from developing excessive muscle mass.

Menstruation is a cyclic event for girls and women occurring approximately every twenty-eight days for about thirty-five years. Gynecology and menstruation have considerably concerned people associated with women's participation in athletic competition. There are conflicting conclusions. Active competition does not seem to have any adverse effects on the reproductive organs. Women can successfully compete in any phase of the menstrual cycle. However, research indicates greater strength from the second to the fifteenth day following the onset of menstruation. A danger that has crept into women's athletics is the use of birth control pills to delay menstruation. This might influence the body chemistry and produce serious side effects.

Some coaches refuse to recognize the dedication and seriousness of women athletes. Many complexities exist for the female athlete such as being labeled "tomboy" or "woman jock."

There has been a lack of opportunity for the female athlete to develop her full potential. Such things as lack of facilities, equipment, coaching, publicity, and funding have contributed to this limitation.

Women coaches are faced with many problems such as sensitivity, insecurity, lack of professional training, male chauvinistic views. Men are dominated by a driving desire to accomplish a particular goal. Women typically are more attuned to feelings involving the rightness of things. Women coaches should strive to obliterate the ills of men's athletic programs.

Male coaches have helped expand opportunities for women in competitive athletics by coaching in the absence of trained female coaches. These men are faced with many complex issues if they lack the basic knowledge of anatomy, physiology, and the psychological makeup of women. Many male coaches are not sensitive to the fears, needs, and limitations of women.

Sports, until recently, have been dominated by males. Recent judicial rulings have decreed that in the absence of a women's team, girls must be allowed to try out for traditionally male-oriented activities. This has had a serious impact on little league, junior and senior high school, and collegiate teams.

Following puberty, women are not as strong as men. Due to secondary sex features, women cannot participate equally in activities requiring frequent contact. Legal and psychological problems may surface because of mixed competition, which can be detrimental to all participants.

References

1. "Any Questions? Women Athletes and Menstruation." *British Medical Journal,* 4:5871 (December 1972), 662.
2. Bentsen, Cheryl. "Women's Sports: There Are Some Growing Pains." *Los Angeles Times,* part 3 (April 23, 1975), 1, 6.
3. *Bradley* v. *Stale.* 83 U.S. (16 Wall.) 130 (1872), 144.
4. Brown, Harmon, M.D. "Weight Training for Women?" *Cramer First Aider for Women 1:2.* Gardner, Kan.: Cramer Products, (January 1974).
5. Clarke, H. H., ed. "Physical Activity During Menstruation and Pregnancy." Washington, D.C.: *Physical Fitness Research Digest,* 8:3 (July 1978), 25.
6. Corbitt, Richard W., et al. "Female Athletics—A Special Communication from the Committee on the Medical Aspects of Sports of the AMA" *JOPER,* 46:1 (January 1975), 45, 46.
7. Cozens, F. W., and F. S. Stumpf. *Sports in American Life.* Chicago: University of Chicago Press, 1953, 366.
8. "Culture and the Curse." *Time Magazine* (February 23, 1976), 58–59.
9. Dalton, Katharina. *The Premenstrual Syndrome.* Springfield, Ill.: Charles C. Thomas, 1966, 104.
10. Dietz, Mary L., and Mary Breen. "Strategies Used by Women Athletes to Cope with Role Strain." *Track & Field Quarterly Review,* 77:2 Kalamazoo, Mich.: U.S. Track Coaches Association (Summer 1977), 53–57.
11. Drinkwater, Barbara L. "Aerobic Power in Females." *JOPER,* 46:1 (January 1975), 36–38.
12. Emert, Phyllis R. "Five Times Fantastic." *The Olympian.* Lynn, Mass.: H. Zimman, (June 1978), 21–23.
13. Engle, Kathleen M. "The Greening of Girls' Sports." *Nations Schools* (September 1973), 27–34.
14. "Final Title IX. Regulation Implementing Education Amendments of 1972, Prohibiting Sex Discrimination in Education," Washington, D.C.: U.S. Department of Health, Education, and Welfare / Office of Civil Rights (June 1975).
15. Gerber, E., et al. *The American Woman in Sport.* Reading, Mass.: Addison-Wesley, 1974, 562.
16. Gilbert, Bil, and Nancy Williamson. "Women in Sports." *Sports Illustrated,* 41:28 (July 29, 1974).
17. Goldstein, S. R. *Law and Public Education.* Indianapolis, N.Y.: Bobbs Merrill, 1974, 168–192.
18. Green, Ted. "Women in Sports: The Movement Is Real." *Los Angeles Times,* part 4 (April 23, 1974), 1, 4.
19. ———. "Women in Sports: Wherever Games Are Being Played These Days, More and More of the Barriers Are Getting Knocked Down." *Los Angeles Times,* part 3 (April 24, 1974), 1, 5.
20. Harris, Dorothy V. "Psychosocial Considerations." *JOPER,* 46:1 (January 1975), 32–36.
21. Hoepner, B. J., ed. *Women's Athletics: Coping with Controversy.* Washington, D.C.: AAHPER, 1974, 120.
22. Klafs, C. E. and M. J. Lyon. *The Female Athlete: A Coach's Guide to Conditioning and Training.* 2nd ed. St. Louis, Mo.: C. V. Mosby, 1978, 341.

23. Malina, R. M., et al. "Age of Menarche in Athletes and Non-Athletes." *Medicine and Science in Sports,* 5:1 (Spring 1973), 11–13.
24. Miller, Donna Mae. *Coaching the Female Athlete.* Philadelphia: Lea & Febiger, 1974, 212.
25. Neal, Patsy N. *Coaching Methods for Women.* 2nd ed. Reading, Mass.: Addison-Wesley, 1978, 281.
26. ———— and T. A. Tutko. *Coaching Girls and Women: Psychological Perspectives.* Boston: Allyn & Bacon, 1975, 235.
27. Nyad, Diana. "Pumping Iron." *Women Sports,* 4:4 (April 1977), 48–51.
28. O'Neill, W. L. *Everyone Was Brave. A History of Feminism in America.* Chicago: Quadrangle Books, 1971, 4–8.
29. Oppenheimer, Valeri K. "Demographic Influences on Female Employment and the Status of Women." In *Changing Women in a Changing Society.* Ed. Joan Huber. Chicago: University of Chicago Press, 1973, 295.
30. Palulonis, Rita A. *19th Conference on the Medical Aspects of Sports.* Monroe, Wisc.: American Medical Association, 1978, 75.
31. Pernice, Sue. "Coaches—Let Your Players Think." *JOPER,* 47:7 (September 1976), 23.
32. Pointdexter, H. B. W., and C. L. Misshier. *Coaching Competitive Team Sports for Girls and Women.* Philadelphia: W. B. Saunders, 1973, 244.
33. Ryan, Allan J. "Gynecological Considerations." *JOPER,* 46:1 (January 1975), 40–44.
34. ———— and F. L. Allman, Jr., eds. *Sports Medicine.* New York: Academic Press, 1974, 735.
35. Shaffer, T. E. "Physiological Considerations of the Female Participant." *Women in Sport: A National Research Conference.* University Park, Pa.: Pennsylvania State University, 1973.
36. Shephard, R. J. *The Fit Athlete.* Oxford, England: Oxford University Press, 1978, 214.
37. Sisley, Beckley. "Professional Preparation of Female Coaches." *The Physical Educator,* 33 (May 1976), 87–91.
38. Vermont, P., and R. Anderson. "Sex Discrimination in Intercollegiate Athletics." Iowa City, Iowa: University of Iowa College of Law, *Iowa Law Review,* 61:2 (December 1975), 420–496.
39. Vernacchia, Ralph A. "Problems of Athletes: A Sociological Observation." *The Physical Educator,* 32:2 (May 1975), 89.
40. Wilmore, Jack H. *Athletic Training and Physical Fitness.* Boston: Allyn & Bacon, 1976, 266.
41. ————. "Body Composition and Strength Development." *JOPER,* 46:1 (January 1975), 38–40.
42. ————. "Exploding the Myth of Female Inferiority." *Physician and Sportsmedicine,* 2 (1974), 54–58.

Ethics in Coaching **12**

YOU'VE GOT IT MADE AS AN OL' COACH...

... when you don't have to prove that "you are a good loser"

... when you can sleep at night before the big game without a tranquillizer

... when you are addressed as "sir" by faculty members and game officials

... when sporting goods salesmen see you at YOUR convenience

For when the one great scorer comes
To write against your name,
He marks—not that you won or lost—
But how you played the game.
                                    Grantland Rice

There are few subjects more complex than ethics in coaching. The te means so many things to so many people. Ethics generally involves behavior described as good v. bad, right v. wrong, and ought v. ought not. It represents a philosophy concerned with moral problems and judgments.

Right action is doing that which produces a good influence psychologically, physiologically, and morally on one's self, family, friends, and associates as well as one's surroundings and environment. Conversely, that which damages one's self or others or the environment is wrong action. Actions that produce a wholesome influence on the performer and his or her surroundings can be learned from three sources. First, from the example and teaching of one's parents. A second source is the scriptural authority of one's religion. And third, from the example of a great man or woman. This may be a person one greatly admires, such as a Helen Keller or an Abraham Lincoln or the charismatic figure of a great coach. One may seek guidance from these sources when one is in doubt about a course of action. Today's society has difficulty knowing right from wrong. This is due, in large part, to the breakdown of the family structure through divorce and the demise of the extended family of grandparents. Hence, the need for codes of ethics has risen sharply in all walks of life.

Interscholastic athletics today need an improved moral climate. A greater effort must be made by coaches to abide by rules and sound moral standards if there is to be a successful fight against unethical practices in the coaching ranks. Everyone concerned with competitive sports must share in this responsibility. Each individual in a leadership position must become aware of proper ethical conduct and abide by it. Ralph Sabock, in *The Coach,* writes:

> There are no degrees of honesty. A coach cannot be just a little dishonest or a
> little bit un-ethical. There are no shades of gray where honesty is concerned.
> The coach who speaks about adherence to the rules only to violate them him-
> self is advocating cheating not by what he says but by what he has done.
> When a coach says one thing and does another, the student will disregard his
> words and assume that his actions are a greater indication of his true beliefs.
> All the words in a coach's vocabulary will not change this fact. (43)

Unfortunately, athletes do not always recognize unethical conduct by their coaches, whom they tend to trust and respect. Thus, those who subsequently enter the coaching profession may unwittingly perpetuate unethical practices. Interscholastic athletics must be conducted in an ethically stimulating environment. The ideals of the coaching profession should be above reproach and serve as an appropriate model for all athletes, especially those who may themselves become coaches.

Objectives ——————————————————————————————

This chapter presents some factors concerned with ethics in the coaching profession:

1. The need for ethics
2. Society's influence on ethics in coaching
3. The definition of ethics: morals
4. Characteristics influenced by ethical standards
5. Professional codes of ethics
6. Win-or-else pressures
7. Unethical practices

The Need for Ethics ——————————————————————

Ethics has become very complex because of the widespread notion that one should not infringe on the freedom, the likes, and the dislikes of other people. The following quote from *The Science of Being and Art of Living* speaks eloquently about the danger of such a concept:

There is a school of thought, accepted by many educational organizations in some of the important countries leading to modern thought which advocates giving freedom to students. Teachers are not allowed to punish them for wrong behaviour. The reason given is that genius grows better in freedom and when it is not suppressed by authority. Such an ideal must have been initiated by very compassionate hearts with only good intentions; but a few decades of experience have proved that it lacks merit. The increase in child and juvenile delinquency and in criminal tendencies in society has alarmed the authorities in almost every country where only a few years ago this principle of growth in freedom was approved of in schools and colleges. It is a very wrong principle. It is cruel and greatly damaging to the interests of society not to guide and shape the thought and behaviour of the younger generation through a combination of love and discipline (33).

It is the responsibility of the more experienced generation to advise the young. Deeper criteria of right and wrong are established when an individual gains experience and has a broader vision of life. An adequate systematic formula of right and wrong for the developing minds of our youth must be established in a code of ethics for athletes. It is a subject that must be taught by both precept and example. It cannot be left to chance and needs to be spelled out explicitly with kindness and authority. It also needs to be enforced. Guidelines should be simple. Ethical practices should be outlined in such a way that all can readily understand them, making it easy to practice and apply them.

It is interesting to note that the press is now proclaiming the value of ethics:

It has become permissible to speak, write and think about "ethics." That represents a healthy advance over very recent times when anybody who talked in such terms was regarded as naive. Now all that remains is to get bureaucrats, union leaders, big business, members of Congress and just plain people to act ethically—which we take to mean with honesty and responsibility toward fellow human beings. The record has not been too good (49).

There is growing evidence in many schools that ethics is becoming the "in" subject. Many professional organizations and big corporations are setting up codes. This growing widespread adoption of ethics codes will be a boon to athletes everywhere. It will deepen understanding and make it easy for the athletes to put into practice the ethical conduct being taught by their coaches.

ESPONSE BY TUTHRES LECTURERS, PROFSORS

Society's Influence on Ethics in Coaching

Many scholars writing about dominant societies in history maintain that the sports and games they played in these societies mirrored their basic structure of life. The Athenian Greeks participated in activities that exemplified grace and beauty. In competition, they awarded an olive wreath to the victor. There was no recognition of those who came in second.

The Romans reveled in sports and contests that were violent and brutal in nature. Too often, the winner was rewarded by survival while the loser faced death.

The United States, as a nation, developed a basic philosophy of sportsmanship typified by the quote, "It's not whether you win or lose, it's how you play the game." Good sportsmanship enacted the ultimate compliment. Unfortunately, this philosophy seems to have been replaced with one reflected by the statement attributed to Vince Lombardi, "Winning isn't everything, it's the only thing."

The competitive urge is deeply rooted in the American character. It is basic to the free enterprise system. Former President Gerald Ford said, "First place is the manifestation of the desire to excel and how else can you achieve anything?" (15). Because of the tremendous importance placed on competition, our nation's citizens seem to view with approval the varied incidents associated with winning. The means and practices employed to gain a victory seem to justify the end. Society looks at business and rewards those who make a profit. Seldom do they question how the profit was obtained. This philosophy has extended into the sports arena. During one of the 1978 World Series baseball games, on a controversial play at second base, the T.V. announcer was heard to say, "He might have violated the rules a bit but he got away with it—good play." Commentators covering the National Football League televised games are heard to say, "Oh! Oh! he ally holding but the officials didn't see it—good play." Victory is paramount. Losing is regarded as humiliating or even disastrous. During 1965–1969, the San Francisco Giants baseball team ended up in second place. To do so, they had to win a majority of their games. Despite this, they were chastised by fans and the news media alike as "born losers" (32).

Sports are thoroughly entrenched in American life. Among the justifications for the promotion of sports in our society is the claim that they contribute to the participants' character development. Unfortunately, there exists many instances where fair play is given only lip service. The opponent is looked on as the enemy needing to be destroyed. An example of this was the high school coach, who on the eve of playing a football game against a team known as the Golden Eagles, painted a chicken yellow and had his players stomp the bird to death. George Sauer, upon retiring from professional football, spoke out against the idea of competitors trying to destroy each other. He suggested that aggression and hate toward opponents had permeated the American sports scene (45).

Interscholastic coaches must not entertain this level of thinking, for they are molding the character of the young. Their players will be the citizens of tomorrow, and the lessons they learn on their way to maturity will influence the basic fiber of American society. Sports should be an idealistic exercise and transcend the psychosocial dysfunction of American society thus offering a more responsible model (37).

The Definition of Ethics: Morals

Any discussion of ethics produces widely diverging opinions about the basic meaning of the word. Behavioral patterns considered ethical by one sector of society might be regarded as unethical by another. Ethics is concerned primarily with human values and becomes the basis for societal relationships. Such relationships, although voluntary in nature, are often governed by constraints imposed by society or by a profession. Involved are acts considered right or wrong, good or evil, honest or dishonest as well as principles of moral conduct that involve accepted customs of conduct in a society.

Webster's Dictionary (19) provides several definitions that are applicable for the coach. These are:

> *Ethic:*
>   1. The discipline dealing with what is good and bad or right and wrong or with moral duty and obligation
>   2. A group of moral principles or set of values

Ethics:

1. The principle of conduct governing an individual or profession—standard of behavior

Because moral conduct is the essence and the end result of ethics, it is essential to include definitions of *moral,* which should influence the coach. These are:

Moral:

1. Relating to principles of consideration of right and wrong action or good and bad character
2. Right behavior
3. Capable of being judged good or evil
4. Conforming to a standard of good and right
5. Actions based on inner convictions
6. Relating to the accepted customs or patterns of social or personal relations

Characteristics Influenced by Ethical Standards

Characteristics illustrating ethical behavior and reflecting character are traits one acquires rather than inherits. People are not born ethical creatures. Behavioral patterns are not built overnight. Rather, they are acquired during maturation as a result of interaction between individuals. Coaches can fulfill a vital role in developing a positive value system through personal example in their daily contact with students. This requires that coaches have a commitment to a strong sense of ethics and that they display characteristics that exemplify sound ethical traits. Obviously, all individuals will possess varying degrees of character development. However, among those qualities that coaches might be expected to have are confidence, courage, honesty, honor, justice, loyalty, perseverance, responsibility, self-control, sincerity, sportsmanship.

Confidence

Confidence in one's own conduct and the general belief that the basic intentions of others are honorable is essential for an agreeable relationship. Those who lack confidence in the actions of others should not expect these individuals to have confidence in them. Confidence is a trait that comes from consistent and steady adherence to acceptable principles of behavior. Such individuals are honestly striving to do the right thing. Ethical individuals will admit to a mistake and attempt to avoid repeating it.

RECTIFY

Courage

Aesop once said it was easy to be brave from a safe distance. Courage implies marching directly into the sports arena with bold-spirited confidence. The athlete who is plucky, gritty, stouthearted, and game to the very end can bear up against all odds. It is easy for one of such heroic nature to bear defeat without losing heart. There are three kinds of courage: physical, mental, and moral. Physical courage involves a lionhearted fearlessness that is honored by many. Mental courage has its basic strength in wisdom of conduct. Moral courage has to do with right and wrong as determined by ethical standards.

Honesty

Truth must be regarded as an accurate statement of fact that has been proved correct. Opinions, though they may have some justification, are not necessarily truths if they lack proof. Honesty opposes deceit and falsification. It involves truth in making and keeping promises and opposes lying or deception. One of the alibis for failing to be truthful in the coaching profession is succumbing to peer pressure and saying that "Everyone else is doing it." Coaches are responsible to themselves and not to others for infractions of the ethical code.

Moral standards are absolute and are not determined by majority opinion. Honesty is a habit acquired by purposeful behavior and comes only with practice. Sometimes, integrity must fly in the face of popular opinion.

Honor

Honor requires action. One becomes honorable when keeping one's word or promise and being one-pointed in doing one's duty. In dealing honorably with players, a coach must draw deeply from the old standbys of patience and tact in telling truths that may hurt. Honor involves the highest principles of the coaching profession and the desire to do what is just and meaningful for an individual.

Justice

The administration of justice is probably the most delicate task a coach handles. One is quickly on the horns of a dilemma unless justice is really understood. Basically, it involves impartiality on a fair field with no favoritism. A coach constantly makes judgments about players and about rules governing participation. There is nothing more invigorating for a player than to have a coach who spares no effort in impartiality and square dealing. It brings confident assurance of results from the very start.

Loyalty

Loyalty is among the most desirable qualities that may be found in any individual. The coaching profession requires individuals to give a full measure of one's ability whether the task is agreeable or not. Coaches must be loyal to the institution, the administration, as well as the players within the program. If an individual is truly loyal, high principles do not conflict with but, rather, reinforce each other. Individuals who become confused regarding loyalty, usually do so because of personal ambition. There is little room in the coaching profession for individuals who do not possess and practice loyalty.

Perseverance

Perseverance steadies and stabilizes character. It usually reflects a long, slow, steady progress toward a definite goal. There seldom is a spectacular or rapid attainment of the end results. Closely associated with perseverance is hard work and a determination to see a task through. It generally implies that there is some progress despite obstacles. Should failure occur, the individual who possesses tenacity and perseverance will start again with renewed determination and without loss of hope.

Responsibility

Responsibility implies first and foremost that one is accountable for one's actions. One does not shift the blame or responsibility on others for any mistake incurred. This has the enormous effect of hastening maturity. The next obvious implication is duty. The coach's duties involve administrative details, team development and public service. Whether such duties are assigned or assumed, the coach cannot evade them or leave them for others to carry out. In fulfilling the ethic of responsibility, the coach at once fulfills the role of reliability.

Self-Control

Self-control is a very important quality to be sought in ethics as well as athletics. It presumes that individuals possessing self-control will conduct themselves in acceptable fashion. These level-headed persons are settled, fixed, and firm. If they lose a game, they do not blame others. When they win, they maintain equanimity. Possessing these characteristics, they become masters of their fate. It would be unthinkable for such coaches to lose control and strike a player or an official, as sometimes happens in the sporting world. School officials may be forced in the best interests of the school to release a good coach who loses self-control. A particular coach's contribution to athletics may be enormous and far-famed. Still, one volatile mishap can ruin a coaching career.

Sincerity

Sincerity implies a behavior that is frank, candid, and honest. It involves telling the truth and speaking plainly with warmth and enthusiasm. Individuals possessing these qualities always have something to give: warm praise for a game well played, elevating advice for a game that was lost, or good news for an injured player. These persons are always giving something of real value. Their sincere action is a wholesome influence on everyone concerned.

Sportsmanship

One of the basic tenets of good sportsmanship is equanimity. Somebody loses and somebody wins every contest. It is healthy to cultivate even-mindedness so that one bears up well under losses and does not boast about victories. Good sportsmanship has its roots in the Golden Rule: Do unto others as you would have others do unto you. This rule requires a fair amount of level-headedness and presence of mind.

Professional Codes of Ethics

A code of ethics accepted by members of a specific professional organization, represents a commitment from individuals to uphold worthy social and moral values and to maintain honorable behavioral patterns. Normally, such codes are developed and refined by the members themselves and express the ideals and goals of the profession. For example, the purpose of the code of ethics for the American Football Coaches Association is stated as follows:

> The Code of Ethics has been developed to protect and promote the best interests of the game and the coaching profession. Its primary purpose is to clarify and distinguish ethical and approved professional practices from those which are detrimental. Its secondary purpose is to emphasize the purpose and value of football and to stress proper functions of coaches in relations to schools, players, and the public.
>
> The ultimate success of the principles and standards of this Code depends on those for whom it has been established—the football coaches. (23)

Some codes of ethics include established procedures to discipline violators of the code. The purpose of the discipline is to suppress the selfish motives of individuals whose violations provide advantages over opponents. The discipline can take the form of a letter of reprimand or probation. In extreme cases, individuals might be expelled from the organization. An example is the football coach who was found guilty of spying on an opponent prior to a championship game. The conference decided that the football team should be placed on a one-year probation, denying them the right of T.V. participation and playing in the championship. The coach was severely reprimanded and restricted in recruiting. The American Football Coaches Association could, if the ethics committee decided, expel the individual from its organization.

Other codes of ethics such as that for the Association for Intercollegiate Athletics for Women (AIAW) do not at this time include methods of disciplining violators. Rather, such organizations look on the codes as guidelines for members to follow in conducting a sports program. There is the hope that such exemplary behavior will add dignity to the profession and encourage desirable human characteristics.

Awareness is growing in modern American society of the need for established moral and ethical standards among its business, government, and professional leaders. Amorality and immorality among governmental officials surfaced during the Watergate scandal of the early 1970s. Corporate morality has been questioned as never before. Amateur athletic organizations recognized, early in their development, the need for codes of conduct to guide their members. Examples of such codes for athletic coaches follow.

The California Interscholastic Federation

Code of Ethics

It is the duty of all concerned with high school athletics:

1. To emphasize the proper ideals of sportsmanship, ethical conduct and fair play.
2. To eliminate all possibilities which tend to destroy the best values of the game.
3. To stress the values derived from playing the game fairly.
4. To show cordial courtesy to visiting teams and officials.
5. To establish a happy relationship between visitors and hosts.
6. To respect the integrity and judgment of sports officials.
7. To achieve a thorough understanding and acceptance of the rules of the game and the standards of eligibility.
8. To encourage leadership, use of initiative, and good judgment by the players on a team.
9. To recognize that the purpose of athletics is to promote the physical, mental, moral, social, and emotional well-being of the individual players.
10. To remember that an athletic contest is only a game—not a matter of life and death for player, coach, school, officials, fan, community, state, or nation.

The National Council of
State High School Coaches Association   ——————————————

National Code of Ethics for High School Coaches

As a professional educator

I WILL Exemplify the highest moral character, behavior, and leadership
Respect the integrity and personality of the individual athlete
Abide by the rules of the game in letter and in spirit
Respect the integrity and judgment of sports officials
Demonstrate a mastery of and continuing interest in coaching
Encourage a respect for all athletics and their values
Display modesty in victory and graciousness in defeat
Promote ethical relationships among coaches
Fulfill responsibilities to provide health services and an environment free of safety hazards
Encourage the highest standards of conduct and scholastic achievement among all athletes
Seek to inculcate good health habits including the establishment of sound training rules
Strive to develop in each athlete the qualities of leadership, initiative, and good judgement

Principles and practices of L/E.

The Association for
Intercollegiate Athletics for Women (AIAW)   ——————————————

The purpose of the AIAW Code of Ethics is to provide a means of assisting personnel and students of AIAW member institutions to identify ethical conduct in intercollegiate sports and to encourage those involved to pursue actions which are appropriate. The Code is not intended to be enforceable rules of conduct, the violation of which would require disciplinary action by AIAW, but rather is a guide for all concerned to apply in various aspects of sport programs. The Code of Ethics cannot be all inclusive but it does identify many areas of concern. AIAW encourages everyone involved to continue to identify and pursue conduct which promotes dignity in sport.

Code of Ethics for Coaches

One of the purposes of intercollegiate athletics is to provide experiences and opportunities for players to develop socially acceptable and personally fulfilling values and characteristics. Competitive sports provide practice opportunities in making value judgments and developing social relationships which will help to determine desirable behavior and personal qualities. A coach has the unique opportunity to influence players in selecting and developing their personal values and desirable qualities.

The philosophy, attitude, and behavior of the coach should exemplify quality human characteristics.

The coach should recognize the uniqueness and worth of each individual and help her to develop confidence, exhibit cooperation, and make a contribution to herself and others around her. Many experiences shared by the coach and player happen under stressful competitive circumstances which require maturity and experience to cope with them. These experiences provide teachable moments in which the coach should share her good judgment and show understanding and control which will influence the reactions of players, spectators, opponents, and the officials associated with the game.

A coach also has a responsibility to provide the information and training necessary for her players to achieve the highest degree of excellence for which they have potential. She also has a responsibility to promote sports and perpetuate the understanding of sports in our society. A basic part of this is the understanding and performance of the game in the true spirit of sport.

Ethical considerations for the coach:

1. Respect each player as a special individual with unique needs, experience, and characteristics and develop this understanding and respect among the players.
2. Have pride in being a good example of a coach in appearance, conduct, language, and sportsmanship, and teach the players the importance of these standards.
3. Demonstrate and instill in players a respect for and courtesy toward opposing players, coaches and officials.
4. Express appreciation to the officials for their contribution and appropriately address officials regarding rule interpretations of officiating techniques. Respect their integrity and judgment.
5. Exhibit and develop in one's players the ability to accept defeat or victory gracefully without undue emotionalism.
6. Teach players to play within the spirit of the game and the letter of the rules.
7. Develop understanding among players, stressing a spirit of team play. Encourage qualities of self-discipline, cooperation, self-confidence, leadership, courtesy, honesty, initiative and fair play.
8. Provide for the welfare of the players by:
   a. Scheduling appropriate practice periods,
   b. Providing safe transportation,
   c. Scheduling appropriate number of practice and league games,
   d. Providing safe playing areas,
   e. Using good judgment before playing injured, fatigued, or emotionally upset players,
   f. Providing proper medical care and treatment.
9. Use consistent and fair criteria in judging players and establishing standards for them.
10. Treat players with respect, equality, and courtesy.
11. Direct constructive criticism toward players in a positive, objective manner.

12. Compliment players honestly and avoid exploiting them for self-glory.
13. Emphasize the ideals of sportsmanship and fair play in all competitive situations.
14. Maintain an uncompromising adherence to standards, rules, eligibility, conduct, etiquette, and attendance requirements. Teach players to understand these principles and adhere to them also.
15. Be knowledgeable in aspects of the sport to provide an appropriate level of achievement for her players. Have a goal of quality play and excellence. Know proper fundamentals, strategy, safety factors, training and conditioning principles, and an understanding of rules and officiating.
16. Attend workshops, clinics, classes, and institutes to keep abreast and informed of current trends and techniques of the sport.
17. Obtain membership and be of service in organizations and agencies which promote the sport and conduct competitive opportunities.
18. Use common sense and composure in meeting stressful situations and in establishing practice and game schedules which are appropriate and realistic in terms of demands on player's time and physical condition.
19. Conduct practice opportunities which provide appropriate preparation to allow the players to meet the competitive situation with confidence.
20. Require medical examinations for all players prior to the sports season and follow the medical recommendations for those players who have a history of medical problems or who have sustained an injury during the season.
21. Cooperate with administrative personnel in establishing and conducting a quality athletic program.
22. Accept opportunities to host events and conduct quality competition.
23. Contribute constructive suggestions to the governing association for promoting and organizing competitive experiences.
24. Show respect and appreciation for tournament personnel and offer assistance where appropriate.
25. Be present at all practices and competitions. Avoid letting other appointments interfere with the scheduled team time. Provide time to meet the needs of the individual players.
26. Encourage spectators to display conduct of respect and hospitality toward opponents and officials and to recognize good play and sportsmanship. When inappropriate crowd action occurs, the coach should assist in curtailing the crowd reactions.

National Association of Intercollegiate Athletics (NAIA)

Code of Ethics

Purpose

A code of ethics is the essential tool with which to protect and promote the best interests of athletics, and the coaching profession. Its primary purpose is to clarify and distinguish ethical practices from those which are detrimental and harmful. Its secondary purpose is to emphasize the values of athletics in American educational institutions and to stress the functional contributions of coaches to their schools and players. Ethics must be defined as the basic principles of right action. Proper ethics in athletics imply a standard of character which affords all America's confidence and trust. The standards emphasized in this code certainly rest in the hands of those engaged in the athletic field.

Enforcement

The Executive Committee shall review any report of violations of the code, collect definite facts, consider all sides of any controversial issue and take such action as may seem appropriate. The committee is empowered by the membership to suspend or expel member schools whose athletic conduct or behavior has clearly violated the Code of Ethics. Such violations shall be reported in detail to the administrative head of the institution in which the incident occurred, together with an exact statement covering the action taken.

Basic Principles

In becoming a member of the athletic fraternity, whether as a school, a member of a coaching staff, or an individual, certain obligations and responsibilities are assumed in relation to your competitors as schools, teams, coaches and student bodies. These relationships are paramount in establishing and holding the kind of friendships which count most in our estimation of athletics in America today.

The essential elements in the Athletic Code of Ethics today are honesty and integrity. Coaches whose conduct reflects these two characteristics will bring credit to the field of athletics and to themselves. It is only through such conduct that athletics can earn and maintain a rightful place in our educational program and make a full contribution to our way of life.

Coach's Responsibility to the Institution

The coach should work with the admissions office of the college and should be permitted to recommend qualified athletes for admission, but should in no way permit the records or transcripts of prospective student-athletes to pass through this office, nor ever attempt to bring pressure upon the admissions officer or committee to admit an applicant merely because he possesses exceptional athletic ability.

Conduct of Administrators and Coaches

The administration of athletics should be carried out in such a manner that the educational aims of the institution will be fulfilled. The administrator of athletics is responsible that both the principles and practices of his program be consistent with broad educational purposes of his institution and the highest ethical and moral standards of sports.

The coach should make every effort to conduct his sports program to give full and active support to the educational aims of the institution. He should have a thorough knowledge of the academic rules and standards of his institution and give active evidence of his full support. He should cooperate fully in support of the faculty on eligibility requirements and insist that all athletes fulfill the same academic requirements as do all other students in the institution.

The coach should actively participate in committees and programs in support of the general educational program of the administration. He should actively participate in programs established by the institution for professional growth.

All coaches should conduct their sports programs in such a manner that both those who participate and those who are influenced in any way through the program be assured of its major emphasis toward building character, sound health, and broad educational aims, rather than merely a publicity medium built on winning.

The coach should insist upon adherence to both the letter and the spirit of high sportsmanship and playing rules. Under no circumstances should he permit evasion of playing rules to gain an advantage.

Officials

Game officials should be selected with care to assure that they be competent and experienced. Once selected, they should have the full support of the administration, coach and athletes in fulfilling their difficult job. Under no conditions should coaches, players, or spectators be permitted to make critical remarks to or about an official during a contest. Booing at athletic contests should be strictly prohibited.

Public Relations

One of the justifiable outcomes of intercollegiate sports is good public relations. Institutions and coaches have a definite responsibility to members of the news media and must furnish accurate and reliable news of public concern at all times. The News Bureau of the institution should be clearly instructed as to the purpose of aims of its intercollegiate program so that it may take every opportunity to inform the public of these aims and their relation to the broad aims of the institution.

Scouting

Scouting of competitors must be confined to regularly scheduled games. Intruding upon practice sessions and the like is to be strictly prohibited. The trading of game movies in lieu of personal scouting is encouraged wherever practicable, provided complete, high quality films are furnished at a mutually agreeable time in advance of the given contest.

Student Recruiting

All student recruiting for athletic purposes should be in harmony with recommended and acceptable practices of the institution and should be controlled by the institution's admissions committee. Where conferences exist, all conference rules regarding recruiting must be observed without favor.

Win-or-Else Pressures

Sports mirror society. The moral fiber of a society is clearly evident in its sports programs. The values of professional sports in America often become the erroneous standards for amateur sports. Violations of ethical standards in amateur sports occur when the precepts of some zealous professional coaches are literally applied to amateur athletics. Examples of quotes attributed to professional coaches are: "Defeat is worse than death because you live with it"; "Life without victories is like being in prison"; and "Winning isn't everything, it's the only thing." If this attitude ruled only professional athletics, it would present no real concern for the interscholastic coach. However, the conduct of professional athletics has a tremendous influence on all sports in America. Its influence filters through intercollegiate, interscholastic, junior high school, and even little-league programs.

The win-or-else philosophy found its roots in professional sports. Professional athletes and coaches are measured by individual statistics, records, and championships. Financial success through gate receipts, T.V. contracts, and play-off games becomes paramount to most owners. In professional sports, winning becomes a matter of financial survival because winning as a measure of excellence has been overemphasized in athletics. Former President Ford in commenting on the importance of winning said, "When you stop winning they not only start booing, they start forgetting" (15).

The win-or-else philosophy has definitely infiltrated the intercollegiate and interscholastic ranks. In many instances, coaches who do not produce winning programs are ousted from their positions. Many communities want and expect to have winners. They look on the athletic program as a source of community pride. Ara Parseghian, Notre Dame head football coach, when he retired in 1975 said, "I find myself physically exhausted and emotionally drained . . . the imperative of winning imposes pressures beyond the experience, perhaps beyond the imagination, of most of us" (34).

Darrell Royal, former head coach of football at the University of Texas, stated that all positions of any significance exert pressures on the individual. In his case, the fear of failure was paramount. He said, "For me the worst thing is fear of defeat. I find more and more I work and push to avoid defeat rather than attain victory . . . defeat is just so unacceptable, too damn tortuous to me" (34).

Motivational factors such as job security, promotions, peer recognition, and fear of failure can cause some coaches to behave unethically. But winning takes precedence over all else. The temptation to violate rules is great when winning becomes all-important. It is at these times that vision and foresight are important, for violations have a way of being discovered and everyone connected with them suffers—coaches, players, and institutions. It is during times of temptation to succumb to pressures that the coach should review a code of ethics. It will shore up his or her basic stability and strength. It will give understanding. It will answer the nagging question, "How far am I willing to go to win a game?" Winning should be a highly desirable by-product of athletics, not the *sine qua non* for the coach's existence.

Unethical Practices

Ethical behavior involving reported violations in both professional and intercollegiate athletics has a tremendous influence on the interscholastic coach.

Dr. Stephen Horn, president of Long Beach State University, after his school was placed on N.C.A.A. probation due to the unethical practices of the coaches, has become a loud advocate of codes of ethics, which include enforcement policies. He points out that high school coaches have a unique opportunity to learn of illicit offers by college recruiters. He strongly advocates the abolishment of a "non-tattle coaching fraternity" and the prompt reporting of unethical action to preserve amateur athletics (24).

Many college athletes become high school coaches. A few, unfortunately, incorporate the illicit practices they learned at the college level, feeling that if they are to win they must employ such techniques. Often, they do not even recognize the unethical nature of some practices. The following are some examples of unethical practices that occur at both the interscholastic and intercollegiate levels:

1. Allowing athletes to participate who are ineligible costs a coach and the school its entire schedule. In 1975, *The New York Times* reported several schools that had to forfeit play-off positions because ineligible players had helped forge winning records.
2. Sometimes the lack of talent tempts coaches to become unethical. A young California baseball player reported that during his sophomore year the school he attended had very little talent. His coach handed an outfielder a ball on a foggy day and instructed him to throw it in if a ball was hit over his head. The next two years, this same coach was a model of behavior because he had highly skilled players.
3. Recruiting at the high school level in most states is illegal, yet more and more interscholastic coaches are approaching prospective athletes. They use ethnic permits, promise grades to qualify for college, move parents from one district to another, or employ any other means they can to secure the services of a promising youngster.
4. Pete and Joe Douglas were identical twins and played on a high school basketball team. They wore jersey numbers 34 and 44. Pete was a better offensive player than Joe. Because of their similarity in appearance, opposing coaches would make defensive assignments by numbers. Their coach would have them change jerseys at half time if the game was close. This unethical practice cost the opposition more than one game and was unknown until the boys graduated.
5. Playing injured players or those with a contagious infection is unethical. A midwestern wrestling coach did not hesitate to use a wrestler even though he knew that the athlete had infectious conjunctivitis.
6. Running up the score on an opponent can cause embarrassment and should not be considered a good coaching technique. During the 1978 football season, a California high school had their opponent down by over fifty points in the first half. At no time during this period was there any attempt by the winning coach to ease the embarrassment of the opposition by playing individuals of lesser ability. As a result, the losing coach

decided he did not want his players to be further embarrassed and refused to play the second half.
7. Exchanging films of games has created some ethical problems. Most conferences agree on the number of films to be exchanged. Some coaches try to circumvent this agreement by obtaining more films than allowed. Another unethical practice is editing exchanged film. One midwestern college coach always provided the exact number of films as agreed on, but the big play prior to a touchdown was always missing. When challenged about this, he always gave the excuse of poor filming or processing.

Other examples of unethical conduct among coaches could be enlarged on, but perhaps a brief statement of them better serves the interests of the ideal coach. These examples are:

1. Attaining a college coaching position by delivering highly recruited athletes rather than by proven coaching ability
2. Forging records so that ineligible players may enroll at a university
3. Practicing deception or cheating in any way because of the peer pressure ("everyone else is doing it")
4. Intimidating reporters and the media about news releases
5. Providing wrong jersey numbers and height-weight data for athletic brochures
6. Organizing workouts or practice sessions that violate fixed starting dates
7. Allowing injured players to participate through the use of drugs that may be physiologically damaging
8. Breaking coaching contracts prior to their legal termination

Every coach is responsible for formulating ideals that teach students right and wrong action, thus making it easier for both coach and students to resist any unethical practices. Athletics should be one of the outstanding training grounds for the most important preparation that one ever makes—the game of life.

Summary

Ethics generally involves behavior described as good v. bad, right v. wrong and ought v. ought not. It is that part of philosophy that is concerned with moral problems and judgments.

There is a great need for ethical standards because of the widespread false notion that one should not infringe on the freedom of others. It is the responsibility of the maturer generation to advise the young.

Competition and the competitive urge are deeply rooted in American society. The United States developed, as a nation, with high regard for sportsmanship typified by, "It's not whether you win or lose, it's how you play the game."

Ethics is concerned with worthy human values that become the basis for honorable societal relationships. Involved are behavioral patterns that are honest and that exemplify high moral conduct.

Character traits influenced by ethical behavior are confidence, courage, honesty, honor, justice, loyalty, perseverance, responsibility, self-control, sincerity, and sportsmanship.

A code of ethics for a profession represents a commitment to uphold correct action and to maintain life-supporting behavioral patterns. Some codes of ethics provide enforcement procedures, whereas others serve as guidelines for conduct by all members.

The pressure of the win-or-else philosophy has filtered down from the professional ranks through intercollegiate, interscholastic, junior high school, and even youth sport programs. Motivational factors such as job security, promotions, peer recognition, and fear of failure can prompt some coaches to behave in an unethical manner. In times of pressure, a code of ethics provides stability and strength. Winning should be a highly desirable by-product of athletics and not the *sine qua non* for the coach's existence.

Most coaches who have been in the profession for any length of time have witnessed unethical practices. Violations of ethical codes are almost epidemic in scope. It is the responsibility of every coach to formulate ideals that give understanding of right and wrong action.

References

1. "AIAW Handbook 1978–1979", Washington, D.C.; AAHPER, 1978, 72.
2. Alley, Louis E. "Athletics in Education: The Double Edged Sword." *Phi Delta Kappan,* 56:2 (October 1974), 102–105, 113.
3. Barrett, Donald H., ed. *Values in America.* Notre Dame, Ind: University of Notre Dame Press, 1966, 182.
4. Black, Stu. "The Most Ruthless Game in Sports." *New West,* 3:24 (November 20, 1978), 81, 83–102.
5. Blackstone, William, and George L. Newsome. *Education and Ethics.* Athens, Ga.: University of Georgia Press, 1969, 135.
6. Boyle, Robert H. *Sport, Mirror of American Life.* Boston: Little, Brown, 1963, 59–60.
7. Brace, David K. "A Code of Ethics for a Dynamic Profession." *JOHPER,* 31:1 (January 1960), 19, 56–57.
8. Bueter, Robert J. "The Use of Drugs in Sports: An Ethical Perspective." *The Christian Century,* 89 (April 5, 1972), 394–398.
9. Camus, Albert. *Resistance, Rebellion and Death.* New York: Knopf, 1961, 271.
10. Combs, Arthur W. *The Myth of Competition—Sport Sociology, Contemporary Themes.* Dubuque, Iowa: Kendall/Hunt, 1976, 239.

11. Cooper, J. M., and D. Siedentrop. *The Theory and Science of Basketball.* 2nd ed. Philadelphia: Lea and Febiger, 1975, 229.
12. Deford, Frank. "Fans to Press: Drop Dead." *Sports Illustrated,* 45:24 (December 13, 1976), 24–27.
13. Dewey, Robert E., and Robert H. Hurlbutt, III. *An Introduction to Ethics.* New York: Macmillan, 1977, 499.
14. Fisher, A. C. *Psychology of Sport.* Palo Alto, Calif.: Mayfield, 1976, 503.
15. Ford, Gerald R., and John Underwood. "In Defense of the Competitive Urge." *Sports Illustrated,* 41:2 (July 8, 1974), 16–23.
16. Franklin, W. K. *Ethics.* Englewood Cliffs, N.J.: Prentice-Hall, 1963.
17. Frost, Reuben B. *Physical Education Foundations, Practices, Principles.* Reading, Mass.: Addison-Wesley, 1975, 507.
18. Fuoss, D. E., and R. J. Troppmann. *Creative Management Techniques in Interscholastic Athletics.* New York: John Wiley, 1977, 494.
19. Gove, P. B., ed. *Webster's Third New International Dictionary.* Springfield, Mass.: G. & C. Merriam, 1971.
20. Harsaniji, John C. *Essays on Ethics, Social Behavior and Scientific Explanation.* Dordrecht-Holland, and Boston: D. Reidel, 1976, 262.
21. Harvey, Buck. "In Pursuit of Cheaters." *Los Angeles Times,* part 3 (August 22, 1975), 1, 10.
22. Hawn, Jack. "Another Side of Recruiting." *Los Angeles Times,* part 3 (May 5, 1978), 1–13, 14.
23. Herbert, Dick, ed. *American Football Coaches Association—Code of Ethics et al.* Chapple, N.C.: Creative Printer, 1978, 88.
24. Horn, Stephen. "Ethics, Due Process, Diversity and Balance." *Vital Speeches of the Day.* Southold, N.Y.: City News, May 15, 1977, 463–468.
25. Hourani, George E. *Ethical Values.* London: George Allen and Unwin, 1956, 233.
26. Keating, J. W. "Sportsmanship as a Moral Category." *Ethics,* 85:1 (October 1964), 25–35.
27. Keenan, Francis W. *A Delineation of Dewey on Progressivism for Physical Education.* Unpublished doctoral dissertation. Champaign, Ill: University of Illinois, 1971.
28. Keith, Dwight. "Standards of Conduct in Athletics." *Coach & Athlete,* 36:2 (October 1973), 14.
29. Kennedy, Ray. "427: A Case in Point, part I." *Sports Illustrated,* 40:23 (June 10, 1974), 87–100.
30. ———. "427: Part II, The Pay Off." *Sports Illustrated,* 40:24 (June 17, 1974), 24–30.
31. Kroll, Walter. "Psychological Scaling of AIAW Code of Ethics for Players." *Research Quarterly,* 47:1 (March 1976), 126–133.
32. Leonard, George B. "Winning Isn't Everything, It's Nothing." *Sports Sociology, Contemporary Themes.* Dubuque, Iowa: Kendall/Hunt, 1976, 84–86.
33. Maharishi Mahesh Yogi. *The Science of Being and Art of Living.* Livingston Manor, N.Y.: Maharishi International University Press, 1975, 334.
34. Maher, Charles. "Bigtime Coach's Life 'Exquisite Tortures.' " *Los Angeles Times,* part 3 (January 6, 1975), 1, 4.
35. Masin, Herman L. "Does the End Justify the Means?" *Scholastic Coach,* 43:4 (December 1973), 5, 73.

36. Meschery, Tom. "There is a Disease in Sports Now." *Sports Illustrated,* 37:4 (October 2, 1972), 56–63.
37. Michner, James A. *Sports in America.* New York: Random House, 1976, 466.
38. Osterhoudt, R. G., ed. *The Philosophy of Sport—A Collection of Original Essays.* Springfield, Ill.: Charles C. Thomas, 1973, 359.
39. Padive, Sandy. "What Kind of Law and Order are Coaches Talking About?" *Los Angeles Times,* part 3 (November 13, 1973), 1, 8.
40. Parsons, Terry W. "What's Right about Athletics?" *The Physical Educator,* 31:1 (March 1974), 49.
41. Purdy, Robert L. *The Successful High School Athletic Program.* West Nyack, N.Y.: Parker, 1973, 263.
42. Ralston, J., M. White, and S. Wilson. *Coaching Today's Athlete—A Football Textbook.* Palo Alto, Calif.: National Press Books, 1971, 471.
43. Russell, L. J., J. D. Maffott, and A. Macbeath. "Is Anthropology Relevant to Ethics?" *Aristotelian Society,* 20 (1946), 61–122.
44. Sabock, Ralph J. *The Coach.* Philadelphia: W. B. Saunders, 1973, 272.
45. Scott, Jack. "Sport and the Radical Ethic." *Quest,* 19, (January 1973), 71–77.
46. Shea, Edward J. *Ethical Decisions in Physical Education and Sport.* Springfield, Ill.: Charles C. Thomas, 1978, 228.
47. Smith, Gary. "Violence in Sport." *JOHPER,* 42:3 (March 1971), 45–47.
48. "Sports Recruiting: A College Crisis." *Readers Digest,* 105:627 (July 1974), 107–112.
49. Stone, Marvin. "Are Ethics on the Way Back?" *U.S. News & World Report* (January 22, 1979), 80.
50. "The Ethics of Competition: Three Viewpoints." *JOHPER,* 42:3 (March 1971), 87–90.
51. "The Newswire: N.C.A.A. Investigating Fund Created for Missouri Coach." *Los Angeles Times,* part 3 (November 11, 1978), 4.
52. "The Rat Race." *Los Angeles Times,* part 3 (May 6, 1975), 1.
53. Wilterman, Marvin. "Winning Isn't Everything." *The Clearing House,* 51 (May 1977), 394–397.

LOCKER-ROOM LORE...

"With a coach's salary, you can be a poor **winner too!**"

"I've forgotten more about coaching than some coaches will ever know... sometimes I think that's my **trouble!**"

DEFINITION OF A COACH — "A FELLOW WHO IS WILLING TO LAY DOWN AN ATHLETE'S LIFE FOR HIS SCHOOL."

"IF AT FIRST YOU DON'T SUCCEED... HAVE THE WIFE PACK AND CALL A MOVING VAN."

SOAP

GLENN ZULAUF

P.S. ————————————————————————

In looking over the information I've presented about various aspects of your future profession, I realize that there are a few additional ideas I'd like to offer you. So, let me add a rather lengthy P.S., which gives practical suggestions about how to apply for a position, hints about teaching and coaching salaries (a topic one unfortunately can't ignore!), and my views on athletic awards and team travel policies.

When you have read and digested all your Old Coach's ideas, you should be well prepared to take on the exciting and challenging position of high school coach.

To find the coaching position that best suits your talents and abilities, the first thing to do is contact your **college placement office,** where, I assume, you registered early in your senior year. As a result of your registration, this office will have on file a confidential record of your academic achievements and extracurricular activities, and letters of recommendation written by people who know your personal qualifications. You can ask the placement office to mail this information to school administrators who might be interested in hiring you. Also, because the office receives data about available positions from many school districts, if you tell them you are looking for a position they can match your qualifications and desires with the specifications of different jobs and recommend that you get in touch with particular schools. When you find a position that looks attractive, the office can give you information about the school district, salary schedules, employment conditions, and the area in general so that you know ahead of time whether or not you might be interested in working in that location. As a follow-up, the placement office will arrange an interview for you with the school representative. Keep in mind, too, that the college placement office offers counseling regarding your career planning and future occupational goals.

A surprising number of positions become available during the school year. Your patience and persistence can pay off. So check with the placement office frequently.

A **personal résumé** is essential, too, because if you hear of a job opening through a friend or a coach you will want to send off some basic information *quickly,* before the placement office machinery begins to work. There are many ways to prepare a résumé, but the best way to look professional is to have your information presented professionally. After you carefully choose a style of type and paper, you can use one of a number of inexpensive printing methods; above all, do not ditto, mimeograph, or xerox your material, because the result will be ordinary, and you want to look unique!

In the résumé, include all pertinent information about yourself, your experience, and your background: your full name, address, phone number, height, age, weight, marital status, number of children, place of birth, and general physical condition. Also describe your educational background— with subjects you can teach and sports you can coach—service record, experience—such as camp counseling—related to coaching, professional affiliations and activities, community activities, and any honors and awards you have received. In listing these things, do not be modest but include everything that will generate interest in you as a candidate. Describe the position you are seeking and your grade-level preference, if you have one.

In most states, it is illegal for employers to accept a job application or résumé with a picture of the applicant attached to the form or printed on it. You should check into the laws of the area where you send your résumé if you are considering sending a picture of yourself.

Once the school has received your résumé, you may be asked for further information. At this point, contact the placement office and ask them to forward your credentials. These should suffice for most situations if you keep them up to date. Be sure to keep your file current by asking your present employer for a letter of recommendation. Even though you have no intention of looking for another job, there are times when opportunities seem to drop into your lap. When that happens, it is helpful to be prepared and not to have to ask friends and coworkers for special letters.

A personal interview is most important for securing a position. Let me give you a few suggestions to consider in preparing for an interview.

Before the interview do your homework. Learn as much as you can about the area where the position is located, the school district, the athletic program, and the philosophy of athletics in the district. The placement office usually can give you information; if not, talk to people who know the area, or contact the local chamber of commerce. If there are things you don't understand or can't clarify in your preliminary work, don't hesitate to ask the interviewer questions. In this way, you will show that you are alert and interested.

Do some thinking about your own philosophy of education and athletics so that you can speak concisely about it. Most interviewers want to know your views on this aspect of the position and will question you either directly or indirectly. Remember, too, that most school districts require coaches to teach an academic subject as well as handle a sport, so be prepared to discuss educational as well as athletic issues.

Review in advance important questions: When would the job begin? To whom would you be responsible? Are there any restrictions on the athletic program? If so, what are they?

Remember that first impressions are lasting. I need not remind you, I'm sure, that a sloppy and unkempt appearance can have a negative influence on the interviewer.

Remain cool and collected at all times. Interviewers vary in their techniques: Some are friendly, while others like to play the devil's advocate and put you on the defensive so that they can find out how you react under pressure.

Before leaving the interview, be sure you know who will take the next step: Will they contact you, or should you call them after a certain length of time?

Following the interview, it is a good idea to write down your impressions as a reminder to yourself. Never take notes during an interview; most interviewers find that offensive. They might also wonder why, in something so important as a job interview, you need written notes to remember what you have talked about.

If you feel it is necessary, you could discuss your interview with your college coach or someone in the placement office. They may be able to clarify some issues or pass along some feedback from the interviewer that can be helpful to you in the future.

Generally, when your are offered a position, you are given a definite period of time to accept or reject the job. If you are uncertain, discussing the pros and cons of the job with other people can help you discover what you really want to do. *Accepting a position,* either orally or in writing, is a serious step, and once you say yes, you are committed to the job. If you change your mind, you will have to deal with hard feelings and possible legal hassles, and that is not only a bad way to begin a career, but also reflects unfavorably on you. After you accept a position, be sure to notify the placement office to take you off the "available" list.

It might be a good idea for you to read an article by Lou Kleinman entitled "A New Dimension in Teacher Selection" (*The Journal of Educational Sociology,* September 1960). It applies to all new teachers and coaches, and it would be worth your time. Kleinman discusses community factors, the school program, organization and administration of the school, personnel policies and practices, facilities, special services, and specific questions regarding particular positions.

Tommy, as you begin your inquiries into coaching and teaching positions, it is very important that you understand salary schedules and supplementary payment for extra duties. You will soon realize that there is no uniform standard of payment for teachers and coaches. Procedures vary among school districts according to basic philosophies and the districts' abilities to pay for desired services.

Most school districts have established *salary schedules* for all grades from kindergarten through twelfth grade. These schedules are based on a teacher's education and years of teaching experience, usually beginning with a B.A. degree and no experience. From this level there is a yearly progression to the top of the position classification. After twelve years in a particular classification, a teacher in most school districts receives the highest salary established for his or her position. To encourage teachers to continue education related to their positions, additional categories or classifications are established, based on the B.A. degree plus a given number of education units taken at the postgraduate level. For example, a district might define the second classification as B.A. degree plus fifteen postgraduate units. There is another classification for every additional fifteen units until the doctorate level is reached.

The base salary for the second classification is higher than that for the first, and so on. For example, Mudville High's salary schedule begins at $9,000 for someone with a B.A. degree and no previous experience; classification 2, which includes teachers with a B.A. degree plus fifteen education units, but no experience, starts at $9,500; classification 3, those with a B.A. degree plus thirty units, or an M.A. degree, begins at $10,000. Each promotion within a classification is represented by a salary increase. For this salary, the teacher is expected to handle five classes of instruction plus normal teaching duties.

How salaries are paid differs widely among school districts. Many districts pay salaries in nine monthly installments that correspond with the academic year; others extend the payments over a ten-month period; and some districts pay salaries in twelve monthly installments that correspond with the school fiscal year. Because financial planning is so important, you should be aware of how the school district handles payment before you sign a contract.

In recent years, many school districts have adopted the policy of giving teachers **supplementary or extra pay** for services that exceed normal duties. Although many districts include all positions—athletic coach, band leader, drama instructor, and publications consultant—in this policy, not all school districts give additional payments for all activities. For example, in Louisville, Kentucky, athletic coaches receive extra payment, but band leaders and others do not. This situation obviously can create problems for a coach's relationships with other teachers.

There are some school districts in the country that handle the supplementary pay problem by giving teachers with extra duties release time instead of money. For instance, a teacher would not be expected to teach five classes daily but rather would be credited with one or two classes for extra duties, depending on the nature of his activity and the hours involved. You remember that I always had the first two periods free and didn't report until the third period. This release time was the way our school district reimbursed me for the many hours I put in after the other teachers had gone home.

Supplementary payment in salary or release time, however, is not a nationally accepted practice. There are many school districts which hold to the premise that all teachers are expected to take on extra duties. In these districts, you will probably find that the salary schedules for teachers are higher than average, to compensate for the extra work expected.

The problem of how to deal with paying extra salaries for coaching or other extra teaching duties is not an easy one to solve. The program needs and financial strengths of school districts differ a great deal, so it is almost impossible to suggest a national solution. In fact, the question of paying supplementary salaries for coaching has contributed to the worries of school districts, which are having a tough time financing the athletic program. They have had to cut back some programs and, in doing so, have deprived students the opportunity to have a rewarding athletic experience. This problem, Tommy, is one you and all other high school coaches must think about.

Tommy, in your new position as high school coach, you may be responsible for deciding which player should receive **athletic awards.** An athletic award is a symbol of achievement, and its value is recognition for superior performance. In the first Olympic games in Greece, winners were given an

performance. In the first Olympic games in Greece, winners were given an olive wreath, the highest athletic honor in Greek society. Now, Olympic winners are awarded medals, and high school athletes receive letters, medals, and various other symbols of high achievement.

In giving interscholastic athletic awards, you should base your decisions on policies that support the aims of education. The monetary value of these awards is limited by guidelines established by the National Federation of High School Athletic Associations and the respective state high school athletic associations. Some states, such as Utah, elect not to give awards but rather stress the value of participation.

Different schools have different policies for awards, depending on the philosophies of the coaches and athletic directors responsible for the programs. Some have very strict participation rules, because they feel that awards should reflect superior achievement and be considered an honor. Other schools believe that an award should be given to each student who makes the squad and that it thus can be utilized as part of the athletic department's public relations program. Tommy, as you know, my own conviction is that there should be a happy medium between these two extremes. You should carefully establish for yourself what you believe to be the best policy.

The criteria for participation differ between team and individual sports. Awards for team sports usually are based on total time a player has spent in competition. If a school does not have a method of keeping accurate records of playing time, the usual policy is to credit an athlete with innings, quarters, or halves, regardless of the actual time involved. Individual sports awards usually are based on achievement in competition or on a point system that takes into account the number of times an athlete has participated and his or her order of finishing.

Regardless of the participation requirements, you should consider two special criteria. **Award standards** should be flexible enough so that a student who doesn't fulfill the minimum participation requirement but has contributed something special or has served with merit can be recommended for an award. I'm thinking in particular of a senior who played on the football squad for several years but, in his last season, failed to meet the participation requirement although he had all other qualifications for the award. It seems to me that this sort of contribution deserves special notice and should be rewarded. Also, you should consider players who undoubtedly would have met the participation requirement if they hadn't been injured. In this situation, give thought to the athlete's grade level in school and whether or not he or she would have an opportunity to achieve the award later in his or her school career.

Tommy, most state athletic associations have suggested criteria for awards. But if you are asked for your opinion about awards, you might want to keep in mind the following suggestions.

Letters should be the same size for all sports. The old concept of major and minor sports is disappearing, and each athlete thinks—and should think—that his or her own sport is as important as any other. If you want to show a distinction within a sport, you can attach a small symbol of the activity to the letter to develop players' pride in their particular achievements.

Captain's awards have merit, since to be the captain of a team is especially significant. In some schools, this position represents the highest athletic award an athlete can receive. Captains of all sports might have special symbols on their letters.

If a team wins an interscholastic championship, you might want to give team members special recognition. These extra awards should cost no more than is allowed by the state and national athletic federations.

When you give athletic awards, don't forget your student managers. They devote many hours to the team and deserve special recognition.

There are two *problems in presenting athletic awards.* Sometimes well-meaning community leaders want to set up special awards for players and teams that have been particularly successful. These people generally are unaware of the financial limitations on awards placed by athletic associations, and it is your responsibility to see that the value of the awards is kept within reason.

You also must decide how athletic awards will be made. You know that I strongly favor award assemblies in the fall, winter, and spring that include all student-body awards for academic achievement, sports, music, leadership, and whatever other categories are designated by school leaders. In this way, athletics are not singled out or given a place of prominence as a school activity. They are included as just one of the educational contributions of the entire school program.

Tommy, some of my ideas might be classified as old fashioned, although you must admit I've tried to stay on the young side in my approach to life. Because I grew up during the difficult years of the Depression, one of my basic beliefs is that things worth having are worth working for. My high school coach set high standards for his players to meet if they wanted to be part of *the traveling squad.* Just because an athlete was out for the sport didn't guarantee a trip to an away game. I can remember times when players were not included for trips because they had been constantly late to practice. Do you remember when I left our starting center behind because he didn't report on time? He told me later he learned a very important lesson from that experience.

As a coach you will have to set your own standards for team travel, and they will depend on your basic philosophy of athletics. Be certain that you fully believe in whatever standards you set, because you can't enforce rules that aren't in accord with your own convictions.

More than likely, your athletic director or state athletic association will propose travel policies which you'll be required to follow. If not, consider the following suggestions.

You should follow the procedure recommended by most authorities and provide *transportation* for athletic teams only in public bonded carriers. Some school districts have their own buses, and these vehicles can be used legally for extracurricular activities. In states where school buses can't be used for this purpose, you will have to rely on private cars; in this case, you must be especially aware of the legal aspects described in Chapter 9 and make sure that cars are driven only by adults who are fully aware of their responsibilities.

If in some rare instance, your players are invited to a school that is so far away that they must travel by plane, use only certified commercial carriers. There is too much risk involved in chartering a noncommercial plane.

For the convenience of squad members and parents, it is important to establish a *travel schedule* with departure and return times. Allow enough travel time to cover unexpected delays like flat tires and heavy traffic. Also, count on giving your players time to walk around and unwind, to dress slowly, and to prepare to play. If they have to hurry, they may not really be ready to perform, and by the time they get going, the other team may have an unbeatable advantage.

Many school districts require that before a player may travel, he must have a *parental permission* slip on file. This permission might take the form of a yearly permit or notes for individual games. Even if no permission is needed, it is wise to let parents know about each trip for their own information and for your public relations with them.

A *list* of squad members who will travel to a particular away game should be posted well in advance of the event. Some coaches make the mistake of posting a list of players who will not be included, an approach that can have a detrimental effect on these athletes' morales.

Give each player the responsibility for his or her own personal playing *equipment* and student managers responsibility for team equipment.

The best general rule is that team members should *dress* appropriately for the manner of transportation and be aware that they are representing their school.

Although, for some reason, players seem to go on *eating* binges when they are traveling, you should encourage them to eat the sorts of meals they normally would eat at home. Consider the requirements of the sport and individual needs when determining the quantity of food that the athletes should have.

If there is an athletic director or faculty representative accompanying the team, he or she should be in charge of all *finances*. But if you are responsible for travel money, make sure that you keep a careful daily record of what you spend. This information will protect you if you are questioned by school officials, and it can help in preparing future budgets. Take time to become familiar with some of the common procedures involved in handling expenses: Cash payment with a receipt, payment by voucher or charge account, and payment made out of a general cash allowance and does not require a receipt. Don't cash contract guarantee checks when you are traveling unless it is absolutely necessary.

Most schools have insurance policies that cover travel for athletic teams. If your school does not have *insurance,* insist on some coverage, because you and your players should not travel without it.

For *an away game,* you should know the exact location, time, dressing facilities, admission prices, regulations on complimentary tickets, seating arrangements, and who will officiate. Also, you should find out if any band or cheerleader arrangements need to be made.

If your school's award policy requires an exact record of individual *participation* in a game, give the student manager the responsibility of writing down playing times for each player. If you don't need such a precise record, the score book or team results will suffice.

You must impress upon all the players that they are a vital part of the group and that their *behavior* will reflect on the team and the school. You should discourage taking souvenirs and state that any destruction is the responsibility of the person who causes it. Close supervision is essential, whether you believe in strict authority or informal checks. One rule you should follow is to make only regulations you are willing to enforce with both your strongest and your weakest players, stars as well as substitutes. If you are fair and present a good example to your students, you will earn their respect and foster in all of them a desire to behave in a manner that will be a credit to their team and their school.

Tommy, from time to time you should sit back and *evaluate yourself* and your athletic program. Look at each success and failure to determine what you did right and wrong, and try to repeat actions and approaches that have produced positive results while eliminating or improving those that have not worked. In analyzing the different causes of successful performance, consider particular emotional forces that helped you achieve desired goals.

Keep in mind the fact that there are people within the school community who constantly are evaluating you and your program, judging the team and you as a coach each time a game is played. Many of their opinions will be formed according to particular interests or prejudices. You will probably not be able to please everyone; but if you have a firm conviction and faith in your own beliefs and methods, you will be respected. A periodic look in the mirror is for your own benefit, Tommy. It will help you judge your progress and give you a perspective on how your coaching efforts fit into the changes that are always taking place in athletics. Perhaps one of the greatest thrills of the profession is the challenge of trying out new ideas. Before you adopt a new method or approach, examine it, weigh it, and answer one very important question: does it contribute positively to the lives of your students, and will it help them deal with experiences beyond the realm of high school athletics?

Coach Art Gallon

A young, enthusiastic coach I once knew accepted a basketball coaching position in a small town in Oregon where basketball had never been very successful. To stimulate interest in the game, he convinced a civic organization to purchase basketball hoops and balls, which he placed strategically in every four blocks throughout the town. He received permission from the electric company to place the hoops on their poles, and then gave basketballs to boys who lived closest to each hoop. In a short time, basketball became an extremely important activity in this town; the high school team improved and soon dominated the state basketball tournament. Because this young coach had imagination and determination, he was able to put his ideas to work and make people become involved in something he believed in.

Use your ingenuity, and draw on your strong background when you meet the challenges of your new profession. Your enthusiasm and belief in the value of athletics will be transmitted to both your students and the people in the community.

Tommy, let me reiterate a few points. When you are applying for a teaching-coaching position, use your college placement office and take advantage of the services it offers; prepare a professional-looking résumé that includes all pertinent information; and think about how you can present a strong impression in a personal interview.

Look into salary schedules of the different school districts that interest you, and make sure you understand how supplementary payments are handled for extra teaching and coaching duties.

Review your philosophy of athletic awards, which recognize outstanding contributions made by the team, individual players, and student managers.

Set careful standards for team travel, taking into consideration the safety of the players, responsibility for equipment and finances, and the conduct of your students as representatives of their school.

And, finally, Tommy, step back and periodically review your own performance as a coach. Analyze your successes and failures so that you can strive to meet the educational goals of athletics and the challenges of your position.

Your Old Coach welcomes you to this rewarding profession and wishes you the best of luck.

Index

Achievement, as motivator, 51
"Act, of God, An" 215, 233
Act of omission, 233
Adams, Sam, 120
Adamson, G. T., 123
Adequacy, athlete's sense of, 54
Additive, drugs, 191
Aerobics, 121
Affiliation, as motivator, 52
Aggression, 9, 44
  and motivation, 52
Agonistic muscles, 77
Alcohol, 201
Allman, Fred, 80
American Medical Association (AMA), position
  on drug use, 190
Amphetamines, 191–194
  Harvard study, 192
Androgenic-Anabolic steroids, 194–195
Anesthetics, local, 197
Antagonistic muscles, 77
Appellate court, 233
Appenzeller, Herb, 222, 228
Aspiotis, Nicholas, 77
Association for Intercollegiate Athletics for
  Women, 30, 35–36
  history of, 35
  membership in, 36
  purposes of, 36
  regions, 35
Assumption of risk, defined, 234
Athletic director, 34
Athletic guarantees, 167–168
Athletic Motivation Inventory (A.M.I.), 44
Atlas, Charles, 96

Attractive nuisance, defined, 234
Awards, athletic, 307–309

Bannister, Roger, 55
Barbiturates, 195–196
Beecher, Henry K., 192
Bench press, 109, 111
Bennington, John, 56
Bent-over row, 109, 112
Beyers, Walter, 39
Bid purchasing, 129–131
Birch, David, 57
Blood doping, 198
Blum, Richard H., 206
Booster groups, 256–257
Bray, Father Kenneth, 59
Brickmore, Lee, 4
Briggs, Paul W., 7
Brown, Harmon, 271
Bryant, Bear, 243
Budget
  approval, 163
  construction, 159–163
  control and responsibility, 156–157
  criteria for, 157–159
  defined, 155
  periodic appraisal, 164
  preparation through data processing,
    169–181
Button, Sherman, 106

Caffeine, 201
Califano, Joseph, 266
California Interscholastic Federation, 291
Cardiorespiratory fitness, 119–123

Care and maintenance, of artificial surfaces, 145–149
Central purchasing, 133
Characteristics influenced by ethical standards, 287–290
Circuit training, 123–124
Coaches, 12–22
  certification of, 15
  educational qualifications of, 15
  as an example, 12
  moral qualifications of, 16
  personality qualifications of, 16–17
  physical qualifications of, 16
  professional qualifications of, 15–16
  school representative, 14
  as a teacher, 13–14
  types of , 19–22
Coachability, 44
Cocaine, 204
Codeine, 204
Codes of ethics, 290–296
  Association for Intercollegiate Athletics for Women, 292–294
  California Interscholastic Federation, 291
  National Association of Intercollegiate Athletics, 294–296
Cokins, Gary, 7
College placement office, 308
Combs, Arthur, 50
Common resistance training methods, 99
  bulk method, 99
  cheating method, 99
  DeLorme method, 99
  double progressive method, 99
  Oxford method, 99
  power method, 99
  superset method, 99
  triset method, 99
Competition, 9, 27, 30, 65
Conditioning, 75, 82–83
  aneròbic, 79
  for the female athlete, 268–271
  fluids and, 90–91
  overload technique, 77, 82
  prolonged training, 82–83
Conditioning programs, 75–125
  circuit training, 123–124
  in-season, 85–86
  isokinetic, 115–118
  isometric, 96–98
  isotonic, 106–115

  mental attitude in, 91
  off-season, 83, 107–108
  post-season, 86–87
  pre-season, 85–86
  strength maintenance, 86
Confidence, 57, 287
Contributory negligence, 216–234
Cooley, E. W., 30
Cooper, Kenneth, H. 121
Cortisone, 196
Counsilman, James, 53, 59, 117
Courage, 11, 288
Court, Margaret, 271
Cowan, Charlie, 64, 189
Criteria, budget, 157–159
Curiosity, and motivation, 52
Curls, 111, 114
Curl-ups, 114, 118
Curtice, Jack C., 12–13

Dangers, coaching practices, 229–231
  advocating violence, 229
  allowing fights between players, 230
  lack of adequate training, 230
  play with injury, 229–230
  use of difficult styles of play, 229
  use of voluntary practice sessions, 230
Data processing, and athletic budgets, 169–181
De Lorme, Thomas L., 98, 99
Defendant, 234
Defense against negligence, 215–216
Dependence, drug, 199–200
Desire, stimulation of player's, 57
Determination, 57–58
Dewey, John, 26
Dimethylsulfoxde (DMSO), 196
Director, *see* Athletic director
Direct purchasing, 129
Discipline, 7, 67
Downers, *see* Barbiturates
Drug abuse, 206–207
Drugs, abused, 195–196, 200–206
  alcohol, 201
  barbiturates, 195–196
  caffeine, 201
  cocaine, 204
  codeine, 204
  hallucinogenic, 201–202
  heroin, 204

Drugs, abused, continued
  lysergic acid diethylamide (LSD), 202–203
  marijuana, 203–204
  methadone, 205
  morphine, 205
  narcotics, 204–206
  opium, 205
  paregoric, 205
  phencyclidine, 205–206
  psychedelic, 201–203
Drug use, in athletics
  as additives, 191
  AMA position, 190
  coach's responsibility, 190–191, 206–207
  and dependence, 199–200
  ethical implications in, 191
  for pain, 198–199
  legal implications for, 191
  professional athletes, influence on, 187–191
  psychological dependence, 199–200
  restorative, 190–191
Due process, 234
Drying room, 140

Educational values in athletics, 8–12
Ego-reinforcement, in motivation, 54
Eisenhower, Dwight D., 6
Endurance, 78–79, 97
  cardiorespiratory, 79, 97
  muscular, 78
English common law, 212
Equipment
  care and maintenance of, 139–149
  defined, 128
  drying room, 140
  issuing, 140
  manager, 139
  marking, 141–142
  measuring for, 138
  player responsibility, 144–145
  reconditioned, 139
  room, 140
  storage, 142
Esslinger, Arthur A., 15
Ethics defined, 286–287
  and drug use, 191
  need for, 284–285
  and society, 285–286

Fabrics, care of, 142–143
Facilities
  defined, 128
  legal problems, 222–223

Faculty control, 27
Failure, and motivation, 54–55
Fatigue, 78–79, 187
Fears, Tom, 117
Female athlete conditioning for, 268–271
  problems of, 273–275
  weight training for, 270–271
Female image, 266–268
Financial support, for interscholastic athletics, 164–167
Fiscal year, 155
Fleming, Peggy, 57
Fluids, and conditioning, 90–91
Flexibility, 75, 78
Ford, Gerald, 285
Foster, Marcus A., 7
Frederick, Jane, 271

Gain, material, 55
Game officials, *see* Officials, game
Garvey, Steve, 53
Giles, John Warren, 217
Gimmicks, *see* Motivational techniques
Gipp, George, 62
Government immunity, 212–213
Grieve, Andrew, 223
Guarantees, athletic, 167–168

Haines, George, 64
Hallucinogenics, 201–202
Hamilton, Brutus, 56
Heroin, 204–205
Hettinger, T., 96
Hofmann, Albert, 202
Honesty, 288
Honor, 288
Hornung, Paul, 106

Iba, Henry, 56
Immunity, legal, 212–213
Independence, as motivator, 52
In loco parentis, 234
Invitees, 223
Initiative, 9
In-season conditioning, 85–86
Interscholastic athletics, 6–32
  development of, 26–28
  educational values of, 6–12
  faculty control of, 27

Interscholastic athletics, continued
  financial support for, 164–167
  girl's participation in, 28
  holding power of, 7–31
  personal values of, 7–12
  state associations for, 31–32
Isokinetic exercises, 115–18
Isometric exercises, 96–98
Isotonic exercises, 98–115
Issuing, of equipment, 140

Jacoby, Ed, 118
Jockums, Dick, 64
Johnson, Patti, 64
Johnston, Willie, 190
Judicial judgments, 214
Justice, 288

Kennedy, John F., 6
Kerlan, Robert, 192
Klafs, C. E., 270
Kreuger, Charlie, 199

Land, Herman W., 203
Law
  and equipment, 221–222
  and facilities, 222–223
  and legal statutes, 213–214
  product liability, 222
  tort liability, 214–215
Leadership, 44
Leather goods, care and maintenance of,
  143–144
Leg development, 106–107
Liability, tort, 214–215
Liston, Emil S., 37
Litigation, defined, 234
Local anesthetics, 197
Lombardi, Vince, 63, 288
Long, Edwin, 169
Lowe, Paul, 187
Loyalty, 289
Lyon, Leland, 44
Lyon, M. J., 270
Lysergic acid diethylamide (LSD), 202–203

MacCracken, Chancellor, 39
Maintenance, equipment, *see* Equipment,
  care and maintenance
Malina, R. M., 272
Mandell, Arnold J., 189
Marciano, Rocky, 57, 78

Marijuana, 203–204
Marking, of equipment, 141–142
Marshall, George E., 32
Masculinity, display of, 54
Maslow, Abraham, 53
Measuring, for athletic equipment, 138
Medical assistance, 226–228
Medical examination, 79–80, 226
Meggysey, Dave, 189
Menstruation, 271–273
Mental attitude, 56–58
  in conditioning, 91
Methadone, 205
Meyers, Debbie, 83
Midwest Federation of State High School Ath-
  letic Associations, 32
Moore, Billie, 243
Morals, defined, 287
Morgan, R. E., 123
Morphine, 205
Moser, Charles H., 240
Motivation, 53–56, 64–68
  competition and, 65
  ego-reinforcement for, 54
  emotional outlet as, 55
  fear of failure, 54–55
  incentives, 51–53
  material gain, 55
  mental preparation, 64
  need for physical movement in, 55
  parental recognition, 54
  personal pride as, 55
  physical fitness as, 55
  practice sessions as, 65–66
  stress addiction as, 55
  techniques, 58–62
Motivation and attitude, 56–58
  confidence, 57
  desire, 57
  determination, 57
  goal setting, 57
Müller, E. Z., 96
Munson, Thurman, 189
Muscle(s)
  agonistic, 77
  antagonistic, 77
  relaxants, 197

Naismith, James, 37
Narcotics, 204–206. *See also* Drugs, abused
Nash, Jay B., 28
National Association for Girls' and Womens'
  Sports, 30, 35

National Association of Intercollegiate Athletics, 37–38, 294–296
  membership in, 37
  objectives of, 37–38
  purposes of, 37
National Collegiate Athletics Association, 38–40
  membership in, 40
  policies of, 39
  purpose of, 39–40
National Council of Secondary School Athletic Directors, 34–35
National Federation of State High School Associations, 32–33
Negligence and the law, 215–216
Newell, Pete, 56
Nutrition, in athletics, 87–90
Nyad, Diana, 271

O'Dell, Griffith C., 133
O'Donnell, Joe, 187
Off-season conditioning, 83, 107–108
Officials, game, 248–249
Ogilvie, Bruce, 44, 56
Olcott, Amy, 271
Opium, 205
Oral enzymes, therapeutic use of, 197–198
Overload principle, in conditioning, 77, 82
Owens, Jesse, 85

Pain, and drug use, 198–199
Paregoric, 205
Parental permission slips, 310
Parent Teachers Association (PTA), 252–253
Parents
  and public relations, 246–247
  recognition by and motivation, 54
Peer recognition, 53–54
"Pep pills", *see* Amphetamines
Pep talks, 61–62
Peppler, Mary Jo, 271
Perceptual method, and motivation, 50
Perseverance, 9, 42, 289
Personal resumé, 304–305
Phencyclidine, 205–206
Physical drug dependence, *see* Drug use
Physical examination, 79–80, 226
Physical fitness, defined, 76
Plaintiff, defined, 234
Players
  and care and maintenance of equipment, 144–145
  and public relations, 243–246

Plyometrics, 118–119
Porter, H. V., 32
Post-season conditioning, 86–87
Power, 53
Practice
  outlines, 69
  sessions, 65–68
Praise, 58
Precedent decisions, 214
Pre-season conditioning, 85
Professionals, athletics and drugs, 187–191
Prolonged training, effects of, 82–83
Prothro, Tommy, 107
Prudence, 216–217
  characteristics, 217
  defined, 216
Psychological drug dependence, 199–200
Psychedelic drugs, 201–203
Psychometrics, 44
Public recognition, and motivation, 54
Public relations, 238–259
  defined, 239–240
  development of, 240–243
  with booster groups, 256–257
  with college recruiters, 250–252
  with game officials, 248–249
  with news media, 253–256
  with other coaches, 247–248
  with parents, 246–247
  with Parent Teachers Association, 252–253
  with players, 243–246
  with spectators, 258–259
  with staff members, 247–248
  with students, 257–258
  and teachers, 248
Purchasing policies, 133–138
Purchasing procedures, 129–133
  bid, 129–133
  central, 133
  direct, 129

Qualifications
  for coaches, 14–18
  for supervision, 218–219

Ralston, John, 18, 56, 64
Recognition, and motivation, 53–54
Recognition, continued
  parental, 54
  peer, 53
  public, 54
Recruiters, college, 250–252
Reeder, W. G., 155

Resistance training methods, *see* Common resistance training methods
Responsibility, 289
Restorative drugs, 190–191
Richards, Jack W., 56
Risk, assumption of, 234
Rockne, Knute, 62
Roosevelt, Theodore, 38
Roth, Dick, 57
Rowland, W. R., 106
Rudolph, Wilma, 271
Running, in cardiorespiratory fitness, 120–121
Russell, Bill, 192–193
Ryun, James, 81

Sabock, Ralph, 283
Saggau, Bernie, 7
Salary schedules, 306–307
"Sanity Code," 39
Sargent, Dudley A., 27
"Save harmless" law, 213
Self-confidence, 57
Self-control, 289
Self-discipline, 9, 65–68
Sensory factors, motivational, 53
Sharman, Bill, 189
Shepherd, R. J., 268
Sincerity, 290
Sit-ups, 112, 116
Smith, Gene M., 192
Smith, L. W., 32
Snygg, Donald, 50
Sources, sporting goods, 149–151
Sovereign immunity, 212
Spectators, control of, 258–259
Sportsmanship, 290
Squats, 111, 115
Staff members, and public relations, 247–248
Standing press, 109, 110
State athletic associations, 31–32
Statute, 235
Staunton, Marshall A., 231
Stehn, Lowry, 218
Stephens, Hubert, 118
Steroids, androgenic-anabolic, 194–195
Storage, equipment, 142
Strength, 75, 76–78, 83–84, 97
  increase, 83–84
Stroke volume, increase of , 121
Students, and public relations, 257–258
Supervision, and the law, 218–221, 224
  necessity for supervisor's presence, 220
  number of supervisors needed, 219–220

qualifications and training, 218–219
  supervision of facilities, 224
Supplementary (or extra) pay, 309
Supplies
  care and maintenance of, 139–144
  defined, 128
Sutton, Don, 64

Teachers, and public relations, 248
Team discussions, motivational techniques, 60
Team rules and regulations, 231
Tension levels, 62–63
Title IX, 30, 168, 264–266
Tort liability, defined, 214–215
Toughness, mental, 44
Training
  prolonged effects of, 82–83
  of supervisors, 218–219
Transportation, and legal problems, 225–226
Traveling squads, 309–310
Trust, 44
Tutko, Thomas, 44, 56
Tyler, Peggy Peterson, 30
Types of coaches, 19–22
  authoritarian, 19
  businesslike, 21
  creative, 21–22
  easy-going, 21
  intense, 19–21
  "nice-guy," 19

Unethical coaching practices, 297–299
Unique problems
  of the female athlete, 273–275
  of males coaching females, 275–276
  of mixed athletic competition, 276–278
  of the woman coach, 273–275
Upright row, 109–110, 113

Values
  educational, 6–11
Values, continued
  personal, 8–11
Veroff, Joseph, 51
Voice, motivational technique, 60

Waiver forms, 226
Walton, Bill, 187

Warm-up procedures, 80–82
Weight training for the female athlete, 270–271
Wellington, Duke of, 11
White, Byron R., 6
Williams, Jesse F., 28
Wilt, Fred, 119
Win-or-else philosophy, 22, 186, 296–297

Women
   athletic competition and myths, 264, 267
   in the olympics, 30
   see also Female athlete
Wooden, John, 56, 68, 69

Zeitz, Harold, 3

Photo Credits

Title Page (clockwise)	Editorial Photocolor Archives Fred Keenan, *The Patriot Ledger* Courtesy of Regis College Fred Keenan, *The Patriot Ledger* Courtesy of Regis College
Figure A	Beth McCampbell
Figure 1.1	Courtesy of Pine Manor College Courtesy of M.I.T. Ellis Herwig, Stock/Boston William Galvin, *The Paper* Courtesy of Boston University
1.2	Courtesy of the Hartford Insurance Group
1.3	Beth McCampbell
1.4	(top) William Galvin, *The Paper* (bottom) Fred Keenan, *The Patriot Ledger*
Figure 2.1	Brown Brothers
2.2	Fred Keenan, *The Patriot Ledger* Wide World Photos *South Middlesex News*
Figure 3.2	Courtesy of the Athletic Department, Iolani School, Honolulu, Hawaii
3.3	Fred Keenan, *The Patriot Ledger*
3.4	(top) Wide World Photos (Bottom) Courtesy of M.I.T.
3.5	*South Middlesex News*
Figure 4.1	Cam Lorentz
Figure 5.1	(in Text)
5.2–5.8	Courtesy of Progressive Weight Training Laboratory under the direction of Sherman Button, University of California at Santa Barbara; models are Frank Cercos and Dennis Mitchell
5.9	Wayne Horodowich
5.10	Wayne Horodowich
5.11	Stuart Cohen, Stock/Boston
5.12	(top) Courtesy of M.I.T. (bottom) Frank Wing, Stock/Boston
Figure 8.1	Courtesy of National Council for the Prevention of Drug Abuse
8.2	William Galvin, *The Paper*
Figure 9.1	Beardsley Ruml, II
9.2	Courtesy of M.I.T.

9.3   (clockwise) Christopher W. Morrow, Stock/Boston
Pam Schuyler, Stock/Boston
Courtesy Radcliffe College
Courtesy of M.I.T.

Figure 10.1   Courtesy of Brookline Public Schools
10.3   *South Middlesex News*
10.4   R. Mills
10.5   Tim Carlson, Stock/Boston
10.6   *South Middlesex News*

Figure 11.1   Pam Schuyler, Stock/Boston
11.2   Arthur Grace, Stock/Boston

ABCDEFGHIJ-H-8210